Innovation
Strategy

047003

Innovation Strategy

Alan West

REGIONAL TECHNICAL COLLEGE GALWAY
2 0 DEC 1994
CASTLEBAR CAMPUS LIBRARY

PRENTICE HALL

NEW YORK   LONDON   TORONTO   SYDNEY   TOKYO   SINGAPORE

658·575

First published 1992 by
Prentice Hall International (UK) Ltd
66 Wood Lane End, Hemel Hempstead
Hertfordshire HP2 4RG
A division of
Simon & Schuster International Group

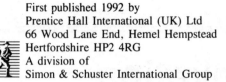

© Prentice Hall International (UK) Ltd, 1992

All right reserved. No part of this publication may be
reproduced, stored in a retrieval system, or transmitted
in any form, or by any means, electronic, mechanical,
photocopying, recording or otherwise, without prior
permission, in writing, from the publisher.
For permission within the United States of America
contact Prentice Hall Inc., Englewood Cliffs, NJ 07632.

Typeset in 10/12 pt Times
by MHL Typesetting Ltd, Coventry

Printed and bound in Great Britain by
BPCC Wheatons Ltd, Exeter

Library of Congress Cataloging-in-Publication Data

West, Alan, 1951–
    Innovation strategy/Alan West.
        p. cm.
    ISBN 0-13-465360-2
    1. Technological innovations — Management. 2. New products.
I. Title.
HD45.W4285   1992
658.5'75—dc20   91-26703
                                                      CIP

British Library Cataloguing in Publication Data

West, Alan
    Innovation strategy.
    I. Title
    658.4

    ISBN 0—13—465360—2

2 3 4   95 94 93 92

Contents

List of illustrations

1

Introduction

Once an angry editor stormed down to the territory of the copy-writers. With him he took the offending copy and a pristine review edition. 'Can't you people write', he fumed. He held up the volume. 'This is an important new title about these issues. This copy makes the whole thing sound like something that you wouldn't give a line of space to, if left to yourselves.' But the perpetrator was unmoved. 'There are only two new things about that book — the title and the publication date. Its contents are identical with the revised edition published under the old title, last year. All the data in this volume was in the last one. Here's the old copy, see for yourself.'

This is a true story told here because on the one hand it concerns perceptions about novelty that will preoccupy readers; and on the other because it helps to explain the approach to innovation taken in this book. The story raises immediate questions in the reader's mind. Who is right — editor or copy-writer? What is new? Who judges what is new?

Classically, the perception would be that the copy-writer rather than the editor was right because the physical contents of the book had not changed. In other words, the book was not fundamentally new. However, examples in today's world tell us that this is not the sole issue, or even the most common view, of innovation. Doubtlessly our editor was more familiar with the publisher's perceptions — that changing the title could alter profits from a financially underperforming text. So a new title, and publication date, which was better received by the market would generate a profitable new response. According to this reasoning, the book's contents are irrelevant to the perception of what is new. Take the example of Collins, the publishers of the famous Agatha Christie paperback list. The company found that simply reducing the violence portrayed on the front cover increased sales by 40 per cent even though Hercule Poirot and Miss Marple continued their unchanging antediluvian pursuits inside.

There is a tendency to think that business innovation is synonymous with pushing back those 'final' frontiers of technology and to disregard the flip cap on the tube

1

of toothpaste. Yet the fact remains that the first is feasible for very few companies because it consumes huge resources; and if we dismiss the second, we risk disregarding the aggregate effect of seemingly insignificant commercial innovations in creating a whole new way of life. We have, for instance, what has been described as a throwaway or disposable society — a result of wide-ranging innovations from Lord Lever's wrapping of bar soap to the disposable paper goods revolution, from nylon tights to throwaway razors, watches, cameras, syringes. The breadth of the throwaway concept has supported innovation over a very wide range of industries and its impact has been so significant that it has generated a whole new outlook unsupported, on the whole, by major technological inventions. By examining examples such as this, the concept of innovation can be clearly seen to extend beyond pure issues of technical change and into promotion, distribution, and many other ways in which businesses can gain competitive advantage over their rivals.

This book looks at innovation as a wide-ranging phenomenon relevant to managers at all levels in very different types of organization. It is as important to business operating in the older, 'mature' industrial sectors and in the service sector as it is to those concentrating on technological advance. At the same time it is as important to the finance manager as it is to the production manager in the same company. There are a number of advantages associated with this broad approach. Firstly, it focuses attention on successful innovation as an issue of sound strategic planning. In a commercial organization this means adopting a systematic approach which will identify the special requirements and the key influences on particular choices of alternatives. Secondly, it highlights the environmental pressures favouring innovation in all sectors, thereby giving further emphasis to the need for sound planning in this area: the broad analysis of innovation across various sectors demonstrates quite clearly that it is only by defining the right type of innovation policy or strategy for specific external and internal forces that the commercial organization can effectively compete at a particular time. Because forces change, so inevitably must innovation policy. A case study approach, valuable in defining how company X succeeded five years ago in introducing product Y, is of mainly historical value as it gives little indication as to how either company X should approach innovation in the changed climate of the present, or what it should do with product Y in the future. To underline this point, many of the companies written about as excellent innovators have proved to be just the opposite in the longer term.[1]

A third important advantage of a broad approach is that it becomes possible to compare and contrast the management of new ideas beyond the R & D stage and into the marketplace between companies that have a consistently good record as long-term innovators. One can analyse the experience of more companies of very diverse backgrounds from the leading and up-and-coming economies in an approach that is quite distinct from the case study of successful innovators. Oddly enough, this broad approach allows us to move from the general to the specific. The specific processes of adjustment demanded by a particular form of innovation become much clearer through this process of comparison. Broad rules and guidelines concerning approaches to managing different types of change emerge but they always reveal the necessity to harmonize structures and control processes with the type of innovation strategy chosen.

A fourth aspect of this approach is that it is forward looking, unlike the case study which is based on historical data. The future demands associated with a particular type of innovation upon the company stay at the centre of the discussion. Innovation is risky and a company must balance risk and return in terms of profit to the organization. Risk minimization effectively means that a company's management of innovation must also be broadly based and should not omit to consider such issues as the availability of the right type of personnel, establishing the right information sources, market analysis, testing and control in addition to the usual high-profile areas associated with innovation like research and development.

By keeping the commercial interest of the company firmly in view a broad analysis reveals an additional facet of successful innovation strategy. Innovation tends to be benefit rather than feature driven or, put another way, it is customer rather than technology driven. Innovations that are technically superior — like the RCA video disc or the Hawker Harrier vertical take-off and landing jet — may not be commercially successful. Looking at innovation from a commercial perspective, that is, return from the level of investment, reveals that technical superiority is not the sole issue in the way companies consider changing their products or services to meet current or future market trends. Returning to our initial argument between the editor and the copy-writer; one or the other will obviously be correct — but it will be the customer that will decide. Such an emphasis moves away from purely the management of technological change towards appreciating where the company should concentrate in developing new ideas and what the broader implications for resource analysis may be.

To survive a company has to be a commercial success and that means producing something its customers want, rather than what the company thinks the customer should want. The company that chooses the right strategy through the correct definition of what the market wants and what the internal resources of the organization (including its management) can achieve and manage will channel its inevitably limited resources into more commercially successful paths of action than one that looks at innovation from a narrow technical perspective. Change is an essential component of business into the new century, and management must appreciate that this is not a simple or single process, but one which will make a variety of demands upon the organization, depending on the type of policy chosen.

This book is divided into three parts. Chapters 2 and 3 describe the essential background against which innovation needs to be considered; Chapters 4 to 7 examine the differing types of innovation and the demands that they make on the organization; Chapters 8 to 10 outline the essential components of the planning to turn concept into reality.

Note

1. In R. Lessem, *The Roots of Excellence*, (London: Fontana, 1985), Sinclair Research was described as a leading innovator — where is it now? Taken over by Amstrad, after a series of disastrous innovations drained the company of resources. Many of the companies identified as leading and successful innovators in the United States in T.J. Peters and R.H. Waterman, *In Search of Excellence*, (New York: Harper & Row, 1982) have since moved either into bankruptcy or dramatic losses in market share. A similar record of changing fortune within the United Kingdom can be found by comparing the subsequent achievements of the companies described in R. Clutterbuck, *The Winning Streak*, (London: Penguin, 1987).

2

Setting the scene: the changing innovation environment

Introduction

The real business environment of the 1990s is likely to be more hostile to the company introducing new products and *this fact must be accepted not ignored.* The sale of more or more profitable products or services is the only viable method of achieving growth and competitive advantage; any firm diverted from concentrating the correct resources in the right areas will be rapidly overtaken. Essentially, it is the pressure of change arising in the external environment over the past fifteen years that makes finding a sound strategy for managing change so important.

The uncontrollable and uncertain facets of business planning have vastly expanded for many reasons — ever-altering interest rates, foreign exchange levels, technical and safety regulations and other legislation, financial markets, commodity prices, price inflation, unemployment rates, labour skills and turnover, training schemes, government grants, taxation and so on. But businesses have coped under such pressures successfully in the past . The German chemical industry was, for example, still developing new products in the 1920s during some of the most extreme inflationary pressures experienced in any Western industrialized country. Though certain trends in the 1970s and 1980s have been more extreme than before they have not introduced any fundamentally new factors into the business planning horizon.

What is really new is a substantial and continuing increase in the competitive environment. This introduces an entirely new set of problems for company long-term investment policies by adding further uncertainty to the evaluation of investment in new products and processes. Because this influence is so new, it is important for businesses to understand the likely implications for investment policy. For example, will the changed competitive environment reduce the overall viability of any innovation policy or will it favour alternative innovation routes?

The main components of this worldwide increase in competitiveness are declining worldwide growth rates, a rise in the number of world manufacturing countries or developed markets, greater ease of access to worldwide markets, international concentration of industrial production among fewer but larger companies, and a more sophisticated and demanding customer in most of the main markets in the world. Each has implications for the development of any innovation strategy.

International growth

Much has been written about the basic slowing of world economic growth but experience in the United States, for long the driving force of the world economy, illustrates the point. From 1960 to 1973, economic growth was on average 3.9 per cent per year. Since that watershed, growth has been a third less — on average 2.6 per cent — and the trend is downwards not upwards. The initial forecasts for the 1990s reveal an even gloomier prognosis. Europe shows a similar halting performance, though the prospects for economic growth improve after closer integration in 1992.[1] Nevertheless, economic chaos in Eastern Europe could make such forecasts optimistic in the short term. The gloom is offset to an extent by the performance of the Pacific basin countries but the rise in the yen has caused a decline in the traditionally higher levels of Japanese GDP expansion which in the 1980s were already significantly lower than those achieved in the 1960s and early 1970s. The effects of rising oil prices in the early 1990s after a period of stability is expected to further reduce growth in many of the oil-dependent economies in the region (Japan, the largest of these, successfully reduced its oil consumption following the oil crisis of the early 1970s). The cost of the Gulf War poses economic and political problems beyond 1991.

The impact on the competitive environment is clear — enterprises can no longer grow solely on the rising tide of demand, but must seek their sales expansion at the expense of other firms in the same sector of the market. Where growth has occurred it has also tended to be accompanied by higher inflation: in contrast with the 1960s when high growth accompanied lower inflation. Higher inflation during the 1980s reduced market attractiveness and added uncertainty to the prospects for long-term investment (a factor discussed in greater length in Chapter 5).

An overall decline in profitability has accompanied declining growth, inevitably generating overcapacity and exerting downward pressure on pricing in a wide range of industries throughout the world. Many of the fortunes of industrial Europe were founded on steel, coal, textiles, and ship building. No one would claim that many such fortunes could be similarly derived in the 1990s. While some of the more severe cases of overcapacity are in these sectors, manufacturing industry has also suffered worldwide from declining profitability since the 1950s, and in periods of high inflation — as the United Kingdom experienced in the late 1970s — will be trading at a loss in *real* terms. Generally, the more mature the market, the greater the pressure on profitability. Thus, the old smokestack industries of the nineteenth century face the greatest difficulties and the new areas of electronics the least. So the new multinationals of the Pacific basin have been able to concentrate generally on higher-margin areas than their competitors in other parts of the world, achieving a 50 per cent higher net margin on sales than companies in traditional industries.[2]

> Even in fairly new industries like aluminium smelting, overcapacity can mean reduced profitability or loss. The analysis of the activities of Pechiney, the largest French aluminium smelter, shows clearly that although a large percentage of company turnover derives from the production of basic aluminium, losses occurred in this part of the business in 1985 and 1986 (see Table 2.1) and most profits came from specialized product. Its continued expansion into innovative and added-value product has been a necessary reaction to high levels of pressure on Pechiney's original business from other large aluminium producers throughout the world.
> The road to financial recovery in ICI was achieved by a rigorous concentration on those areas that could yield higher returns than those possible in the supply of basic industrial chemical feedstocks.[3]

As might be expected, changes in the value-added component in the major world economies also reflect this decline in profitability. All leading industrialized countries have seen a significant decrease in the value added to their goods since the 1960s. Trends in the main markets between 1960 and 1985 are shown in Table 2.2. The overall decline in these markets during this period has been 18.5 per cent, but some countries have managed a significantly smaller reduction — Japan and Italy heading the league table. The decline of the United States, a reduction of 28 per cent, and, in the worst case, of the United Kingdom at 30 per cent, are at the foot of the table. Indexing the data in Table 2.2 to take account of the

Table 2.1 Pechiney turnover and profitability by activity, 1986 ($000 million)

Activity	Turnover	Profit (loss)
Basic aluminium	2640	(40)
Packaging material	2141	272
Components	707	(3)

Source: Company annual accounts, 1986/87

Table 2.2 Value added as a percentage of GDP

Year	US	Japan	West Germany	France	UK	Italy
1960	28.3	33.9	40.3	29.1	32.1	28.6
1971	24.9	35.2	37.0	28.5	28.5	27.4
1979	23.0	29.3	33.8	27.0	25.8	30.6
1983	20.6	29.1	31.3	25.2	21.6	27.1
1985	20.4	29.8	32.3	25.4	22.6	26.2

Source: OECD

Table 2.3 Indexed changes in valued added, 1960—85

Year	USA	Japan	West Germany	France	UK	Italy
1960	100	100	100	100	100	100
1971	(12)	4	(8)	(2)	(11)	(4)
1979	(8)	(17)	(9)	(5)	(10)	12
1983	(10)	(1)	(7)	(7)	(16)	(11)
1985	(1)	2	3	1	4	(3)

Source: Adapted from OECD data

Table 2.4 Marginal efficiency of investment, 1961—84

Country	1961—73	1974—79	1980—84
Japan	0.35	0.10	0.14
USA	0.20	0.15	0.10
Europe[1]	0.19	0.11	0.05

Note: [1]Europe consists of West Germany, France and
the UK
Source: OECD

decline in percentage terms from the previous period (see Table 2.3) shows that
the rate of decline has also varied, with the UK showing the most consistent
reduction in value added through the period and with an acceleration after 1979.
Though recent improvements in value-added performance suggest that the rapid
decline in profitability has been halted, it is yet unclear whether the value-added
performance levels of the 1960s are re-attainable. Table 2.4 shows a similar decline
in the marginal efficiency of investment over the same period.

The implications for international competitiveness of this fairly universal decline
in value added and marginal efficiency of investment is clear. Companies and
industrial sectors will come under increasing pressure to maintain margins and
profitability. They will have to compete more effectively, both within their core
markets and in other sectors, for additional revenue. Added value will be more
difficult to achieve, and only those companies that concentrate on an effective
competitive policy which continually revises and alters product or service offerings
will attain a satisfactory rate of return from an international market that is exerting
a downward pressure on profitability and added value. A continually expanding
world economy will no longer provide growth. With reduced returns from
investment, companies will have to be more and more precise in how they develop
new activities and interests.

World manufacturing patterns

The rise of manufacturing industry in the developing world adds another dimension
to the competitive environment. Access to international markets has eased and

the growth in the number of countries involved in international manufacturing has inevitably intensified the degree of competitive pressure both in the home markets — where the nationally based companies have a natural advantage — and in the wider international arena as well. Though the world economy has expanded overall many of the new rapid-growth areas have been dominated by nationally based corporations. This is understandable because historically national governments and other buying groups have favoured local suppliers and initially most industrial corporations concentrate on the home market, protected by a variety of legislative or non-legislative barriers from extensive competition from overseas. There follows a period of overseas expansion.

In other areas access to markets has tightened, however. Latin American and African debt hangs over world banks, with the result that trade with these markets has steadily declined since the mid-1970s. With the drop in oil price and the consequence fall in revenues, OPEC members ceased to be such important alternative markets for trade development. Other events have also helped to alter the trade patterns of certain countries. The United Kingdom, for example, had historically a considerable protected trade with Commonwealth countries, but membership of the European Community (EC) meant that this trade had practically vanished by the mid-1980s with a re-alignment towards Europe and North America (see Table 2.5). By contrast, Japan and the other industrializing countries of the Pacific rim were largely excluded from such protected markets and were forced to concentrate on developing business at home and then in developed markets overseas (especially in North America). This inevitably sharpened their world competitiveness, when compared with those countries that received a substantial proportion of their business from their protected markets.[4] UK governments, however, continued to encourage trade with developing countries via 'soft' loans rather than the more complicated and demanding task of creating viable opportunities in the more competitive developed world markets. Gaining the contract for the construction of a bridge across the Bosphorus may indeed provide valuable short-term work for particular industrial sectors, but the evidence suggests that it does little to improve long-term industrial competitiveness.

So though world markets have grown, the increased opportunities have been largely offset by the increase in the number of players. The effect of this is significant for competitive policy, with a steady reduction in the number of markets

Table 2.5 Destination of UK export trade by percentage, 1953–87

Area	1953	1987
North America	10	16
South America	5	2
Asia	13	9
Europe	40	58
Other	32	15

Source: UK Department of Trade and Industry/OECD

Table 2.6 OECD shares of the world market in manufactured goods: percentage market share, 1963−87

Market	1963	1979	1987
West Germany	20.5	19.0	17.0
United States	17.0	14.0	13.0
UK	11.0	7.0	6.0
France	8.0	9.5	10.0
Italy	6.0	7.5	7.0
Total (excluding Japan)	65.0	57.0	53.0
Japan	4.0	12.0	15.0
Total (including Japan)	69.0	69.0	68.0

Source: OECD

with low levels of competition. The Pacific basin is a good example. Table 2.6 shows that since the early 1960s there has been a considerable increase in its share of world manufacturing. As its importance increased so has the number of companies that can be considered as major manufacturers. This is most marked with the emergence of Korea and the large trading companies such as Goldstar, Hyundai, Samsung and Daewoo.

The Sony Corporation is one of the most successful new manufacturers of the Pacific rim. Its insistence on large-scale investment in high-added-value products in consumer electronics has seen its turnover and profitability rising since the early 1970s. By 1990, its entry into the American market with the acquisition of CBS records and Columbia pictures made the company one of the entertainment giants of the world. Sony is, however, only one of the many manufacturers established in this market sector and faces extreme and rising pressure from other electronics companies throughout the Pacific rim.

Improved access to world markets

Since 1945 there have been immense improvements in international access to world markets. Though overall world GNP has increased by 488 per cent since 1950, world trade has grown at approximately double the rate (928 per cent) over the same period. It is noticeable that in the higher-growth areas of the Pacific basin this growth in inter-country trade over individual output is an even greater multiple than the overall rate of increase in world trade during the 1980s.

GATT, The General Agreement on Tariffs and Trade, and other world regulatory bodies have also been crucial in identifying and attempting to remove barriers to international trade. Given the extreme nationalism and provincialism of the early twentieth century, it has been extremely successful, though there have been and will continue to be individual set-backs, with some areas advancing more rapidly than others. For example, by 1988 a global market in financial securities had become an established reality, and appeared likely to continue regardless of the problems caused by such temporary set-backs as the market collapse at the end of 1987. The volume of this trade is enormous — Barclays bank estimated the *daily* currency flows at around £200 billion — far in excess of the demands caused by international payments for goods or services. Other markets will change more hesitantly and reluctantly, with West Germany, for example, continuing in 1988 to resist EC attempts to open the beer market to foreign imports. The problems of the Uruguay round of discussions under way during the late 1980s and early 1990s, centring around improved access to agricultural and fabric markets may also prove to be an exception to the general success of GATT initiatives.

European integration has progresed with the gradual lowering of trade barriers improving EC members' access to more markets. The planned single market of 1992 may or may not occur exactly as planned or precisely on time, but the general trend towards greater integration and ease of internal EC trade cannot be ignored. For example, the market sectors most likely to see substantial increases in competitive pressure within the EC following the removal of barriers are in telecommunications, transport, financial services, food and drink, where national regulations have acted to restrict cross-border access for particular types of innovation or product development by demanding specific modifications for particular markets. This is one major market region where the effects of so-called non-tariff barriers will further decline throughout the 1990s. Pressure on other markets to minimize regulations that hinder the free flow of goods will also reduce the impact of such factors in international trade. Claims that Japanese snow is unique (implying that foreign ski manufacturers — which dominate the Japanese market — should meet onerous design regulations) or that the Japanese digestive system cannot cope effectively with beef (thereby maintaining restrictions on foreign imports) will become more difficult to maintain. Other major markets such as India and Taiwan are already discussing or implementing specific proposals to reduce the impact of such restrictions on the access to their markets.

These changes mean that fewer countries within the EC and elsewhere will be able to maintain monopolies or quasi-monopolies through formal (tariff) or informal (non-tariff) barriers where the rate of innovation, whether public or private, is always slow. (Observers of certain industrial sectors can be pardoned for not wholly believing that many oligopolies are truly competitive.) The number of environments where companies such as British Telecom exist, laboriously and slowly introducing digital equipment, will become the exception, rather than the rule.

Markets will tend towards the other extremes: for example, those of the Japanese consumer electronics industry or the US car market. In the first, there exist companies like Mitsubishi introducing 257 new products in 1986 while its two main competitors produced a similar number: Hitachi (243) and Toshiba (223). All these products initially appeared in the highly competitive environment of Tokyo's Akihabara district where shoppers in the 300 electronic shops have over 70 models of compact disc players, 80 video recorders and nearly 200 different types of colour television. Such an environment approaches the 'ideal' competitive climate postulated by the earliest writer on competition, Adam Smith. However, it remains exceptional in the sale of goods, whether consumer or industrial, throughout the world. Akihabara is indeed maintained as a testing ground for new products for sound commercial reasons which will be discussed in later chapters. In the US car market the variety of models and the price competitiveness are exceptional when compared with other trading blocs, with over 400 models available in 1990 at prices well below those of the EC, even when allowing for tax. (The European standard model of General Motors, sold under the Ascona or Cavalier badge, retailed at around £7000 net of tax throughout the EC in comparison with $8500 in the US at 1990 prices.)

Improved access to international markets implies that the zone of influence within which even the largest companies have effective control will continue to shrink. Foreign well-resourced competitors will be able to gain access to core markets more easily and more cheaply, though it is likely that such competitors will tend in the short term to come from nearby markets rather than from a distance, leading to the development of trading blocs in the 1990s (see Tables 2.7 and 2.8). These alterations in world trading patterns inevitably have consequences for competitive policy. They mean that in the short term most firms will experience a rise in competition from firms that in the majority of cases are located nearby and have substantial knowledge of the company's own home market. Such firms will be able to respond rapidly to any action taken by their competitors and will have an expanded vision of what is in effect their 'home' market. This change can

Table 2.7 Patterns of world trade in 1988 between major blocs

	Percentage excluding inter-bloc trading	Percentage including inter-bloc trading
East Asia	22.9	20.5
North America	16.1	16.1
EC	24.3	39.3
Other	36.7	24.1

Source: OECD, DTI, Bank of England

Table 2.8 Intra-trade as a percentage of total trade by trading bloc, 1982–88

	1982	1985	1988
European Community			
Exports	53.9	54.4	59.5
Imports	50.1	52.7	57.7
North America			
Exports	28.3	38.0	34.6
Imports	27.4	28.0	26.7
East Asia			
Exports	31.1	25.9	26.9
Imports	31.1	32.2	35.7

Source: Bank of England, *Quarterly Bulletin*, August 1990

already be seen in the pronouncements of car companies such as BMW and Peugeot in reaction to Japanese European manufacture, where the Japanese are perceived as invading their home (i.e. European) market, rather than narrow national boundaries. To gain competitive advantage a firm will therefore have to operate within much wider boundaries and appreciate the implications of change introduced by other manufacturers in any part of its international network because it will rapidly and inevitably affect the majority of its major markets. As the size and effectiveness of the competitive pressures increase, so must the sophistication of the response that the company makes.

Concentration of international trade

An important issue for the world economy is the concentration of productive power among fewer and fewer companies, with over 25 per cent of world manufacturing controlled by 600 corporations, and over 60 per cent of employment in European manufacturing companies provided by multinational corporations.[5] Even in areas like steel manufacture which developing world governments consider essential to manufacturing strategy, the sector is still dominated by companies established within OECD member countries. The chemical industry established in the early part of the twentieth century also shows the same continuing power of old established companies. Of these the most important are the three component companies of the original IG Farben monolith, Hoechst, Bayer and BASF, which still dominate the world markets with a combined turnover of $73 billion and around 27 per cent of the world production. The turnover of these companies is of an order of magnitude greater than their nearby competition such as DuPont and ICI. Even within specialist sectors of the chemical industry like paint manufacture there has been increasing concentration, and in detergents Unilever, Procter & Gamble and Colgate Palmolive are market leaders throughout the world with the exception of parts of Europe where Henkel hold market shares approaching 25 per cent. Photographic film, another extension of the chemical industry is dominated by Kodak, with companies such as Fuji and Agfa making up the remainder of a highly competitive world market. Other examples of consumer products and international concentration include denim jeans, alcoholic spirits (Seagrams, Allied Lyons, Grand Metropolitan), chocolate and soft drinks, frozen food, packet soups, and many others.

In the supply of computer hardware, IBM and Fujitsu lead mainframe systems and IBM and DEC supply 45 per cent of the world's mini-computer systems. Fujitsu's 1990 acquisition of ICL — the last UK computer systems manufacturer — from STC, its parent company, further increased its market share in this sector as well. Concentration of production has progressed significantly further in the component industries where the costs of establishing a semiconductor production line were in excess of $200 million at the end of 1987. Such cost levels have the common effect of further reducing the number of manufacturers in many high-technology industries. Though the process of international concentration has been most marked in highly capital-intensive manufacturing, similar changes are apparent in consumer goods and services. A few major operators dominate in hotels, fast food, cinemas, insurance, airlines and tourism. Western European retailing is also following the trend towards greater concentration.

There are various explanations for the phenomena of contraction and concentration. Higher investment levels for new production plant and research is an obvious one. General Motors, which by any corporation measure has vast resources, decided to withdraw from the heavy-truck market dominated by European firms because of the substantial investment required to maintain a competitive product. Volvo alone spends over £100 million per annum on research and development. The staggering costs of new drug development (see Table 2.9) partly explains drug company reluctance to invest in significantly new pharmaceutical families and the preference for concentrating on existing ones whose toxicology is better understood. One study suggested that overall development costs for new drugs had increased twentyfold since 1963.[6]

But research and development costs are not the sole area where costs have significantly increased. Many companies with international images use the television broadcasting of the Olympic games for promotional purposes, for example. The cost of Olympic TV rights rose from $4.8 million in 1964 — the first games broadcast by satellite — to over $300 million at the Seoul Olympics in 1988. Sponsorship of the Olympic games by nine companies including Federal Express and Coca Cola cost a further $120 million. It has been estimated that the cost of fully backing the nationwide launch of a consumer goods product in the United States would be in excess of $50 million and may reach $100 million in highly competitive sectors like toiletries. Legislative and technical control has lengthened the period of investment payback in many industries and often it is only the larger companies that can finance long-term developments. In addition, greater access to markets encourages the development of large companies able to spread the development overhead across a wider range of markets. It has been suggested that for many types of manufactured products it is the non-tariff or informal barriers that are now more important than the formal tariff barriers.

Table 2.9 Estimated costs of new drug development by stage

Stage	Cost of stage (£m.)
Drug synthesis	14
Biological screening	12
Pre-clinical tests	50
Controlled tests	5
Final tests	4
Gaining approval	2
Launch	1

Source: Pharmaceutical trade estimates

The processes of contraction and concentration also imply a concentration of resources; capital, knowledge, and skills. Competing directly with resource-rich organizations is an almost impossible challenge: the margin for error in world markets is steadily diminishing. A smaller competitor once remarked of Procter & Gamble that 'even though one can see the steamroller coming does not mean that you will not be squashed'. This perception of the weakness of market followers is supported by research that suggests that market followers are likely to see a much lower return on capital employed (ROCE) than either those that specialize or those that dominate a mass market.[7]

The experience of the Rover car group typifies some of the issues of increased competitiveness resulting from the reduction in the numbers of players in a particular sector. Around three-quarters of total world car volume are produced by nine manufacturers, and it has been suggested that for a mass car manufacturer to be viable it will need to produce in excess of 500,000 units to cover the high tooling costs and research and development expenditure.[8] This industrial logic means that a relatively small company like Leyland cannot effectively compete in the mass car market and has to devise a competitive strategy that is not based on volume production. This lesson is exemplified by Mercedes Benz in West Germany which only makes around 500,000 units per annum yet remains firmly wedded to the concept of concentrating on a relatively narrow specialist sector. Because of this policy it can direct its resources effectively into an area where it enjoys a significant competitive advantage. By contrast, the continuing insistence on a mass market presence by Rover will place it under increasing strain.

Given the continuance of trends in concentration, market position will exert a considerable and often overriding influence on the type of competitive strategy that a firm can follow. Competing against very large internationally based corporations will mean that the firm with more limited resources must define carefully and specifically the realistic opportunities that exist to differentiate it from such competitors. If it does not succeed in so doing the inevitable consequences are declining profitability and eventual closure. For the large company the existence of large well-developed competitors has different implications. The first is that the speed of technology transfer will be substantially increased. Large well-resourced companies will be able to copy or better competitive technology within a shorter and shorter period of time. Sony, for example, considers that its technological period of grace — the length of lead that it held over the competition following the introduction of advanced products — has dropped from an average of three years in the 1970s to an average of six months in the mid-1980s. Competitive products to the Sony Discman were in Tokyo's shops four-and-a-half months after its introduction. This decrease in the market advantage enjoyed by a changed product has inevitably affected perceptions of the speed at which projects are expected to become profitable (the payback or payoff period, the date by which the project will enter into profit). Surveys of firms' expected repayment periods in the 1940s, 1950s, 1960s and 1980s suggest that the average pay-off period has shortened since the 1950s even though the companies and the industries surveyed differ.

As the speed of technology transfer increases, the organization must also examine non-technical areas as sources of potential in achieving and maintaining a competitive edge. Pure technical excellence will not last long unless the company is in the position to clearly protect a particular product or product group with unassailable patents. Speed into the market will be of increasing importance. Shorter pay-backs require greater attention to detail as the margin for error is correspondingly smaller. An economic model developed by the management consultants McKinsey suggests that for high-technology products with a limited payback period coming to market six months late but on budget would cut potential returns by 33 per cent, whereas coming in on time but 50 per cent over budget would only reduce profitability by 4 per cent. This perception is strengthened by other research which is included in the following chapter.

The problem facing the larger company is therefore very different to that of the smaller. Either it increases the level and/or effectiveness of R & D or capital expenditure to maintain competitive advantage or it seeks to decrease the level of potential competition in the market. Many cross-border agreements in industries with high degrees of concentration (for example motor cars, electronics, aerospace) have the stated aim of sharing research and development costs across a broader base of sales. There is, however, an implicit understanding establishing zones of influence to reduce competition in specific markets or market areas. Where this trend will end will largely depend on both the attitudes of the regulatory bodies and the severity of conditions within particular market sectors. In the late 1980s world airlines were increasingly forming alliances to transfer passengers from one 'hub' to another, with British Airways and United Airlines entering into one such agreement. These agreements have come under pressure from both the EC regulatory bodies as well as from market changes, resulting in the proposed takeover by United Airlines of Pan American routes involving its entry into the market zone previously dominated by British Airways. The conclusion that can be drawn from this and other examples is that these 'terratels' (world cartel agreements) are inherently unstable. But where regulatory authorities are weak certain of the major players in any particular market will attempt to control the market position through alliances with other firms in specific market sectors. Such alliances on the basis of current experience are likely to be an unsatisfactory response to competitive forces within the market over the long term.

Rising sophistication

Affluence, education, and mounting pressures for greater industrial efficiency favour continual novelty and steady improvements in available product performance. To the consumer, novelty has become a steadily more important factor in product purchase. Whereas the average British woman owned about two blouses in the late 1940s, by the mid-1980s she had sixteen. A man expected eight years' wear from a suit in 1960 but less than three years' wear in 1980.[9]

Leisure footwear manufacturers can only expect one particular line of running shoes to last a single season in the 1990s — the previous pattern of the 1970s had been for two or three years' continual production. This climate is relevant to products requiring much higher manufacturing investments like motor cars: the Morris Minor and Volkswagen Beetle were largely unchanged over twenty-two and twenty-five years respectively; their replacements, the BL Metro and the Volkswagen Golf are updated every three years. The pressures are obvious: the moment the new product is launched the company will start planning for the introduction of the later variants. Product change cannot be considered as an intermittent process but one requiring continuous attention.

The close attention given to the interrelationship between product and customer has created awareness of more sophisticated consumer demands for greater variety of product and for improvements to existing products. Markets have therefore become more segmented. For example, the US car market had increased the number of clearly defined segments from nineteen in 1978 to twenty-six in 1985 (see Table 2.10). These expectations are almost certainly set to rise. A 1983 poll found that 26 per cent of Americans considered a second car as a necessity; 60 per cent frozen food, and 70 per cent facial tissues![10] Similar changes are occurring in the industrial sector. Hewlett Packard, for example, obtains over 60 per cent of its sales from products introduced in the last two years in contrast to the position in the early 1980s where over 60 per cent of sales were from products introduced over three years previously. The demanding industrial equipment manufacturer is also requiring more and more specific components. This trend towards shorter manufacturing runs and more specific designs can be shown in the production patterns of semicustomized chips (see Table 2.11), with a clearly defined trend towards both a greater diversity of types produced and a greater specificity of use.

The competitive impact of rising expectations has certain far-reaching implications for competitive strategy. The first is that the volume of production relating to one specific product type will go on declining. The manufacturer producing continually the Model T Ford — a single product in a single colour,

Table 2.10 Segments in the US car market, 1978—85

Category	No. of segments by year	
	1978	1985
Microcompact	—	2
Subcompact	2	2
Midsized	—	2
Intermediate	2	2
Full size	4	—
Luxury	2	2
Truck	3	6
Van	2	5
Station wagon	1	1
Sports car	1	2

Source: Ward Automotive Yearbooks (US)

Table 2.11 Production patterns in semicustomized chips, 1975–91

	1975	1980	1986	1991 (projected)
No of designs '000	0.1	1.1	10	100.00
Average production run '000	750.0	50.0	3	0.25

Source: Business Week, 6 March 1989

immortalized by Henry Ford's comment that 'you can have any colour that you want as long as it is black' — is indeed a thing of the past. The modern motor car manufacturer such as BMW faces the production constraint that an identical model with the same engine size, colour and internal options, will be rare: at one BMW plant it is estimated that precisely the same model will only be made at three-week intervals. Clearly, such variation makes significant demands upon the production process and the emphasis for manufacturing plant is on continual improvements in flexibility. In order to be competitive modern commercial organizations must be prepared to meet a wide-ranging and diverse manufacturing strategy.

The second obvious issue is that any competitive strategy relating to product change depends on a better, more effective understanding of market conditions than one's closest rivals. To achieve this a company must have the right organizational set up in place: one that can respond to change with satisfactory new product concepts. The larger firms will require structures that are capable of identifying market change and responding to it within the shortest possible timescale.

The third implication of rising expectations is less obvious, but relates to the effects of greater variety on the overall economies of scale. Typically, the perception has been that the greater the production run of a single unit, the greater the economies of scale, with fixed costs of production spread over a wider volume. With a greater demand for change, these economies of scale are no longer feasible. Even though companies can offset the effects of rapidly altering demand by flexible manufacturing systems and identifying the maximum number of components that can be left to the last moment to modify according to market demand (a distribution concept known as 'postponement'),[11] the overall effect must be to press companies to identify market opportunities that provide a higher level of return on individual items to offset the overall reduction in the economies of scale.

Models of economic development and the future

The crucial questions for the businessman of the 1990s are whether this identified state of competitiveness will increase or whether improvements in economic conditions are likely to be sufficient to benefit profitability and expand growth, thereby changing the environment back towards one that poses less severe problems to the majority of businesses.

Forecasts always rely on some form of model where a relationship between what has happened in the recent past is used to predict future trends. Attempts to analyse the post-1945 environment suggest that the concept of economic cycles provides a sort of framework for understanding the present and forecasting the future. The simplest formulation of the economic cycle argument belongs to a Russian economic historian, Kondriateff, who described long-term economic cycles relating growth and depression to technological introduction, expansion and over supply. Other analyses have produced a variety of three-, five-, seven-year or longer-term cycles. The Kondriateff model suggests that since the start of the industrial revolution there has been a steady increase in the number of mature industries. These will become more and more competitive as manufacturers with high levels of existing investment seek marginal improvements in profitability and product performance in areas that are fully understood by a large number of companies (see Table 2.12).

According to the model the technological possibilities of the main sources of post-war economic expansion — specifically electronics, petrochemicals, and

Table 2.12 The stages of post-1945 economic development

Factor	Stage 1 1945−55 Early stages	Stage 2 1955−69 Growth	Stage 3 1970−80s Maturity	Stage 4 1990s? Decline
Research emphasis	Basic patents	Expansion of patent concepts	Emphasis on manufacturing efficiency	Reduction in new product
Return on R & D expenditure	Low	High	Declining	Low
Growth method	New products	Modifications to new products	Company acquisition	
Design	New use of materials/ concepts	Increasing duplication	Emphasis on cost contribution	Minor cosmetic changes
Production	Craft emphasis Few economies	Economies of scale more important	Economies of scale vital	Over-capacity Industrial re-structuring
Capital requirements	Low	Growing	Extremely capital intensive	Limited new investment Old industries breaking up
Competitive structure	Small local	National consolidation	International companies	Global agreements Cartels
Labour skills	Limited	Trained personnel	Emphasis on skills	Many jobs replaced by automation
Growth	Slow	Rapid	Slowing	Declining

Source: Adapted from R. Rothwell *Futures*, 13(1), 1981

composite/synthetic materials — will be exhausted and similar downturns in activity to those seen in earlier downwaves will occur in the 1990s. Like all models which use historic data to develop some common view of the future it begs a number of questions, which opponents have used to question the main conclusions. From a practical standpoint, one can develop from these models a range of predictions about future events in the economy and by measuring the reality against the theory come to some decision about the validity of their broad conclusions.

Using wave theories to predict future economic changes might suggest that a number of conditions should be met before the hypothesis can be regarded as totally 'proven'. The key components considered might be whether the following factors apply:

1. Growth rates are declining.
2. Overall industrial profitability is decreasing.
3. Industrial overcapacity is growing.
4. Employment in manufacturing is decreasing.
5. Job replacement by automation is increasing.
6. Returns on R & D are declining.
7. Companies are growing by acquisition rather than organic growth.
8. Global agreements are increasing.

Available figures make clear that worldwide growth rates and manufacturing profitability are declining and that industrial overcapacity in many areas is a major problem. What is not clear is whether these are short- rather than long-term phenomena. There is also further clear evidence that manufacturing employment is declining. In the US, manufacturing and agriculture combined ceased to provide jobs for the majority of the workforce in the 1950s and by the 1980s it was the service sector that was providing a steadily greater percentage of overall employment (see Table 2.13). The point at which the service sector provided the majority of employment has been described as 'post industrial society'.[12]

Initially it was thought that the service sector would provide a viable long-term source of economic growth and employment. Though this had certainly been true in the 1960s, 1970s and early 1980s, with the majority of the new employment in the United States concentrated in this sector (there were over 133,000 fast-food outlets in the United States by the end of 1989) it is unlikely to continue. Service companies are not immune to the forces affecting the industrial sector

Table 2.13 Declining importance of the industrial sector as an employer in the United States

Sector	1870	1920	1940	1980	1988
Agriculture	57	27	18	3	3
Industry	25	34	33	28	24
Service	18	39	49	69	73

Source: US Department of Employment

and are showing many of the same characteristics favouring increased productivity, concentration of activity, and automation — all tending to reduce employment. British Airways management, for example, has reduced its labour force from 59,000 to 36,000 during the 1980s, has taken over its main UK rival British Caledonian, and invested heavily in electronic booking and control systems. Though large retail stores are often welcomed for the employment they bring, their overall effect is to reduce the numbers employed within the overall market sector and the area in which they operate. The 1991 recession has also hit service sector employment much more harshly than manufacturing.

Estimates of losses of several hundreds of millions of pounds suffered by the City of London in the year following the October 1987 crash inevitably point to further reductions in staff and withdrawals from the market by a large number of companies previously enthusiastic about the possibilities of deregulation. These examples suggest that in retrospect the expansion of the service sector will be seen to have experienced the same employment dynamics as the manufacturing sector, and is unlikely to provide a long-term buffer against the need to maintain and improve competitiveness in manufacturing. Investment in advanced manufacturing systems in Japan, with the growth of flexible manufacturing systems and the increased number of robots used in capital-intensive plants, provides clear evidence that the level of automation in industrial manufacture will increase into the new century.

Evidence of decreased returns from research and development is harder to find. Though overall research and development expenditure increased substantially for many countries between 1965 and 1987 (see Table 2.14), it is noticeable that in lead innovative markets like the United States the rate of growth has slowed since the mid-1980s, with higher rates of growth in Japan (Table 2.15). When total R & D investment is considered, the United States had been the major source of new product innovations in the 1950s and the 1960s and this is reflected in its share of world expenditure. The continued growth in investment by Japan in research and development since the early 1970s has fundamentally changed the balance of the share of expenditure between the top five industrialized countries with substantial reductions in the share of the United States and the United

Table 2.14 Total research and development expenditure as percentage of GDP

Country	1965	1987
Sweden	1.5	3.0
USA	3.4	2.8
Japan	1.5	2.8
West Germany	1.4	2.7
UK	2.3	2.5
France	1.6	2.4
Canada	1.0	1.5
Italy	0.6	1.4

Source: OECD

Table 2.15 Growth rates in industrially funded R & D, 1967−88

Area	1967−83	1967−75	1975−83	1980−88
Japan	10.8	10.6	10.9	11.2
USA	4.1	2.4	5.7	6.9
W. Europe	4.4	4.3	4.5	5.7

Source: OECD

Kingdom, and increases by West Germany and France. The increase in the overall level of expenditure on research and development by the main industrialized countries over the last fifteen years suggests that overall returns per dollar, yen or Deutschmark invested are declining which supports the view that overall marginal returns on investment have decreased since the 1960s. However, as the numbers of mature markets rise they need continued high levels of investment in research and development; this view is supported by the Profit Impact of Market Strategy (PIMS) database finding that returns on research and development expenditure are likely to be highest in mature industries.

Finally, there are indications that organic growth is declining in importance as a method of international expansion: a rise in takeover activity in mature industries especially; and more international agreements between major companies to expand their presence in one or more of three main trading areas, Europe, North America or the Pacific basin, with the growth of 'triad power'. It is interesting that the historically low level of Japanese takeover activity before the 1970s altered steadily during the late 1980s. This was partially due to the strength of the yen in international markets but was also a reflection of the reduced opportunities for growth in the main trading blocks.

Conclusions: downwave or upwave?

The use of wave theory as a model of economic activity to forecast future changes in the world economy is supported, at least in part, by changes in the market in the late 1980s. Whether the downwave will be as bad as is suggested by some authors is debatable.[13] Opponents of wave theory suggest that such models are no longer valid, for a variety of reasons. First, the professional approach of management will ensure that research is more effectively focused than it was in earlier economic periods, and secondly, new technologies will continually evolve Phoenix-like from the ashes of the old in a never-ending upsurge of economic activity. To support this view they mention new developments like the breakthroughs in the development of superconductivity, and the growth of biotechnology.

Their role ranks high in the potential contribution to future product evolution. One futurology survey in 1988 gave potential changes in order of probability (see Table 2.16). Another suggested that the most likely developments could be separated into the further development of four technologies, biotechnology, energy, advanced materials, and information, highlighting progress in certain key

Table 2.16 Potential product
developments by 2000

Computers recognizing handwriting
Voice-controlled telephones
Colour fax
Combined telephone/computer/TV
Voice-controlled computers
Picture telephones
Gesture-controlled computers
Flat desktop computers
Translation telephones
Defeat of heart disease
Defeat of Aids virus
Defeat of rheumatoid arthritis
Defeat of leukaemia and lung cancer

Source: Fortune, November 1988

areas (see Table 2.17). Those sceptical about the contribution of such areas to economic growth point quite rightly to the failure of the biotechnology companies to make major commercial advances since the discovery of the genetic code in 1953 by Watson and Crick; and to the progressive downturn in growth in the computer industry — one of the key growth generators of the 1960s, 1970s and early 1980s — with a decrease in revenue growth from an annual 30 per cent in 1983 to a pedestrian 8 per cent in 1988. As a result, profitability declined from around 20 per cent return on equity in 1983 to 14 per cent in 1988, a figure below the average returns for leading firms in the United States.

More realistic perhaps is the argument that a more highly skilled and technically competent labour force will more effectively exploit minor technical advances and change in other product areas to produce new variants. Thus, changes in

Table 2.17 Developments to 2000

Biotechnology:	Single cell protein
	Bioengineering
	Biomass
	Medical diagnostics
	Pharmaceuticals
Energy technology:	Heat pumps
	Solar energy
	Coal gasification
	Renewable energy sources
	Monitoring and control
Advanced materials:	Biocompatible material
	Advanced composites
	New materials for electronics
	Superconductivity
Information technology:	Electronic office equipment
	Fibre optics
	Satellite developments

Source: R. Rothwell, 'Engineering Technologies', *Second International Technical Innovation and Entrepreneurship Symposium, 1987*

the type of paints and the design of household fittings and fixtures has meant a vast expansion in the variety of DIY tools — no longer is it possible to have a single piece of equipment with a variety of attachments. Opponents to the theory of universal decline also point to the connection between technology and minor alterations in technical standards and regulatory pressures which inevitably create opportunities for major change in many areas of business. Any business will be aware of how alterations in operating systems affected the demand for new computers and software. Another example is the development programme to improve the quality of television picture reception, High Definition Television (HDTV). Japanese proposals to change television screens from the current 625 lines to 1,125 threatens to make an estimated 700 million television sets obsolete. The development of reusable compact discs, similarly offers up whole new market sectors.

On a more mundane level, proposed changes in regulatory climate would have forced the UK Football League to introduce identity cards and electronic turnstiles to reduce football hooliganism. Above all, sceptics point to the fact that no product sector can ever be considered unchangeable, with advancing technology continually making an impact on even the most apparently stable sectors, and the fact that futurology has never been a science — many commentators would question whether it was even an art. Thus, futurologists of the early twentieth century failed to identify any of the growth areas perhaps because they were preoccupied with possibilities that still remain at best theoretical. Even the most basic products offer significant scope for product change (see Table 2.18).

Perhaps economic historians of the future will be able to point to a single factor

Table 2.18 Changes in deodorants since the 1880s

	1888	1900	1930	1940
Development	Launch of Mum	Everdry antiperspirant	Arrid antiperspirant	Stoppette Spray
Advantages	Zinc oxide kills bacteria	Aluminium chloride reduces wetness	Dried rapidly	Easy to apply
Disadvantages	Messy	Stinging, staining, messy	Had to be applied with fingers	Cold and dried slowly

	1950s	1960s	1970s	Present
Development	Ban Roll On	Gillette Right Guard	Deodorant sticks	Antiperspirant solids
Advantages	Fast drying	Not sticky	Controls wetness easy to apply	Controls wetness easy to apply Environment-friendly
Disadvantages	Poor control on wetness	Harm ozone layer	White residue	White residue

Source: Trade and Author

and clearly identify the exact point at which economic prosperity peaked or started to regenerate. Corporate planners of the late twentieth century do not have that advantage. Uncertainty is the only certainty when forecasts of product change and economic growth are considered. Twelve years ago there were no compact discs, no video recorders, no personal computers, and no fashion sportswear. Three years previously there were no fax machines; five years, few portable telephones. The next twelve years may provide examples of similar industrial sectors developing from often unfortunate beginnings. On the other hand they may not, which is perhaps comforting for the philosopher but useless to the businessman. For them the economic reality is clear; increasing competition and a hostile business environment will demand greater and greater attention to the new-product development process, and more concentration on understanding the environment in which the organization is operating, and what potential avenues for change in reality exist.

Notes

1. P. Cecchini *et al.*, *The European Challenge 1992*, (Aldershot: Wildwood House, 1988).
2. K. Ohmae, *Triad Power*, (New York: The Free Press, 1985).
3. H. Pickersgill, *ICI: The Awakening Giant*, (Oxford: Blackwell, 1986) J. Harvey-Jones, *Making Things Happen*, (London: Collins, 1988).
4. For a comprehensive discussion of developing competitiveness see M.E. Porter, *The Competitiveness of World Markets*, (New York: The Free Press, 1990).
5. For an excellent example see P. Dicken, *Global Shift*, (London: Harper & Row, 1986).
6. National Economic Development Organisation, *The Chemical Industry*, (London: NEDO, 1987).
7. M.E. Porter, *Competitive Strategy*, (New York: The Free Press, 1980).
8. P. Dicken (1986), p. 289.
9. J.C. Blackburn, 'The UK Clothing Sector and the Relaunch of BHS' in A. West (ed.), *Handbook of Retailing*, (Aldershot: Gower Publishing, 1988), pp. 44−62.
10. L. Watkins and R.M. Worcester, *Private Opinions, Public Polls*, (London: Thames & Hudson, 1986), p. 150.
11. A. West, *Managing Distribution and Change*, (Chichester: Wiley, 1989), p. 141.
12. The post-industrial society is discussed at some length in D. Bell, *The Coming of Post Industrial Society*, (London: Penguin Books, 1976).
13. R. Beckman, *The Downwave*, (London: Pan, 1983).

3
Setting the scene:
the demands of innovation

Introduction

A hostile environment means that businesses and other institutions must actively intervene to try to manage both their responses to change from the outside and to be ready to support and nurture change from within. There are two main issues: what type of change, and what is its management component?

Historically, the impetus for innovation came from alterations in the pattern of customer demand or from the activities of competitors in the market. A 1950s survey clearly identifies this pattern of product change (see Table 3.1). Here we see that most product innovation was *reactive* with the company accepting a product development agenda imposed by its rivals, or by changes in the market place. This accounted for the majority of reported innovations. Only a small percentage of the total was *active* or *entrepreneurial* with the organization leading the market, with other types of change occurring because the organization has *planned* to cope with the demands of customers, material shortage, or labour problems. (This supports Hutzler's Refutation that desperation rather than necessity is the mother of invention!)

Similar surveys for the 1980s reveal that, if anything, the competitive or reactive influence has increased — recent recessions reducing the importance of innovation in meeting increases in demand or shortages of raw materials. Changes in overall demand will remain an important factor in driving certain types of innovation, but what is clear from these surveys is that the key factor determining most innovation is the effect of competition. However, the only conclusion to be drawn from the earlier analysis of the competitive forces operating in the market is that the entrepreneurial component of innovation will become more important, and that companies should attempt to control the market by looking for and introducing changes that are entrepreneurial rather than merely reactive.[1] Though change is unfortunately inconvenient, and for most managers, whether in small or large

Table 3.1 Reasons for innovation

Component	% of reported innovation
Demand led innovation:	
Desire to overcome labour shortage	5
Desire to overcome materials shortage	12
Desire to meet excess demand	10
Competitive led innovation:	
Demands by customers for new product types	12
Direct pressure of competition	10
Force of example of firms in other market sectors	33
Internally generated innovation:	
Desire to use work of research and development dept	18

Source: Carter and Williams, *Investment in Innovation*, 1971

companies, thoroughly upsetting and to be avoided wherever feasibly possible, it will become more and more a part of corporate and national existence; but inevitably some will persistently fail to adjust.[2]

As the level of competition increases so does the level of risk — markets become less attractive investments because they promise a lower level of profitability and greater uncertainty about the pay-back period on investments. Businesses will therefore need to be much more careful in defining and controlling innovation, and national governments more sensible in their approach to encouraging and supporting innovative enterprise. Though there is a significant degree of overlap the main issues in need of consideration are as follows:

1. The type of innovation strategy that the firm should consider — what area of product change it should concentrate on.
2. The resource requirements for achieving particular types of innovation.
3. The overall complexity of innovation.
4. The management demands of achieving planned levels of performance, with the change occurring on time, on budget and to specification.
5. The acceptance of the overall level of success and failure inherent in any investment, and particularly in the introduction of change.

Strategy

Much that has been written about innovation has concentrated on the 'major events' — the romantic discovery of the penicillin mould in a contaminated Petri dish; the largely accidental discovery of radiation sources in pitchblende by the Curies; and the fact that a worker at Raytheon had his foil-covered chocolate bar cooked while working on radar research, leading to the development of microwave cookers. Far less attention has been given to the strategic implications of either the slow accretion of small changes to established products or product concepts:

the way they are manufactured and brought to market, although this constitutes the vast majority of alterations in the physical nature of products or other innovative components. Even far less interest is apparent in considering changes that do not involve physical alterations in the product yet substantially improve the firm's position.

This inattention stems from a fundamental misconception about the true nature of the 'product'. Business managers tend to concentrate solely on a product's physical or performance characteristics as being of paramount importance. In some sectors and at some periods this is undoubtedly true. However focusing on such issues hides the fact that the product is much more than the sum of its physical characteristics. It includes to a greater or lesser extent additional perceptions of non-technical value, such as price, delivery, after sales service, and attitudes to the product as well, such as trust, image and perhaps aesthetic issues. Marketing man is often fond of describing a product as a 'bundle of benefits', a point that will be returned to as crucial for the definition of effective innovation management, as all new directions will need to start with an accurate description of what the eventual customer wants.

The myopia about the real nature of the product explains to a large extent why to the business manager technical innovation is not, and cannot be the sole criterion of success. Seemingly major discoveries or innovations may not have much impact, or worse for the profit-making organization, little return on the investment. For example, one of the most interesting innovative concepts of the 1960s was the hovercraft which promised a substantial market for air-cushion vehicles and their derivatives. The concept nearly 30 years later is still restricted to a very limited number of short water crossings and has yet to repay much of the substantial investment in developing the technology. RCA invested millions of dollars in the creation of the video disc, and similarly DuPont in the development of synthetic leather and silk. There are many other examples among the many armed services research projects throughout the world, producing substances such as silly putty which flows when hit and then re-solidifies, a compound which has yet to find a use (other than in the centre of a trial number of golf balls).

By contrast, a minor alteration in the configuration of a product may dramatically alter its commercial fortunes. Take, for example, the Sony Walkman. Here a product, simple in concept, required no new components or assembly skills but merely a reorganization of existing materials and techniques to produce a personal stereo. It is estimated that over 5 million units were sold in the United Kingdom alone, with a worldwide total of 27 million, by the end of 1988. Or consider the tremendous growth in leisure footwear, a new industry developed by Nike and Adidas; repackaging by Cadburys of their plain chocolate assortments into a new triangular blue box (Biarritz increased sales by 30 per cent in the first year). Heinz introduced the plastic sauce bottle to similar rapturous applause from both trade and consumer. A flexible plastic device to prevent snoring is set to become an international best seller. Rank Hovis McDougall long claimed the reformulation of Bisto gravy products in granule form as the most successful product innovation amongst a range of new sauces, extruded biscuit products and others. In the early

1980s Birds Eye, faced with a declining share of the frozen pea market, succeeded in branding the product via an innovative advertising campaign which largely stabilized its market share for the rest of the decade. Or consider a company like the small French ski company Degre 7, which carved out a profitable niche by producing fluorescent coloured figure-hugging ski suits which sold throughout the skiing world.

All management operating in the competitive, rapidly changing world, must accept that there is no golden continuing rule for a successful change, or as Carl Lagerfeld, the founder of Lagerfeld Perfumes stated, 'there is no logic in innovation'. The value of the innovation must be rooted in its commercial viability, and its ability to capture a greater share of a competitive market place, rather than in some intellectual perception of its value as a 'new concept'. Any commercial organization must view innovation as a continuum from the highest levels of investment in basic research to the smallest changes in the format or presentation of particular existing products, their manufacture or support in the market. In effect this means appropriate types of innovation strategy being applied at particular times for individual companies, but no single type of innovation being inherently 'better' or 'worse' than any other. Even the most apparently mundane innovation can receive substantial attention which will be reflected in sales. The Central Office of Information which handles press releases for UK products overseas, identified two products that had received substantial attention in 1987; one was a plastic cap with a lip that could fit over soft drink cans to prevent spillage while drinking, the other was a new type of bird scarer. Even a new form of canine repellent (with the trade mark Dogoff) had received more attention than the traditional concepts of innovative machinery and equipment. Long-term commercial success or profit must therefore be the innovation yardstick rather than some concept of business prestige. Emphasis by Apple Computers on the Mackintosh as a direct competitor to the IBM PC almost brought the company to its knees; but a successful marriage of hardware and software systems enabled the company to practically create and continue to lead a desktop-publishing market with a forecast value of $12 billion in 1992, of which Apple's share is 20–25 per cent.

The service economy adds a further dimension to the perceptions of the value of innovation; the McDonalds fast-food concept, has been in commercial terms highly innovative, as much so as the development of nylon by DuPont, and no observer of the impact of innovation should attempt to value one above the other, even though there still remains a lurking belief in many quarters (especially governmental) that the only real innovation occurs in highly capital demanding ventures. The Japanese, however, recognize the equality between service and product innovation and the Nikkei awards for excellence in new product development normally include a range of services. The items for 1985 were no exception, and those receiving the highest commendation 'Most Excellent' are included in Table 3.2.

The narrow historic view of innovation affects major institutions/governments and individual companies alike. Within a company it can lead to a blinkered

Table 3.2 Nikkei awards for innovative excellence, 1985

American Family Life: Senile Dementia Assurance Policy
Aucnet: On-line computer videodisc network for buying and selling second-hand cars
Calpis: Hicellent — wine and fermented drink product
Casio: Pella — ultra-thin watch
Fresh System: Telephone order/home delivery system for fresh food
Fujitsu: VP50 supercomputer
Hoya: Optic fibre junctions
Japan Tourist Bureau: 'Tabi Tabi' — tourist ticket system
Minato Sangyo: Anico household deodorant
Minolta: Alpha 7000 autofocus camera
Matsushita: Panamemo 107 telephone
Plus Corp: Copyjack-photocopier
Shin-Etsu: Pheromone Insecticide
Sony: CCD-M8 Video System
Sumo Hall: New wrestling venue

Source: Asahi Daily News, March 1986

approach which causes it to ignore the many alternative paths that may exist.
Rolls-Royce, for example, had a board of directors entirely made up of aero engine
engineers before 1970. Their philosophy was that success lay in designing bigger
and bigger engines. This insistence on the continuation of a single investment
route eventually led to one of the largest company failures in post-war British
engineering and the company being taken into public ownership. The general point
is that profitable innovation can be achieved through a number of different
approaches, and that success with one project or one project direction will not
automatically lead to similar successes in the future. Attitudes and approaches
to innovation must be constantly reviewed and no potential avenue ignored merely
because some other approach worked in the past. Preconceptions about effective
innovation and a dedication to the old and trusted approaches which succeeded
in the past will often be a recipe for failure. It is common to find that the story
of dynamic company success trumpeted in one popular management book of last
year is often heralded as the current problem story in a management book of the
current year. Strategies for change cannot therefore remain static, and must reflect
the interrelationship of business resource and market. The changing market will
present continually different problems which will require different solutions. By
matching the market demands with the available resources a commercial
organization will be able to define the most appropriate route for the development
of new products and concepts.

Resource requirements

Strategy relates to resources in two ways; an organization must be aware of its
resource base to define strategy, and then it has to have the resources in place
to implement it. Resource analysis goes beyond the purely financial to include

personnel and systems.[3] It has recently been summarized as the concept of core competence which will be further discussed in Chapter 7.

Because of the complexity of the resource-base issue any interrelationship between gross expenditure on research and development and the level of financial return is likely to be fairly tenuous. First, few studies indicate a clear relationship between R & D investment and profitability which is supported by the analysis of the levels of expenditure and return in any one particular sector. For example, in the electronics industry there is a much wider variation in profit margins than there is in levels of investment on research and development, as Table 3.3 indicates. Secondly, though there is evidence for the linkage between R & D expenditure and profitability in the large PIMS study, the relationship is an indirect one. The database has clearly shown a strong relationship between R & D expenditure and growth in market share, higher relative product quality, and a higher rate of new product introduction.[4] Other PIMS studies indicate a strong relationship between high levels of market share and improved profitability, together with the fact that higher quality enables the firm to charge higher prices, so potentially improving profitability.[5] It should be noticed in passing that the PIMS studies have been subject to whole series of criticisms, with the result that many of the findings are suspect.

However, it is clear that the highest rates of research and development expenditure have been in the most rapidly growing industries, suggesting a potentially strong link between research and development and sales. This is supported by a ten-year study which still failed to find a strong relationship between R & D expenditure and profitability (see Table 3.4). In the short term in some

Table 3.3 Some examples of comparable R & D expenditure and profit margin, 1988

Company	R & D margin on sales	Profit margin on sales
Siemens	10	3
GE	10	9
IBM	10	10
Fujitsu	9	2
CGE	8	3
NEC	8	3
A.T.&T	7	6

Source: Business Week, 20 February, 1988

Table 3.4 Relationship between R & D expenditure and ten years' sales growth

R & D expenditure %	Leaders	Also-rans	Laggards
4+	55	42	1
3–4	48	33	9
<2	28	33	39

Source: G.K. Morbey, Journal of Prod. Innov. Management, 5, 1988

industries such a relationship can be established. For example, in UK clothing retailing, companies classed as innovative had a higher return on capital employed from 1982−87. However, since 1987 such companies' performance has been significantly below the market average. This suggests that the inevitable time lag effects in research and development expenditure will make any clear relationship even more difficult to define. Such effects have been identified in many industries.[6] One can therefore conclude that though there is a broad link between sales and research and development expenditure, exact relationships change over time and differ greatly from industry to industry and from firm to firm.[7]

The absence of a clear relationship between expenditure on research and development and effective new product performance lies in the 'how' of the investment, rather than its total level. This is underlined by the choices governments make in national investment policy, with many directions yielding poor results even though expenditure has been maintained at a very high level over a number of years. The role of the national government in setting national strategy and helping with the provision of resources is described in Chapter 6.

The various elements within the 'how' of expenditure yield more positive relationships. There is a strong connection between sales and level of patent activity as revealed in detailed analyses of UK industry in the early 1980s.[8] The studies showed a close connection between patent activity and sales in a whole range of high-technology industries. The main sectors and the degree of correspondence is included in Table 3.5. It is clear that in high-technology areas, industrial investment in developing new patent concepts will have a significant effect on the overall level of economic performance. Such patent activity does imply a significant level of expenditure in research and development and, as might be expected, the number of companies or organizations involved in significant levels

Table 3.5 Relationship of per capita patent activity to per capita export sales (ignoring defence technology)

Significant relationships	Non-significant
Special industrial machinery	Misc. electrical
Drugs	Plastic materials
Metalworking machinery	Radio and TV receivers
Engines	Household electrical
Instruments	Rubber products
Electrical industrial apparatus	Farm machinery
Industrial organic chemicals	Textiles
Soaps and cleaning products	Misc. transport equipment
Misc. chemical products	Non-ferrous metals
General industrial machinery	Agricultural chemicals
Fabricated metal products	Stone, clay, glass products
Motor vehicles	Food
Railroad equipment	Bicycles
Misc. machinery	Paint
Refrigeration products	Ship and boat building

Source: K. Pavitt, *Technical Innovation and British Economic Performance*, 1980

Table 3.6 Percentage of US patents by UK-based company 69—72 and 81—84 by company

Rank	1969—72	1981—84
1	ICI	ICI
2	Lucas	Lucas
3	GEC	NRDC
4	NRDC	Beechams
5	ITT	Rolls-Royce
6	Rolls-Royce	GEC
7	BP	Ciba-Geigy
8	Dunlop	ITT
9	Philips Petroleum	BP
10	Pilkington	Unilever
11	Plessey	UKAEA
12	Molins	MOD
13	UKAEA	NCB
14	UIS	Thorn-EMI
15	Ciba-Geigy	Plessey
16	Thorn-EMI	Glaxo
17	UK Govt	Dunlop
18	British Steel	Molins
19	Courtaulds	IBM
20	Dowty	Shell
Total percentage of patents	37.22	35.84

Source: National Institute for Science and Economic Research

of patenting are relatively small. This is confirmed in an analysis of the concentration of patent activity within the United Kingdom which shows the top twenty organizations contributing nearly 40 per cent of total patent activity (see Table 3.6). As might be expected, there are also strong correlations between the investment that the company makes in specific levels of scientific performance. For example, research suggests that the greater the number of elite scientists the greater the chance of effective sales growth especially in high-technology companies (see Table 3.7). The resource implication for the company is that recruitment and maintenance of a strong and effective science base should emphasize concrete performance measurement — patents, research papers and the like. The importance of this particular factor and how the company should

Table 3.7 Correlation between patents, publications (papers), sales and elite scientists in three groups of companies

	Patents/sales and papers/sales	Scientists/sales and papers/sales	Scientists/sales and patents/sales
Company type			
High tech.	0.30	0.63	0.33
Capital intensive	0.67	0.67	0.61
Resource intensive	0.15	0.63	0.17

Source: R.G. Cooper, *R & D Management*, 28(2), 1987

develop an organization that encourages such concrete performance will be discussed in later chapters.

This pattern has significant implications for both national and corporate investment in change. It clearly defines the role of national governments in supporting large organizations as the prime source of technical advance; small companies cannot realistically be expected to provide the sort of effective resource base essential to wide-scale research and development programmes. At the corporate level it makes the issue of specialization in the area of technical change and the concentration on non-technical factors to gain competitive advantage even more important.

An example of a major industrial sector in the late twentieth and earlier twenty-first century demonstrates the implications of resource base. By the year 2005 European high-speed rail networks should consist of around 30,000 km of line, 19,000 of which will be upgraded or new. The total investment involved is estimated to be £70 billion with an additional £20 billion in rolling stock. The companies that will be able to take advantage of such a market and meet the demands for more efficient and effective products are those that are either broadly resourced across the entire range of specialization required such as CGE of France or Siemens of Germany, or those that specialize in specific areas of component supply (Allusuisse of Switzerland is a world leader in the design and construction of high-performance railway bogies). By contrast, an organization such as British Rail lacks the resources either in skills or finance to develop and introduce high-speed rail systems. This is most clearly shown in a report of the first return Glasgow—London trip of the £37 million APT (Advanced Passenger Train). On its initial journey the tilting mechanism (designed to allow it to corner at high speed) failed three times, customers' drinks were continually spilt and interconnecting doors jammed. After further abortive trials the fleet of trains was withdrawn from service.

Table 3.8 Factors in successful commercialization and product development

Main roadblocks to commercialization

Identification of consumer needs
Understanding of political and business motives within the organization
Company communications
The isolation of the research and development department
The failure to involve the appropriate people early in the process
Lack of early commitment to the project

Crucial factors in success/failure

Technical execution
Appropriate skills/resources for the type of change
The setting of appropriate objectives
Management involvement

Source: M. Wolf, *Research Management*, issue 4, 29, 1986

Table 3.9 'How vital have you found various factors in a major new product?'

Factor	%
Top management commitment	72
Development into consumer proposition	66
Initial idea	59
Sales force commitment	59
Distribution	57
Financial evaluation	48
Consumer research	48
Liaison throughout company	46
Pricing	46
Detailed implementation	44
Technical development	42
Consumer advertising	36
One senior executive leading project	32
Project champions within company	26
Monitoring after launch	26
Production efficiency	26

Source: KAE, *Financial Times*, 4 March 1985

Most of the quantitative research into the main causes of success and failure in developing and commercializing new products concentrates on other aspects of the resource environment.[9] For example, one in-depth study of a large number of projects suggested that the main 'roadblocks' to commercialization were people-oriented, as were the main factors in success and failure (see Table 3.8). These findings are consistent with those of many other studies; one in 1985 shows the involvement of management and interaction between members of the company as crucially important (see Table 3.9), and more detailed research looking at the importance of particular factors within the company as a correlation for possible success (Table 3.10). Time and again such surveys related success with how well the company understands the market, how committed it is to change at senior levels and how well the entire company is structured to communicate and develop new product concepts, rather than on pure financial or production capacity. These

Table 3.10 Correlation of new product performance with corporate resources

Resource factor	Success	Killed	Failed	% sales by new products	% sales to R & D efficiency
Financial	ns	ns	ns	ns	0.191
R&D	ns	ns	ns	0.242	ns
Engineering	ns	ns	ns	0.310	ns
Market research	0.324	−0.177	−0.293	ns	0.223
Management	0.287	−0.242	ns	ns	0.211
Salesforce/dist	0.265	ns	−0.254	ns	0.233
Advertising	0.359	−0.243	−0.262	ns	0.249

Source: R.G. Cooper, *Research Management*, 26(6), 1983

findings support anecdotal and personal experience that appropriate personnel policies are a fundamental resource for change — a point that is considered in more detail elsewhere in the text.

The resource demands of innovation are complex but identifiable. Understanding this makes it possible to define the type of resources needed for particular types of innovation policy and to allocate such resources in a sophisticated and committed way. The small company can adopt effective innovative policies to achieve competitive advantage as well as the larger, better-resourced organization. The large organization, though it can invest more heavily in the market than its smaller competitor, must still appreciate how its larger resources can be most effectively spent.

Complexity

The need for effective management of a complex process is very much in evidence in much of the literature on innovation.[10] Fundamental to this is the importance of a detailed understanding of the various stages through which a typical new or improved product can pass, and the demands that it will make on the organization (see Table 3.11). Defining the appropriate direction for innovation and creating the necessary resource environment is only part of the picture; organizations will have to set specific responsibilities for particular parts of the innovation process and effectively manage and monitor the transition from one stage to another. Though it may seem that the overall complexity of the task is self-defeating a number of studies show that the more detailed the analysis and preparation at the early stages of the introduction of new product, the greater the chances of success.[11] This means the correct resources being available at the right time and management skills and policies of a high quality to ensure that the organization can maximize its chance of success.

The complexity of new aircraft development is enormous, and success at a firm such as Boeing makes substantial demands upon management. Company staff must be able to define the performance requirements of all the tens of thousands of components that make up the finished product — electrics, electronics, airframe, engines, and internal fittings. They must also consider the interrelationship between these components and each other, and the demands of the external environment such as passenger and freight-handling requirements. Two examples are illustrative. Extending the range of the 747 in the development of the 747–SP obviously meant major changes in fuel storage, engine performance and total passenger load, to achieve the average thirteen-hour continuous flight. Such changed performance had, however, less obvious implications in other areas. One was in the design of the toilets which suffered from what was called 'odour fatigue' over the longer flight. Or take the potential implications of changing forward seating to rear-facing seats which are claimed to improve safety. Such seats would need to have higher backs to prevent whiplash effects, and these higher backs

Table 3.11 The main management components of innovation

Stage	Market issues	Business issues	Skills required	People involved
Concept	Does market exist?	Initial decision to develop	Market analysis Technical	Research Information manager
Concept Analysis	Define market	Funding for initial stage	Technical Marketing Engineering Finance	Development team Senior management
Working model	Define key improvements Contact key customers		Engineering Key accounts negotiation	Technicians Production Research development team
Engineering Prototype: • test • refine	Define barriers	Patent Start business plan	Engineering Legal Marketing Finance	Development team Senior management Production staff
Production Prototype: • test • refine • design for assembly	Marketing mix: • price • promotion • place • competition • segment service support	Compete business plan Finalize funding	Engineering Research Market analysis Finance Distribution Legal	Shopfloor Production engineer Sales force Senior management Marketing Advertising Distribution management
Limited production: • refine	Key customers Advertise	Monitor Control	All above, plus specialist engineering Market analysis	All company
Full production	Monitor	Monitor	All company	All company

Source: Adapted from H.C. Livesay, *Journal of Product Innovation Management*, 6, 1989

would make it nearly impossible to show in-flight entertainment on central video screens!

Meeting targets

A crucial factor in success is that companies make their innovation planning systems *work* to achieve those desired end results as identified in all the strategic planning, organization design and resource allocation systems. Those companies that cannot meet the required level of specification, cost, development timing and development budget will be unsuccessful in achieving effective new product development. The most important factors appear to be the ability to meet the required specification and to get to market on time, as the Kinsey model mentioned in the previous chapter suggested. A more detailed study suggested that cost is also important (see Table 3.12).[12] Achieving performance targets means concentrating on the effective management of product change instead of assuming that expenditure on research and development will automatically lead to new product success. As competitors increasingly install new manufacturing equipment the technological period of grace (see pp. 15–16) is decreasing steadily, while the costs of failure rise.

Cultures, both national and corporate, where numeracy and planning are favoured tend to be more successful in both setting and achieving specific targets. Many Japanese companies by their recruitment and internal personnel policies have reinforcing systems whereby planning and implementation procedures are maintained to a high order. Specific industrial skills and market understanding is then built onto a basic core competence that exists to achieve specific goals within a defined time span. The combination of these two elements provides certain Japanese companies with a significant competitive advantage over organizations

Table 3.12 Success parameters in new product innovation

Performance specifications		Factory cost	
Exceed by 20 per cent	100	20 per cent below target	97
Exceed by 5 per cent	90	5 per cent below target	75
Fall short by 5 per cent	54	5 per cent over target	56
Fall short by 20 per cent	0	20 per cent over target	16
Development schedule		Development budget	
4 months early	83	Underspent by 20 per cent	74
6 weeks early	78	Underspent by 5 per cent	63
6 weeks late	60	Overspent by 5 per cent	63
4 months late	24	Overspent by 20 per cent	40

Source: M.D. Rosenau, *Journal of Product Innovation Management,* 5, 1988

that lack either the specific market skills, the ability to define accurately performance criteria and to meet particular market demands on time and price.

Success and failure

A major problem in the management of change at the corporate, national and academic levels is how to identify success or failure. One is faced with differing concepts as to what measurement should be used to identify performance, and gross differences as to the impact such failure can have on the corporation. An example of the first is a study of the various criteria that have been used to measure new product performance (see Table 3.13). Any student of company or national politics will know that changing the base for evaluation will often lead to a reappraisal of the success of a particular venture, and when there are at least ten possible alternative reclassifications, the field for 'creative adjustment' is wide indeed. Because of the complexities of costing systems and the problems of applying strict financial analysis to one product among many that normally share the same production plant, rule of thumb assessments tend to be used to categorize products instead of strict accounting principles.

Management concepts of success may also lead to a substantial overrecording of 'successes' in those products that have passed through all the development stages and have been fully launched. A great deal of management prestige and authority rests upon these products and many of the most costly product failures are the responsibility of management reluctance to accept the reality of marketplace rejection of the product. The problem is further complicated by different companies' perceptions of what is 'new'; the addition to frozen cod of basil rather than parsley sauce may be seen by one company as novel, whereas the replacement in a boiler of a cast-iron with an aluminium heat exchanger, a rather more difficult engineering problem, is not considered novel by another.

Once such issues have been resolved there is even dispute on the gross statistics of new product failure, with some studies suggesting that failure rates are

Table 3.13 Measures of success for new product introduction

Profitability
Pay-back period
Domestic market share
Foreign market share
Relative sales
Relative profits
Sales versus objectives
Window on new opportunities
Window on new markets

Source: Author

substantially lower than has previously been reported.[13] The historic view has been that new product developments have a very high failure rate, with the result that one is tempted to suggest that firms should never attempt to innovate; the potential risk and loss of investment are often so high that spare cash should be more providentially hidden under the mattress in the form of gold bars or converted into Impressionist paintings. The argument is often also a sterile one in that success or failure has very different implications for different sizes of company, and vary according to the type of market sector and company practice. It is always necessary to relate failure to the costs associated with that failure. An unsatisfactory range of speciality frozen food, such as the Green Dragon range of Chinese meals produced by Birds Eye, do not often involve the company in large losses, as the investment in research and development is limited and the manufacturing plant will be shared with other products. In such an instance a high rate of product failure may not be catastrophic in the short term, though annoying, expensive and time wasting. In contrast, the costs associated with failure of the float-glass system developed by Pilkington would have been very severe — the company had, by the time success was achieved, produced over 100,000 tons of unuseable glass, and invested millions of pounds in the process. If the process had not been ultimately successful, it might easily have led to the collapse of the company, something which Birds Eye did not face with the failure of frozen sweet-and-sour pork. So, although companies across different product sectors may show the same overall rate of product failure at various stages of the development process (see Table 3.14), the financial implications of this failure may be very different.[14] For the small company the problems of the innovation process are far more acute; they have fewer resources to spare than the large well-established company which may survive an unsuccessful or disastrous product introduction, whereas such failure will often be the death of the small company.

To illustrate the point that different sectors, regardless of their overall similarity in areas of product failure, experience very different investment outcomes, one can compare two extremes: the development of a pharmaceutical drug and the introduction of a new toiletries product. For the drug the cost emphasis is very clearly during the initial stages when safety and toxicity trials are completed. The relative costs of introducing the drug into the market are insignificant. In contrast,

Table 3.14 Rate of commercial success: the percentage of products that pass through each stage that are eventually classified by the company as 'successful'

Sector	New product ideas	Development phase	Commercialization
Chemical	2	18	59
Consumer goods	2	11	63
Electrical machinery	1	13	63
Metal producers	3	11	71
Non-electrical machinery	2	21	59
Raw material processors	5	14	59

Source: Booz, Allen and Hamilton, *Management of New Products*, 1968

for the consumer goods company the vast majority of the cost load occurs during the commercialization phase, when substantial sums can be spent on advertising and promotion. Even here the situation will vary from company to company. Thus Procter & Gamble will have an entirely different approach — because of its philosophy of heavily supporting brands — to Black & Decker with its emphasis on the ability of the product to find its own place in the market, accepting a higher rate of product failure with a lower level of investment during the commercialization phase. This partly explains some of the difference between companies in the consumer goods sector — Procter & Gamble — that achieve a higher success rate in commercialization of their products than others. But though Procter & Gamble's 60 per cent success rate with products that have passed through the entire testing procedure is substantially higher than other competitors in the grocery/toiletries sector (comparatively 16−20 per cent), the investment reality is that Procter & Gamble *must* have a higher success rate to survive because of its much heavier investment during the commercialization phase. Again, profitability is the important factor to be considered, rather than some hypothetical scoring rate. To underline the importance of financial return rather than numerical success in product introduction, one can note that Black & Decker in the United Kingdom is a highly profitable operation whereas Procter & Gamble is not.

Despite these variations in assessing product change a number of common threads can be identified. As might be expected, the highest numerical rates of product failure occur right at the beginning of their development, but as the investment at this stage is normally limited the cost of failure is small. Far more substantial is the level of loss incurred in the development phase of the project, which accounts for nearly half of the total lost investment in new product development. It is only during the commercialization phase that 'success' outweighs 'failure', and even here perhaps some of the reported difference may not be so great. One survey of expenditure patterns at various stages of development is included in Table 3.15.

For the company considering new product innovation in the 1990s the matching of resource to different types of change will become more and more important. As the organization becomes more able to direct such operations effectively, success is much more likely than failure; where the organization fails to appreciate the different opportunities that exist each with their own resource requirements failure is probable.

Table 3.15 Expenditure within category as a percentage of total overall expenditure on innovation

	Analysis	Development	Testing	Commercialization	Total
Successful	1	12	4	11	28
Unsuccessful	14	45	6	7	72
Total	15	57	10	18	100

Source: Booz, Allen and Hamilton, *Management of New Products*, 1968

Knowledge wars

It has been suggested that the majority of companies are likely to double the rate of new product introduction during the next decade.[15] As companies assess their potential for profitable innovation in this climate it is inevitable that the management of knowledge will become more and more important. At the corporate level, the maintenance of a knowledge edge will be crucial to accurate assessment of all the factors involved in innovation management, enabling the company to generate high levels of value-added products and services to achieve higher profits, higher wages and greater dominance in the marketplace. Service companies will survive and prosper through their skills in identifying requirements for new developments and allocating the appropriate resources, as will the most advanced manufacturing concern. The common characteristics of investment management and detailed planning of innovation will become one of the most crucial skills of the late twentieth and twenty-first centuries. The successful competitor will be the one that is able to build and maintain competitive advantage in an increasingly competitive world, and this competitive edge will be defined by knowledge — the ability to understand the market better, the way in which the firm can provide higher-value-added products, and the management of the change that has been decided upon. Such alteration in attitudes will require a substantial change from traditional approaches to product development towards new concepts of management (see Table 3.16).[16]

Table 3.16 Directions for change in the new product development process

Old concepts	New concepts
Strategy	
Reliance on technical change	Perception of range of alternative, technical and non-technical benefits
Focus on product features	Focus on product benefits
Concentration on low or high risk projects	Balanced portfolio of projects
Projects geared to long-term returns	Increasing emphasis on speed and effectiveness in many areas
Intermittent demands for new product concepts	Continuous demands for new product concepts
Evaluation	
Narrow information base	Information base appropriate for strategy
Single disciplinary R & D team	Wide-ranging group relevant to product needs
Limited customer involvement	Much closer customer contact in most projects
Lack of internal supporting structures	Increasing emphasis on structures automatically encouraging change
Commercialization	
Commercialization separate from evaluation	Process integrated
Rigid process	Flexible commercialization process differing for each project

Source: Y. Wind and V. Mahajan, *Journal of Product Innovation Management*, 5, 1988

Table 3.17 Strategic approaches to new product development

1. Develop an understanding of the demands of different types of innovation.
2. Appreciate the market dynamics and what constitutes an attractive market for innovation investment.
3. Consider the resources, both corporate and national, that are available to support particular innovation routes.
4. From these facts decide on the most sensible area in which to concentrate investment for new product development.
5. Develop the appropriate organizational response to this innovation route.
6. Organize the appropriate information to identify the best possibilities in the market within the innovation area.
7. Match product benefit to customer demand.
8. Identify appropriate testing procedure for the chosen innovation route.

Source: Author

Management must concentrate on developing strategies to identify specific areas of new product development, and from that develop the necessary organization, information framework, design, development and testing procedures to gain and maintain competitive advantage. These steps are itemized in Table 3.17.

Notes

1. The role of political systems in opening markets to competitive influence is discussed in M.E. Porter, *Competitive Strategy*, (New York: The Free Press, 1980). The point is emphasized in P. Drucker, *Innovation and Entrepreneurship*, (New York: Harper & Row, 1985). C.F. Carter, B.R. Williams, *Investment in Innovation* (London: Macdonald, 1971).
2. Interesting studies of these organizations are in M. Meyer, *Permanently Failing Organisations*, (New York: Sage Publications, 1989).
3. For a detailed check list of the issues involved in the development of a business or marketing strategy see A. West, *Cases in Marketing Techniques*, (London: Paul Chapman, 1988). G.D. Smith, D.R. Arnold and B.G. Bizzell, *Strategy and Business Policy*, (Boston, Mass.: Houghton Mifflin, 1985). D. Collier *et al.*, 'How Effective is Technological Innovation?' in *Research Management*, issue 5, 27, (1984), 61−87.
4. For a detailed discussion of the PIMS findings see D.F. Abell and A. Hammond, *Marketing Strategy*, (Englewood Cliffs, NJ: Prentice Hall, 1982).
5. A. Parasuranan and L.M. Zeren, 'R & D Relationship with Profit and Sales', *Research Management*, issue 1, 26 (1983), pp. 37−42.
6. A detailed analysis of UK industry over a decade failed to find any clear correlation in this area. See G.A. Luffman and R. Reed, *Strategy and Performance in British Industry 1970−1980*, (London: Macmillan, 1984).
7. Two empirical studies of UK innovation found that there was a relationship between the past growth rate of the firm, its overall size and the technological opportunity apparent in the industry. See N. Kay, *The Innovating Firm*, (London: Macmillan, 1979) and N. Kay, *The Emergent Firm*, (London: Macmillan, 1982). It is thought that the size of a firm can be a limiting factor in effective innovation, with organizations having more than 11,000 employees showing a reduced rate of radical new product

innovation. See J.E. Ettlie and A.H. Rubenstein, 'Company Size and Effective Innovation', *Journal of Product Innovation Management*, issue 2, 4, (1987), pp. 159—80. The relationship between expenditure and effectiveness is further confused by the fact that as the overall level of expenditure increases, the rate of return declines, with an optimum existing for each industry which will change from time to time as competitive pressures alter. Thus it has been suggested that the optimum level of expenditure for the chemical industry is likely to be around 4 per cent of sales; on electronics 6 per cent; and computers around 10 per cent. See C.C. Wallin and J.J. Gilman, 'Interrelationships between R & D Expenditure and Effectiveness in Certain Industrial Sectors', *Research Management*, issue 2, 30 (1987), pp. 28—37.

8. K. Pavitt (ed.), *Technical Innovation and British Economic Performance*, (London: Macmillan, 1980).

9. M. Wolf, 'Commercialisation Factors in Product Development', *Research Management*, issue 4, 29 (1986), pp. 54—69.

10. R.R. Rothberg (ed.), *Corporate Strategy and Product Innovation*, second edn (New York: The Free Press, 1981). G. Foxall, *Corporate Innovation*, (London: Croom Helm, 1984). N. Koncaglu, in R. Loveridge (ed.), *Managing Technological Innovation*, (Chichester: Wiley, 1989). H.C. Livesay *et al.*, 'Management Control and Innovation', *Journal of Product Innovation Management*, 6 (1989), pp. 365—81.

11. J. Hise *et al.*, 'Technical Development and the Innovation Process', *Journal of Product Innovation Management*, 6, (1989), pp. 327—40.

12. M.D. Rosenau, 'Success Parameters in Product Innovation', *Journal of Product Innovation Management*, 5 (1988), pp. 243—56.

13. C.M. Crawford, 'Levels of Success in Research and Development', *Research Management*, issue 4, vol. 30 (1987), pp. 16—32.

14. Booz, Allen and Hamilton, *Management of New Products*, company report, (Booz, Allen and Hamilton, 1968).

15. Booz, Allen and Hamilton, *New Product Management in the 1980s*, company report, (Booz, Allen and Hamilton, 1982).

16. Y. Wind and V. Mahajan, 'Management Perspectives in Innovation', *Journal of Product Innovation Management*, 5, (1988), pp. 270—84.

4

Innovation opportunities

Introduction

Because innovation is not a simple clear-cut process limited to simple technological advance in product management, approaches must be tailored to the demands of the market and company resources. No single solution will be suitable for all business areas and no organization should limit its thinking to one of the many options that exist across the entire range of its markets. We have, moreover, seen how rapidly company markets are changing as competition becomes fiercer and single and unchanging solutions within a particular business unit will often bring about eventual disaster. Each type of innovation policy will place different demands upon the organization, both financially and structurally. A company has a great deal to gain from an understanding of the demands of, and opportunities provided by, each particular type of innovation. From this base it will acquire the ability to evaluate the potential for each innovation type for each market and product area in which the company is involved, helping to define those areas where the company should be concentrating to maximize its available resources.

Main types of innovation

Any complex phenomenon is difficult to subdivide into neat, clearly separate packages, and innovation is no exception. Most analyses define it from the perspective of the marketplace instead of viewing innovation as a process involving a range of investment possibilities. Innovations have thus been separated variously into those that are continuous — involving little change in behaviour or product; those that entail change in customer behaviour but little change in product — termed dynamically continuous; and those requiring changes in both — discontinuous innovations. Other methods of division include a separation of innovation into those that are revolutionary, or those that are evolutionary. A further method of analysis is to consider innovations as occurring from either 'discovery push' or 'need pull', or incremental, technical, application derived or radical.[1]

However valuable such divisions are academically, they do little to aid the business in deciding on the investment policy appropriate to particular circumstances. It is surely more valuable to define types of innovation from the perspective of the organization instead of attempting to fit them into preconceived categories. For the business planner it is essential to identify the problems posed by different types of innovation in relation to resource requirements both of capital and skill, to the level of risk, to the rate of potential return, to the speed at which the innovation must be brought to market, to the problems of controlling the development process, and most especially to the type of market conditions best suited to different types of policy. This approach to innovation is pragmatic and practical. It measures the value of an innovation in purely commercial terms, identifying organizational needs and the likely advantages. It attempts to define innovation as a market-led issue, but one that *leads to the development of competitive advantage*, not one that concentrates on duplicating the activities by licensing or other forms of technological transfer. When considering the demands made by a programme of innovation within an organization it is possible to identify nine broad categories of change which are distinct in their demands from others (see Table 4.1). Though the majority of innovation can be placed within single categories, a continuum of activity will inevitably mean that some innovations will overlap with other categories.

Sector creating innovations

Sector creating innovations essentially 'break the mould' and open up new markets. The replacement of the vacuum tube by the transistor is a case in point — the durability of the transistor meant it could be used in a much wider range of product areas. Penicillin also opened up an entirely new sector of the drugs market, as have cortisones and steroids. Companies innovating in this way achieve profitable returns by producing a product that is so significantly different from the competition that the time that the development takes is less crucial than in other types of innovation, providing *uniqueness is the sole criteria for product introduction*. Innovations that take many years to produce and are not sufficiently distinct will be extremely expensive mistakes.

Sector creating innovations are often characterized by the development of new types of materials — ceramics, artificial fibres, semiconductors, steel, crystals, organic compounds are all examples of products that have been fundamental in generating significant economic development. Innovations of this type rarely if ever have a smooth path to universal acceptance — the phrase 'build a better

Table 4.1 Types of innovation

Sector creating innovation	Performance extending innovation
Branding innovation	Technological reorganization innovation
Reformulation	Process innovation
Design innovation	Packaging innovation
Service innovation	

Source: Author

mousetrap and the world will beat a path to your door' does not work in practice. The slow penetration of dramatically different products is caused by market conservatism, the slow acceptance by consumers of the potentialities of the product, the initially high costs of the innovation, and the limited awareness of the manufacturer of the broader market potential. The development of the integrated circuit is one of the best examples of these phenomena. Since its discovery in the Bell Laboratories in the 1950s, costs per processing unit have fallen over 100,000 times — with a 100 times reduction in cost forecast to the end of the century. At the same time, the microprocessor has entered more and more market sectors — watches, cars, televisions, aircraft and even by the mid-1980s, the humble lawn mower.

These changes in product cost and usage have made a nonsense of initial market estimates; RCA in the mid-1950s estimated the total world demand for computers was unlikely to be more than 5,000 per year by the end of the 1960s. Though the recent growth in the practically universal application of the microprocessor has been staggering, it suffered in common with other sector creating innovations in having a long period in gathering momentum in those manufacturing sectors where it was eventually accepted. The result of this slow initial acceptance phase is that the growth pattern of sector developing innovations tends to occur in a series of steps, as the product finds wider and wider applications. A classic example of such a development is the growth in the consumption of nylon. The result of the slow growth in demand characteristic of such products is that companies must accept this as a fundamental part of the planning process when directing their strategy into such areas; long pay-back periods will be the norm rather than the exception.

The characteristics of sector creating innovations are clear. They can provide the originator with a substantial protectable property via patents, or in certain instances copyright, enabling a long run of profitability before the patents exhaust. The effectiveness of such patents depends on the broadness of their original scope. Polaroid managed to win a long and expensive — for the loser, Kodak — court battle on the protection of the instant film, but other patent protections have been less effective. One example was working through the US legal system in 1988 — the attempt by biotechnology companies to gain protection for particular genes produced in their laboratories, which up to now have had no protection once they enter the broad animal or plant population.

Regardless of patent protection, the research lead that can be established allows the company a period of technological superiority over the competition and an often longer period of market domination in areas such as price and distribution. A favourite remark on the career of Lord Lever, the founder of the Lever empire in the nineteenth century was, 'where he led, he conquered, where he followed, he failed'. There are many examples of a company establishing a strong position by technical innovation which continues after the initial technical lead is established. Xerox, creating a new market sector of dry document copying was able eventually to cope with Japanese competition; if it had been second in the market it is unlikely that such a recovery would have been possible. Such anecdotal reports are supported by the PIMS database which shows clearly that return on capital employed increases in line with market share — a direct consequence of being first in the market with an innovation. The changing competitive climate outlined in previous chapters has obviously altered the pattern of a period of technological leadership followed by a period of market leadership, making fundamental research less attractive to all but the companies with the greatest resources.

To gain such clear defendable market positions the company has to invest heavily and continuously in skilled personnel, equipment and time — for all the blind alleys and turnings of the research process. Readers will have already noticed the enormous expenditure involved in the development of new pharmaceutical drugs (see p. 14). This takes no account of the substantial timescales that such developments involve: ICI in 1987 estimated that a new company entering the pharmaceutical business could not expect any worthwhile products or return on investment for over 23 years. Often, the investment will be increased by the production requirements of the new product which frequently cannot be made using existing manufacturing methods. However, this route remains viable even in the 1980s: Merck introduced five new treatments in 1987 alone with products for hypertension, ulcers, a new hepatitis vaccine, a new broad-spectrum antibiotic and a drug for certain urinary infections.

Companies like Merck have been far more successful than others in maintaining a flow of new concepts measured both by the rate of patent introduction and successfully commercialized products; other examples include Bell, 3M, DuPont, and the German chemical companies. The research groups employed by such companies show similar characteristics. Firstly, they are large — it seems that there is a clear minimum number of research personnel necessary to generate worthwhile synergistic effects. Studies of the development of new concepts within Silicon Valley suggest that a research staff of thirty may be the minimum viable within that industry with fifty to sixty in the chemical industry (see Chapter 6).[2] Unilever employs large research staffs in central locations to provide research support to its wide-ranging international operations, similarly finding that the concentration of research staff is essential for effective results.

Secondly, it seems essential to effective research groups that they operate in an atmosphere which maximizes conceptual rather than specific project progress.[3] Such an approach obviously entails sufficient flexibility to develop any particularly valuable product of the research group without excluding specific targeting of research areas and approaches to problems. Merck research, for example, concentrates on identifying the biochemical changes caused by disease and finding ways of preventing them from occurring. The staff who work best in such an environment are those most attracted by theoretical concepts — the 'pure' rather than 'applied' scientist. This type of individual will often work at a distance from the manufacturing centres of the company. The picture of the IBM researcher sitting under a tree and, it was claimed, thinking — a favourite corporate advertisement of the early 1980s — bears some resemblance to reality, as sector creating innovations can only rarely be translated directly into full-scale manufacturing and this encourages the separation between research and production. Thirdly, the open transfer of information within the research group is very important. Göttingen in Germany, and the Cavendish Laboratory at Cambridge both proved major centres of new concepts in the development of atomic fission, and both were characterized by open discussion and the flow of ideas.[4] The contribution of IBM research laboratories to the development of superconductivity and hard discs in the early and late 1980s is thought to result from improved internal communication between researchers. It is said that the failure of some pharmaceutical companies to develop new concepts is at least in part due to the obsessive, often pathological, secrecy within their research facilities reducing flexibility and interchange among researchers.[5] One comment made to the author on one such organization was that one set of researchers were frightened to greet each other during coffee and lunch breaks in case they might be exchanging information.

The role of publication in sector creating innovation is also important. German chemical companies concentrate on academic results, encouraging their research staff to publish and move between the pure academic environment of the universities and the research departments of major companies. This obviously has the effect of enhancing the effective size of the research pool of chemical companies since they can draw on individuals from academic institutions. Similar transfers occur in the United States. These interrelationships place a high value on innovative and, more importantly, independent thought rather than adherence to strict organizational guidelines. For the organization concentrating on true innovation the issue of speed to market is rarely a crucial one, as patent protection gives a clear period of technological advantage.

The result of these interacting components is that this type of innovation is subject to extremely high levels of risk and high levels of investment. Success may come — nylon for DuPont — but so may costly failures — artificial leather and silk. As the competitive environment intensifies, the risk will increase. Moreover, as the level of governmental support declines in many areas of fundamental research the risk becomes even more substantial for the commercial enterprise. Nuclear and renewable energy research is an area where the withdrawal of government support substantially increases risks for the commercial organization and is likely to reduce fundamentally the viability of such areas for successful commercial innovation. (The role of the national governments in developing and supporting research and development in specific areas is outlined in another chapter.) No commercial organization would be able to cope with the losses of the Dungeness B nuclear power station which started construction in 1963 and had yet to produce viable quantities of power in 1988.

Developments during the mid to late 1980s that may prove to be sector creating breakthroughs include the progress with superconducting materials spearheaded by IBM's research laboratories, the announcement of the optical chip by the glass company Pilkington, the production of a plastic material that will store electricity from BASF, the German chemical multinational, and the continuing research on low-weight battery systems, and perhaps further developments of the aeroglass concept, GE's further development of artificial diamonds as a possible processor, and the development by Bayer of replacements for transmissions, shock absorbers and other mechanical devices with a colloid that changes consistency in a controlled fashion in an electric field.

Glaxo has been one of the most rapidly growing pharmaceutical companies in the world. Its turnover has increased from £397 million in 1979 to an annualized rate of over £2.5 billion in 1989. It has achieved this substantial progress by becoming a focused research and development company concentrating on gastrointestinal, respiratory and infectious diseases. The number of research scientists employed has increased from 2,000 in 1985 to 5,000 by late 1989. Spending on research and development grew at a compound rate of 45 per cent per year, with a total expenditure between 1984 and 1989 of $1.7 billion. Once a drug with promise has been isolated, the research staff are set specific tasks to aid the drug through the complex regulatory procedure. Though heavily dependent on an anti-ulcer drug Zantac the company has developed a list of new products: Sumatripin which relieves migraine headaches, an estimated $750 million market, and Salmetrol, relieving asthma attacks, an estimated $500 million market, being two of the more important.

Performance extending innovation

The history of technical advances reveals that they tend to follow a similar pattern. A product innovation is seized upon by a number of companies which then attempt to increase the performance of the new discovery. The means by which competitors can gain access to the technological lead established by another company will either be based on the insights provided by their own research and development departments, which enable them to duplicate the underlying concept without facing patent or copyright difficulties, or via a process of licensing the existing concept from the initial developer. Once the concept is understood, the competitive firms in the market will attempt to gain competitive advantage by improving on the performance of the existing product.

Such performance advances are difficult to achieve initially, but there follows a period of rapid improvement, then a final levelling off as performance limits are reached. The pattern of investment return versus performance extension is called an S-curve, and has been clearly demonstrated in a number of product areas, including optic fibres with a 400-fold increase in carrying capacity since their introduction, and in a wide range of chemical products. It has similarities to biological systems where selective breeding reaches a plateau. For example, the winning times of racehorses over similar courses have not improved since the 1950s, and the number of new breeds of dogs accepted by the Kennel Club has also shown a similar plateau effect.[6]

The relationship between performance and price does not relate always to a single criteria such as speed, which has been the important criteria for the performance extension of data-processing systems as one microprocessor replaces another (see Table 4.2). Other dimensions such as power, durability, weight and flexibility may also be important. Ceramics are currently under development to reduce brittleness and liability to fracture, to take advantage of their high heat

Table 4.2 Changes in performance by microprocessor type

Year	Microprocessor	Speed in MIPS (millions of instructions per sec)
1974	Intel 8080	0.1
1977	Zilog Z-80	0.25
1981	Intel 8088	0.5
1984	Intel 80826	1.0
1987	Intel 80386	4.0
1990	Intel 80486	8.5

Source: Business Week, October 1988

resistance. Stretching the performance of ceramics may enable them to replace a lot of jet engine metal. A clear example of another type of performance extension is Kodak's larger lithium batteries. Lithium as a power source has power/weight advantages over typical alkaline batteries, but has been limited by the size of the battery that could be safely produced. Kodak engineers overcame this restriction and are likely to establish the company firmly in the $6 billion battery market as a result. Performance can also be extended by reducing power, durability or some other component. For example, the development of lasers using gallium arsenide semiconductors has been associated with reductions in the power output which, combined with the reduction in size, has enabled them to be used for localized skin treatment.

Sector creating innovations must be perceived as providing a central core area of product expertise which can be extended as a locus for performance extension along a number of different dimensions, each with its own S-curve and performance plateau. It is argued that once the performance plateau is reached, not only will additional improvements be extremely expensive to achieve, but the industry will be extremely vulnerable to new technologies providing improved performance — with one S-curve being replaced by another. There is ample evidence to support the first contention: the tyre companies, for example, investing hundreds of millions of dollars for marginal improvements in overall performance.

The use of the plateau to forecast possible technological change is, however, of little value, and operates mainly with hindsight. Hindsight tells us it was 'inevitable' that the clockwork watch industry, led by Timex, would be destroyed by the integrated circuit; that vacuum tube manufacturers that persisted with the tube were doomed to failure with the advent of the transistor. But recent military research on the effects of electromagnetic warfare has highlighted the value of the vacuum tube over the transistor, and a revival of clockwork mechanisms at the premium end of the Swiss watch industry, shows that the straightforward replacement of one technology by another is too simplistic. In contrast the S-curve concept is very valuable in providing information on the likely return for further investment in product development. It implies that when performance plateaus are reached the attractiveness of the environment for further development is significantly reduced, and the company should consider other options, and must realize that alternative new technologies introduced by potential entrants are a major threat to continued investment.

Improving performance of already established products makes far less stringent financial demands on a company. Firstly, the company's expenditure on research and development is likely to be lower than that of the company attempting to establish new product sectors. For example, Sony, with corporate goals emphasizing technological leadership, spends around 9 per cent of turnover on research. Sharp, in contrast — with a record of successful performance extension including the introduction of the first large-screen liquid colour crystal display in 1988 — spends around 4.5 per cent of its total turnover on research and development. Secondly, performance improvements have a much more rapid market acceptance as the barriers to diffusion, present with the original product, are substantially reduced. The groundwork for product acceptance has been cleared by the initial innovation — customers are aware of what the item is and what it can achieve, and the presentation of improved product performance is a much easier task.

This reduction in the barriers to diffusion means that the pay-back from performance extension is more rapid; though the fact of a more competitive market with other manufacturers entering the sector means that individual product margins will tend to be lower. It is likely that the advantages obtained by the manufacturer will be quickly overcome by leapfrogging improvements from competitors. Thus, investment must be maintained to ensure a competitive edge as few of the developments will be patentable in a way that is effective enough to control a particular market segment over a long period. The manufacturer relying on performance extension will often have to run very hard to stand still. Companies operating in such environments have to concentrate on speeding the product to market, as lengthy product development and testing procedures allow the competition to establish a clear market edge. For example, though the Philips VCR 2000 series was technically superior, the slow process of product development — in contrast with its Japanese competitors — and modification made the company lag behind and lose market share.

Emphasis on performance extension has other implications. First, the necessary work can be carried out with a smaller staff than required for sector creating innovation. Secondly, the research staff need to work to specific and highly structured research briefs, with progress being regularly monitored. The disadvantage is that these development 'tracks' — to borrow the terminology of the Manhattan project where particular programmes were labelled Tracks, 1, 2, 3, etc. — are highly vulnerable to changes in competitive action or managerial indecision, in contrast to the successful fundamental research-based operation where management or market changes are unlikely to have major repercussions on the effectiveness of the research programme. Because the work is so directed, managements eager to reduce the amount of interaction and maintain secrecy in the research departments can still achieve a high level of effective output. The staff employed will also tend to differ from those found in sector-creating innovation. Performance extension is often an engineering problem and the structured approach necessary to the definition and resolution of the problem requires engineering related skills, particularly in chemical and mechanical engineering. Where theoretical skills are employed they will be applied rather than pure research directed. Because of the competitive environment, improvements must be brought rapidly into effective production. This demands close interaction between development and production staff — often described as 'downstream coupling' — another contrast to sector creating innovations where theoretical concepts are far more important. As a result, performance extension will tend to be implemented most competitively in companies with large manufacturing volumes, and with centralized and large-scale production facilities.

Compaq is one of the most successful companies to arrive with the personal computer, and retains the record for reaching the top 500 companies in the shortest period of time. Its expertise lies in maximizing the potential of any given microprocessor technology. Compaq machines were faster, easier to use, and more powerful than their competitors. Corporate and individual users prized the technology that the company offered being prepared to pay significantly higher prices for Compaq equipment as a result. This performance edge is achieved through detailed planning; Compaq studies the competition in detail and develops systems maximizing the performance of existing hardware. From a detailed specification of the operating performance required, Compaq engineers and designers produce the level of performance necessary in a shorter time than the majority of the competition, producing significantly superior 386 microprocessor-based and laptop equipment.

Technological reorganization

Technological reorganization involves the import of additions or materials from other areas of industrial development to produce a new product. It differs clearly from both performance extension and reformulation (see p. 70) in that the resulting combination of technologies can often build a product differing substantially in application, and nearly always providing higher levels of performance at lower than existing prices. The First World War tank was one of the earliest examples of technological reorganization making a product differing substantially in application. Here, advances in diesel engines developed for heavy trucks, tracks initially built for agricultural vehicles, and the new lighter breech-loading guns were combined to build a new product: the armoured fighting vehicle. Many of the early successes of Japanese industry rested on the ability to reorganize technology effectively in order to develop new concepts. Four-stroke easy-starting engines were not technologically new — but they were to the motor cycle industry renowned for difficult two-stroke engines. The introduction of four-stroke technology was effective and enabled Japan to gain world market leadership in this market sector.

Examples of recent innovations involving technological reorganization range from the new combination of materials to produce new fastening systems in a company such as Avdel, the market leader in industrual fastening systems; simple combinations of portable workbench and vice to produce the Black & Decker Workmate; the highly successful Amstrad word-processing system, the Amstrad PCW 8256; to the range of computer-numeric-controlled cutting equipment, one of the many applications of combining microprocessors with existing equipment produced by such companies as AEG and Siemens; and the personal products of Sony such as the Watchman — portable miniature television, Discman — portable compact disc player, and the highly successful Walkman. The food industry continues to produce many examples of technological reorganization. It has been suggested that around 70 per cent of the food that will fill the supermarkets in the year 2000 has not yet been produced. Synthetic compounds such as polydextrose, under investigation by food companies as a replacement for fat in many food products, will mean continual change for the industry.

When one considers the success of the Amstrad PCW 8256 it is apparent that though the technology used was outdated (both in terms of the hardware and more significantly, in the CPM operating software), the combination of components in a particular configuration made the product highly successful. The acid test of success in that particular market is measured not just in the overall sales achieved — an estimated 750,000 in the United Kingdom alone — but in the fact that in a highly price-competitive market the company was able to maintain the introductory price for nearly two years. The success of the Workmate shows that even the most basic changes to a product, introducing a mechanical vice into a portable work surface, can produce a viable and highly profitable product. Black & Decker, the licensees of the Workmate concept, have also had a number of other highly successful technological reorganization projects, including the Lawnraker. The Epilady, a new form of depilatory equipment, also provides an example of a highly effective product developed from existing concepts.

Computer-numeric-controlled equipment provides a further example of the amalgamation of product from one technology — microprocessors with basic mechanical lathes. A growth area of medicine, endoscopy, involves the combination of optic fibres with lasers allowing medical staff to direct laser beams internally to seal ulcers, remove tumours or destroy gall stones — this is a combination of laser and optic-fibre technology. Similarly, a rapidly growing market in the United States is the voice phone, which can be programmed to record and then transmit messages to a selection of telephone numbers until they are finally received, a classic example of technological reorganization combining existing technologies in a new product concept with market sales approaching one billion dollars in 1988.

A similar growth market in prospect for the 1990s involves the rapid expansion of the cordless telephone market at the expense of cellular systems. The development of the facsimile or fax system provides yet another example of the potential of technological reorganization, with a forecast UK company base of 150,000 units by 1990. Valuation of the desktop publishing market — another area of technological reorganization — has risen from $100 million in 1985 to $700 million in 1988 with 1992 forecast at $1,200 million. The entire graphics market is set to expand rapidly as a result of such technological reorganization (see Table 4.3). Changing usage of compact discs (CDs) as data storage devices is likely to provide another substantial growth area provided by a basic technological reorganization using the concept in another area.

Certain forms of technological reorganization involve substituting the materials

Table 4.3 Graphics application market size by sectors ($bn)

Market sector	1988	1993 (est)
Printers	6	2
Displays	4	11
Graphic software	1	10
Misc. hardware	1	3

Source: Business Week, November 1988

traditionally used for certain products. The experience of the Japanese manufacturer Kao shows this at its simplest level. Attack is an effective combination of biotechnology with detergent powder which enabled the company to wrest much of the Japanese powder detergent market away from Procter & Gamble. With a similar combination of chemical technology from two diverse fields Kao has also developed a new bath salt, called Babu which produces a miniature 'jacuzzi' effect and now dominates the Japanese bath-additive market.

There are more complex changes in material technology. French metal producers have developed increasingly sophisticated metal and plastic 'sandwiches' to revitalize one sector of the economy. Other material composites were important in the evolution of aircraft engines from turbojets in the 1950s, to turboprops and turbofans in the 1980s and the propfan promised for the 1990s. Composites are also very important in technological reorganization at the premium end of the consumer goods market: Japan's Yamaha company transferred ceramic technology in developing a range of tennis rackets which are thought to be superior to the synthetic fibre rackets — an illustration of how materials technology developed for particular applications can be transferred into totally new ideas. Yamaha has also created a new industry and effectively destroyed an old one by the continued investment in the development of electronic music with its highly successful range of pianos and keyboards. The development of colour photocopying by Mead in the United States is another example of this process. The company uses a polyester film coated with microscopic capsules containing the three primary colours, which react to light of different frequencies. When passed through a standard roller these capsules break and blend the dyes to produce a full colour image.

As a route to product innovation, technological reorganization has the advantage of normally rapid market penetration in common with performance extension policies. In both cases the dynamics of the product are fairly well understood. In many cases the market penetration will be extremely rapid. For example, the replacement of both cross-ply tyres by radial and manual cash registers by electronic was extremely fast. The advantages for the customer were fairly obvious: greater mileage in one case, greater accuracy and ease of use in the other. But one advantage of technological reorganization over performance extension is that the company is not involved in the creation of new technical concepts but is rather using the tried and tested in a new way. The normal implication of such a product change is that development costs will be lower than in performance-extending innovation.

There are, however, disadvantges. The market lead obtainable by investment in this area is often shorter than in other types of innovation, simply because the costs are lower, other manufacturers also understand the existing technology being used, and the end results are rarely effectively patentable — though there are exceptions. It is clear that companies operating in such areas need to bring the product quickly to market. The use of computer-aided design and manufacture (CADCAM) techniques to model the proposed product will be important in such developments to define cost and to determine production schedules. For example, 3M developing a heart pump based on new plastic materials used computer-aided design to simulate the flow of blood in the circulatory system to reduce the risk of blood clot formation. This enabled the firm to reduce substantially the product development time and bring the item into production before its competitors.

The main management requirements for technological reorganization innovations are close links between engineering and production staff, with product development teams staffed by engineers from a variety of backgrounds, so that the necessary cross-fertilisation of ideas, crucial for technological reorganisation can be effectively achieved. The manufacturing system also has to be responsive to the need for continual re-adjustment of product, being flexible enough to rapidly retool and redirect the entire operation.

> The watch industry is a good example of companies being faced with both design and technological reorganization issues. The initial introduction of the integrated circuit led to Pacific rim domination of the watch market in the 1970s, a classic example of technological reorganization providing a higher level of performance at a lower price. However, the Swiss response was to concentrate heavily on design, both at the top end of the market 'designer' watches and at the lower end 'Swatch'. By 1989, Switzerland controlled nearly 50 per cent of the world watch market by value (total $8.7 billion).
>
> Since the mid-1980s there has been a steady increase in the variety of additional technology combined with the basic timepiece. These include telephone pagers, calculators, and a wide range of sports-related features (compasses and depth gauges, for example). With the continuing reduction in size of cellular telephones, it is likely that this technology will become available to the watch manufacturer in the late twentieth century.

Branding innovation

We have seen that the product concept extends beyond the purely technical into areas such as support and attitude and that innovations can be made as easily in these areas as in the development of new technical concepts. Branding is one such potential innovative concept. In simple terms, it involves the creation of increased propensity to purchase for a particular product which is independent of any objective assessment of performance. Research suggests that around 24 per cent of consumer products sales relate to promotion (see Table 4.4) and there are similar findings for the industrial and service sectors. Studies on the most famous branded

Table 4.4 Underlying purchase decisions

Factor	Percentage
Product appeal	49
Seasonality	27
Trade promotions	17
Advertising	6

Source: A.C. Nielsen, 1988

products in the soft drinks sector are a good example of how branding can effect sales. Blind tastings of cola drinks reveal that most consumers do not automatically choose either Pepsi or Coca Cola from a range of alternatives. When the product is presented packaged and identified, clear preferences are stated.

Branding is an investment in building a customer franchise with various important benefits for the company: it increases sales levels and improves the amount of repeat purchase; the product can be sold at a premium over non-branded competition; and it allows the company to introduce other innovations, such as reformulation. To continue with the example of Coca Cola, the strength of branding has facilitated the introduction of new variants — Cherry Coke, Diet Coke, Caffeine Free Coke — as well as the re-establishment of the old formulation 'Classic', which is sold alongside the new formulation developed to combat the sweeter Pepsi Cola but which consumers initially disliked.[7]

Branding can also significantly improve market position by changing consumer perceptions of a particular product and this can be just as innovative. The branding exercise carried out by TI Raleigh, the British manufacturer of bicycles, in the early 1980s transformed perceptions of children's bicycles for several years. The BMX racing bike concept — alluringly named 'Striker' and 'Drifter' — allowed Raleigh to increase substantially both volume and profitability in a market sector hitherto suffering from slow but steady decline. Even companies following branding in commodity areas can see substantial improvements in buyer perceptions and profitability.[8]

In the competitive 1990s, branding is likely to become a more attractive innovative route as market concentration of buyers strengthens. This is most clearly demonstrable in the consumer goods sector where much of the branding investment has traditionally occurred. The growth in the power of retailers in the United Kingdom was mentioned in Chapter 3 as an example of industrial concentration. Similar trends are occurring throughout Europe (see Table 4.5). Because they control a large percentage of the grocery retailing market, multiple chains can often improve profitability by either manufacturing product themselves or by contracting a third party to produce under their own or 'private' label. This buyer concentration steadily increased the percentage of own-label products in the grocery market as a whole (see Table 4.6). The pattern of private label growth is far from even: certain sectors show a much smaller growth than others, and there are major variations between sectors (see Table 4.7).

Table 4.5 Multiple grocers' percentage
share 1988 (includes co-operative groups)

Country	Share
UK	83
France	64
West Germany	70
Belgium	59
Italy	26

Source: A.C. Nielsen, 1989

Table 4.6 Private labels' percentage share of UK
grocery market

1983	1984	1985	1986	1987	1988
27.1	27.4	27.7	28.7	29.4	29.4

Source: AGB/TCA

Table 4.7 Private labels' percentage
market share by product sector, 1988

Sector	%
Canned foods	27
Cigarettes	3
Packet foods	17
Confectionery	1
Pet foods	7
Toiletries	10
Paper goods	40
Detergents	11
Perfume	2

Source: AGB/TCA

The close connection between strong and innovative branding, and the degree of private label penetration is inescapable. Pet food in the United Kingdom is dominated by one group, Mars, with a commitment to continuous branding; similar emphasis is to be found in confectionery, toiletries, perfumes, detergents and cigarettes. Private labels dominate those areas where there has been little continuous investment in branding; frozen food, tinned foods and paper goods, though there are exceptions in each of these sectors — Bowater Scott has managed to maintain market share by high levels of continuing investment in building the brand image of the market leader, Andrex. Various other companies also acknowledge the importance of consumer goods branding by attempting to put a value on their branding investment. Rank Hovis McDougall has followed a policy of including three years' earnings from each brand as the 'conservative' value of the brands in its portfolio; the figure for the 1987 accounts was £678 million.

A statement by the United Biscuits chairman, Sir Hector Laing, sums up the current popularity of brands: 'The most important assets are brands. Buildings age and become dilapidated. Machines wear out. Cars rust. People die. But what lives on are the brands.'

Though most commonly associated with consumer goods, branding has been most innovative in industrial and service sectors in the 1980s. In the industrial sector the creation of a customer franchise by IBM for its personal computer range was important in securing the company's ascendancy in its early expansion in a market that it continues to dominate (though not so impressively) in the late 1980s. No one would claim that the technology offered by the company in the initial PC was at all revolutionary; when compared with other systems then available, the machine was slow and the design was poor. Yet the product was an enormous success — much greater than the company had forecast — and has gone on to establish a series of industry benchmarks. The largest component of the success was the promotional emphasis that was given to the concept by one of the largest companies in the world; in other words, the IBM PC can be seen as a great branding success. As a result, IBM could maintain its high share of the market even though production lagged far behind demand, which for the majority of companies would constitute disaster. It could also sustain a price advantage over the competition, even after competitors introduced reformulated products, and extended the technology. No individual figures on the PC profitability were released, but comparison with Commodore whose Commodore 64, with the same amount of memory as the initial PC though without the disc drives, was costing £35 to produce by the mid-1980s, would suggest that the profit levels of the PC were generous at least and enormous as best! IBM's PC branding exercise enabled it to introduce variants such as the AT, XT and PS/2 and catch up with the processing technology inside the machine that was being offered by other companies.

Similar investment by Kimberley Clark in the paper towels and cleaning materials market — till then an industrial commodity — has slowly improved its market position and profitability within this sector. A similar decision by the DRG group to build up a dominant position in the paper market led to the successful positioning of their Conqueror brand in the corporate letterhead market. Turner & Newall's branding strategy established the Ferrodo products in a premium position in many world markets. In the service sector, the investment made by McDonalds has been part of their international success, with a far higher brand awareness than their main rival Burger King. During the mid-1980s British Airways have concentrated on building up branded consumer products, including Super Shuttle and Club World, both of which, it is claimed, helped achieve better occupancy than their main competitors.

The problems of branding investment are primarily associated with the time scale of the expenditure. Brands that do not receive support will wither and die. A product such as Omo or Lifebuoy, old-established and dominant brands of their time will slither from the consumers' minds without continued support. Establishing effective brands requires continued high-level support. A survey of

Table 4.8 Brand perceptions by market: top ten brands in each market 1988

Ranking	US	Japan	Europe
1	Coca Cola	Takashimiya	Mercedes-Benz
2	Campbells	Coca Cola	Philips
3	Pepsi Cola	National	Volkswagen
4	AT&T	Matsushita	Rolls-Royce
5	McDonalds	Sony	Porsche
6	American Express	Toyota	Coca Cola
7	Kelloggs	NTT	Ferrari
8	IBM	JAL	BMW
9	Levi Strauss	Nippon Airlines	Michelin
10	Sears	Seiko	Volvo

Source: Economist, March 1989

international brand awareness in Europe, the United States and Japan showed only one brand, the ubiquitous Coca Cola, appearing in all three market lists (see Table 4.8). Though brand perceptions in this survey were perhaps unduly weighted towards the 'esteem' in which they were held, it nevertheless provides powerful evidence for the substantial long-term investment required, and supports the view that branding as an option has to be carefully assessed in relation to long-term market attractiveness and the level of resources within the organization. This is also supported by the fact that in many consumer sectors the leading brand in 1925 is still the leading brand in the late 1980s (this rule covers sectors from biscuits to soup).

The organizational requirements of a successful branding exercise extend beyond a long-term commitment to continuing and substantial investment. A company will have to understand how cultural factors affect the message required, the value of the available promotional channels, the creativity of commercials, and the structuring of advertising to maximize return from investment. For example, high consumer awareness of Mars confectionery is closely associated with the company's understanding of how media advertising works; the worldwide market penetration of Marlboro cigarettes is partly due to the type of sponsorship activity undertaken. This view is supported by figures showing a wide difference in the awareness of different types of sponsorship (see Table 4.9). An important facet of the examples quoted is that creativity in branding gives an innovative edge. The success of the Nescafé 'Big Romance', featuring an upwardly mobile couple meeting over cups of instant coffee, was reflected in a substantial shift towards Nescafé and away from the main competitor, Maxwell House, in what had traditionally been regarded as a mature and highly regulated market.

There are fairly obvious staff requirements connected with a branding policy: a high level of marketing and advertising expertise — an ability to use and develop market research; planning skills to maximize the potential return from the investment — close contact with the customer; perceptive monitoring of the development of the brand image — whether the chosen media are achieving the goals set; and a willingness to experiment with new forms of promotional channels.

Table 4.9 Awareness of
sponsorship: percentage naming
any sponsor

Snooker	54
Soccer	49
Motorsport	47
Marathon	44
Cricket	42
Tennis	38
Cycling	34
Athletics	28
Darts	28
Rallying	28
Classical music	6
Theatre	6
Ballet	4
Opera	3

Source: RHL Associates, 1989

The bottled water market demonstrates clearly the dynamics of branding. In what can be considered the ultimate commodity market, a number of companies have established long-term customer franchises by heavy investment in branding. The market leader, Perrier, has achieved dramatic growth outside its home market, France, by concentrating on heavy promotional activity to create an image of sophistication and style which has now become so closely part of the product as to be effectively inseparable.

Process innovation

All manufacturers have to replace worn out machinery with new capacity. This will require alterations in working practices and operating methods, and will be at the most basic level, innovative. Much of the new gross capital formation that takes place within the economy reflects this underlying replacement of existing equipment. The rate at which this gross capital formation occurs can provide one indication of the speed at which the industry is improving productive capacity. Figures for 1987 suggest that the United Kingdom continues to lag behind its major European competitors (see Table 4.10).

Table 4.10 Expenditure of GDP by use:
1983−87 proportion of GDP concerned
with gross capital formation

Country	1983	1987
Switzerland	23.3	25.2
Italy	18.0	17.4
France	19.6	19.4
West Germany	20.8	19.4
UK	16.5	17.3

Source: OECD

Though it can be argued that replacement of existing equipment involves changes in working practices which may be innovative, they will be mainly of a minor nature and are often referred to as 'passive' innovation. In contrast there are many opportunities for the organization to actively seek out potential methods of improving manufacturing processes, thereby gaining advantages over the competition. Firstly, companies can get a competitive advantage by increasing the speed of the manufacturing process. As volumes of detergent consumed within the United Kingdom rose, Levers moved from manual to automatic filling of cartons to meet the growing demand. Low volumes of Export Surf in contrast continued to be hand-packed until the middle of the 1970s. Secondly, investment in process technology can substantially improve the flexibility of production by enabling it to move from the manufacture of one product to another. Comparisons of the German and UK kitchen furniture industry reveal that by insisting on the introduction of sophisticated numeric-control cutting equipment the German industry has gained maximum flexibility of design and the ability to cope with more complex materials than their UK competitors. As a result, companies such as Poggenpohl and Miele have become established internationally as premium suppliers of kitchen furniture, having shown how it is possible to innovate effectively in a basic industry.

Thirdly, process innovation may substantially decrease the time taken in moving from initial concept to final finished product. Computer-aided design and manufacture and flexible manufacturing systems (FMS) have become important in many market sectors, and are significant influences on the development of other types of innovation, especially performance extension and technological reorganization. This advantage has been labelled TBC or time-based competition. A comparison between the speed of the Toyota plant in carrying out certain operations and a similar plant in Detroit shows the considerable edge that FMS can provide, both in the speed of introduction of new products and overall production (see Table 4.11). Similar time saving has been identified in a number of other companies that have introduced advanced process technology. Fourthly, process innovation may improve the ability of the production process to deliver product of a certain quality, or at a lower price. At the time, Henry Ford's motor car production line was highly innovative. The company could then make a product at a price which dramatically undercut its competitors and still yield a very handsome profit —

Table 4.11 Comparison of FMS[1] performance in certain areas of operation

Factor	Toyota	Detroit
New car development	3 years	5 years
Vehicle manufacturing time	2 days	5 days
Scheduling dealer orders	1 day	5 days
Stock turn	22.8 days	45.6 days

Note: [1]Flexible Manufacturing Systems
Source: Adapted from R. Thomas in *HBR*, 3, 1988

tunnel kilns were introduced by large pottery manufacturers for the same reason. A comparison between a conventional system and a company utilizing FMS technology shows clearly where the advantages lie (see Table 4.12).

Just-in-time (JIT) manufacturing systems developed by large volume manufacturers in consumer durables and industrial markets are an evolution of process innovation investment strategies.[9] At their most innovative there are attempts to totally automate production such as the investment by General Motors at Sagenaw in the United States to build the new range of compact cars. Many innovative approaches in process innovation will attempt to improve quality at the same time as lowering cost. Many German chemical industry successes and their patent activity lie in this area. Japanese industry has concentrated on this route to improve competitiveness in the electronics sector with a range of process innovations that have made important contributions to overall improvements in profitability (see Table 4.13).

The value of process innovations depends on the attractiveness of the market and the resource position of the company. The majority of process innovations are not patentable but where they are — as in the case of Pilkington's float-glass process — they can create substantial control over an industrial sector. Such control is achieved because the high levels of investment reduce the ability of competitors to enter the market. A good example of this is in the motor car market: as mentioned on p. 15, the substantial investment in process systems implies that manufacturing volumes in excess of 500,000 units are necessary to compete effectively in the world mass car market. The costs of process innovation in the production of microchips are increasingly acting as a similar barrier with the investment in 'clean' manufacturing environments in excess of $150 million. It

Table 4.12 Superfast innovators and producers

Superfast innovators

Company	Product	Development time	
		Old	New
Honda	cars	5 yrs	3 yrs
AT&T	phones	2 yrs	1 yr
Navistar	trucks	5 yrs	2.5 yrs
Hewlett Packard	computer printers	4.5 yrs	1.8 yrs

Superfast producers

Company	Product	Order to finished goods time	
		Old	New
GE	circuit breakers	3 weeks	3 days
Motorola	pagers	3 weeks	2 hours
Hewlett Packard	electronic testing equipment	4 weeks	5 days
Brunswick	fishing reels	3 weeks	1 week

Source: Fortune, 13 February 1989

Table 4.13 Comparisons of FMS[1] with replaced systems in Japan

Factor	Original system	FMS
Number of parts produced (index)	100	100
Number of untended systems	0	18
Number of machine tools	133	253
Number of operators	601	129

Note: [1]Flexible Manufacturing Systems
Source: R. Jaikumar, *Harvard Business Review*, 6, 1986

is likely that the investment in dry-clay technology to produce pottery will produce similar raised barriers in the pottery industry, which has traditionally had fairly low barriers to entry, and acceptance of irradiation of food within the EC will create higher investment barriers in food manufacture as producers invest heavily in new production systems.

In many mature industries process innovation is becoming more important in speeding the introduction of new products. It has been suggested that the advantage of Japanese car companies over their American competitors is that their flexible manufacturing systems enable them to bring new products more quickly to market; the process innovation has enabled them to shorten their decision cycle, thereby reducing their response time to market changes. In a competitive and fashion conscious market such process innovations may become more and more relevant (see Table 4.14).

One scenario suggested for the fashion industry in the late 1980s is the rapid transfer of market information from marketplace to manufacturing point. First, point of sale computers will transfer information to head office on demand patterns. Orders then pass automatically to manufacturing plants whether they are in the home market or overseas. Rapid manufacturing techniques will reduce the production process to three or four weeks, after which the product is despatched to the warehouse system where it will be shipped to the relevant outlets. Such

Table 4.14 Performance of one factory before and after automation (original production levels indexed at 100)

Factor	Before	After
Types of part produced per month	100	100
Volume produced	100	100
Floor space	100	40
CNC machine tools	100	58
Other machine tools	100	21
Machine operators	100	21
Distribution/control operators	100	12
Processing time:		
machining	100	9
unit assembly	100	50
final assembly	100	48

Source: R. Jaikumar, *Harvard Business Review*, 6, 1986

interlocking manufacturing and despatch system will, it is suggested, reduce the re-order cycle from the current six months to around sixty days.

With continually changing exchange rates and relative labour costs, the value of process innovations may become increasingly apparent to many companies, even those operating in labour intensive markets. The recent rises in the yen and other Pacific rim currencies has forced American companies to reconsider much of their low-cost subcontracting strategies. Companies like the American carpet manufacturers that invested in process innovation by developing equipment that could offset rising labour costs are relatively unaffected by changing labour costs and currency rates, and can, as a result, plan and cost more effectively. Many Japanese manufacturers have also realized that shifting labour intensive parts of their production to low-cost labour markets only puts off the day that they will have to manufacture cost effectively by investment in process equipment and have not, in 1988, attempted to deal with the rising yen (up 20 per cent against the dollar) by substantial shifts in manufacturing location. Instead they have attempted to cope with the problem by innovative approaches to reducing cost within the home factory (see Table 4.15).

Process innovations will require substantial investments and often long periods of development, and, as a result, will only be viable if the investment can be spread across a large production volume. Michelin has invested a higher proportion of its research and development in improving the efficiency of the production process rather than in attempting to extend the performance of radial tyres, and has seen its share of the world tyre market, already impressive, further expand in addition to improving profitability. Pirelli, one of the few competitive manufacturers in Europe, has suffered from years of low profits in an attempt to match this investment from a much lower sales volume base.

Managing the effective introduction of process innovation will be highly demanding on specialized engineering skills and operations management, including the skills of the buying staff, as this area in particular is put under strain in the development of close and effective co-operation with component suppliers. The ability of Japanese manufacturers to manage such types of change is strengthened by the preponderance of production and process engineers that the Japanese educational system produces — seven times the per capita level of the United States. As the manufacturing process becomes more complex, the skills of the entire workforce will have to be raised to cope with the demands of the equipment,

Table 4.15 Comparison of US and Japanese manufacturing industry

Factor	US	Japan
Working stock/inventory	Up to 9 months	Under two months
Time from order to shipment	5–6 months	1–2 months
Quality defects/rework	8–10%	1% or less
Average age of equipment	17 years	10 years
Annual investment per worker	$2600	$6500

Source: Business Week, June 1988

and the types of operation involved. This is a crucial factor largely separating the demands of process innovations from other types of innovation. In the comparison of the UK and West German furniture industry mentioned above, the main limiting factor to the installation of comparable equipment within the UK economy was the shortage of skilled labour (and the universal, often unstated, unwillingness of management to train individuals to a high enough standard).

Illinois Tool Works (ITW) is one of the largest component suppliers in the United States, with sales of $2.2 billion in 1989, and profits of $164 million. Facing serious competition from the Pacific rim in all its low technology component supply operations the company has decentralized (employing only 100 staff at the headquarters servicing thirty countries) and concentrated on maximizing production efficiency in all its individual units. Changes have included reorganization of the factory towards in-line production (assembly line systems) for large orders and subcontracting specialized orders to outside firms. Such simple approaches to the management of the manufacture of basic components has led to the company achieving steady growth in profitability, substantially lower inventories, and greater employee satisfaction.

Design innovation

Though able to change dramatically the viability and success of companies in consumer, industrial and service sectors, innovation through design tends to be disregarded by many companies and often by entire industry sectors. It is accepted wisdom that most UK manufacturers are 'bad' at design, whereas Italian equivalents are 'good'. Much of this assessment hinges on the difficult problem of what constitutes good design. Apart from the aesthetic issues which have been and continue to be a subject of much debate, the marketplace is the sole arbiter for the commercial organization. Unfortunately, what the marketplace chooses as good design will vary from year to year, and in certain sectors often from month to month. Analysis of products that have succeeded in the 1980s indicates that there are both general components of successful design and specific areas towards which companies can direct their design activity. In general, the close relationship of form to function is important — cookers with controls at the same level as the hotplates, however stylish they appear, will not be successful products. Distinctiveness in design is another important component: it adds value to the product by separating it from the competition.

Flexibility of design also means that the product can be modified for market conditions and changes in consumer preferences, substantially increasing the potential life of the product in the marketplace. One classic example is the Aga cooker, invented in the early twentieth century, which has survived changes in types of fuel used in the home, changes in construction material and alterations in consumer colour preferences, to retain a specialized niche in the cooker market over eighty years later. Exceptional designs of this type may enable the company to trade off a certain lack of technical or component advantage, with customers willing to purchase well-designed products even when competitors are providing a more technically advanced product.

Successful design innovations tend to be concentrated in four main areas. There are design successes that concentrate on *image*. The innovative use of design in sportswear has achieved dramatic increases in profitability and market size by creating a fashion market in what had previously been regarded as grubby, dirty and cheap — the unenlightened era of the gym shoe, cotton singlet and shorts. RayBan dark glasses, produced by Bausch and Lomb, have similarly created a premium market with sales of two million units in 1987 producing revenues of around $40 million. But this image perception also supports areas other than clothing: 'rugged' lines to Japanese four-wheel-drive vehicles have done much to ensure their popularity throughout the United States and Europe in the late 1980s. The minivan has also appeared as a successful appendage to the car market illustrating the potential role of design in developing new sectors within mature markets. In offices, better design by Olivetti computers was partly responsible for initial success versus the major competitor, IBM. Xerox similarly lost market share to much better designed Japanese copiers which could fit into smaller spaces throughout the 1980s. In an era of expensive office space, the Japanese equipment was better suited to the prevailing environment. The early acceptance of the Mackintosh as a personal computer for the home was due partly to the 'sophisticated' design which out-competed the basic box of the IBM PC. Apple is notable in having a design team reporting direct to the chief executive.

The role of design in improving market position is again clearly seen in the watch industry. Here, the Swiss with their middle-range watch industry collapsing under Japanese competition survived by initially moving up-market with ranges of costume watches, and then re-entered the lower range of the market with the highly successful Swatch — which depended upon sophisticated design not technological innovation for its market position. The success of this move can be seen in the increasing share of the world watch market that the Swiss have managed to acquire — without sacrificing profitability as it is estimated that the production cost of each Swatch had dropped to $10 by early 1987 — while maintaining a UK retail price of over $30. The introduction of a new range of designs in 1988 permitted still further increases in the retail price.

For many service companies the image component of design is crucial. Appropriate design allows retail stores to create unique atmospheres; intimate for the specialist store, clean and well organized for the food store. Design is such an important component that major groups invest vast sums in upgrading outlets — J.C. Penney and Sears Roebuck investing nearly $5 billion over the period 1985–87 to improve their ageing store layouts. Other service companies such as hotels, caterers and entertainment centres all emphasize design in their attempts to differentiate from the competition.

Another important criteria for design is *user friendliness*. Customer requirements such as convenience, comfort and safety are often met by companies that insist on a high-design component. Electrolux vacuum cleaners with built in attachments rapidly gained market share against the market leader Hoover. A classic example of improvement in comfort is the Ergon 2 chair which allows the user to alter heights, angles and the shape of the seat cushion. This chair remains one of the top selling items of office equipment in the United States. Digital's edge over its main rival IBM in the microcomputer sector is its concentration on user friendly and comprehensive software development. User friendliness is now one of the most important factors for commercial vehicles, especially heavy lorries where companies such as Scania (part of the Saab group) increased their European market share by concentrating on the ergonomics of driving to reduce driver fatigue, and improve safety and efficiency thereby. JCB, the world market leader in the specialized sector of the construction equipment market, the backhoe loader, concentrates on producing machinery that can be rapidly and safely mastered by relatively low-skilled personnel.

Design can also increase a product's *efficiency*. The use of wind tunnels to steadily reduce the drag coefficient (CD) of cars has become commonplace. The Wilson profile tennis racquet increases the power that the player can impart to the ball, achieving first year sales of $25 million with a racquet retailing for around $250. For many manufacturers design is crucial in controlling *cost*. There are two main components. The manufacturer can look for manufacturing cost reductions through new design — as in the case of Potterton, the central heating boiler manufacturer, redesigning the central heating boiler. A Japanese manufactuer of personal stereos similarly reduced costs by redesigning its product as a result of price competition. The comparison of the two different designs and the benefits of the redesign is in Table 4.16. This data shows how changes in design can speed production significantly and reduce component cost. Where used, this design for assembly (DFA) has a major beneficial impact on the competitive structure of the firm.[10] A survey of twenty-nine consumer products showed that DFA could yield benefits in a number of manufacturing areas (see Table 4.17). The integration of design at this stage can also improve quality significantly and reduce waste.

Table 4.16 The effects of improved design on the manufacturing efficiency of the Sony Walkman (all indexed to original design)

Factor	Before	After
Number of parts	100	46
Assembly workers	100	17
Assembly time	100	33

Source: International Business Week, 6 June 1987

Table 4.17 Investigation of 29 consumer durables undergoing DFA

Factor	Before	After
Number of parts	100	75
Number of sub assemblies	100	65
Number of operations	100	70
Assembly time	100	72
Costs of machining	100	60

Source: H. Jensen, Harvard Business Review, 2, 1988

Changes in design significantly improve a company's ability to introduce new product variants and standardize components in a wide product range. It may be more effective for a manufacturer to introduce a product stage by stage — Model 1 being followed by Models 2 and 3 as the concept is increasingly refined. It is obviously most cost effective to plan design with such updated concepts already incorporated. An example of such clear thinking was the Amstrad PCW, initially introduced with a single drive but with the space for the second disc drive. Similar design innovation has been responsible for the speed at which new video recorders in the Amstrad range have been introduced. Companies can also use design to reduce the number of problems that the company may encounter during the development phase. Thus, Compaq can speed new product variants into the market because it uses standard components in as many parts of the new equipment as possible, reducing the amount of time that the company has to test the entire product.

Design innovation requires a degree of emphasis which separates it from other types of innovation. It requires close contact with the marketplace, the creation of an independent design team that is involved at each stage of product development, and a commitment by top management to use design as a competitive weapon. Because much of the perceived value of design is non-quantifiable in strict performance terms — the product may not be demonstrably faster or more durable — design innovations will demand that the company carefully tests and monitors consumer perceptions at each stage of the development process. Increasing the design component in a company's product range will require additional investment. However, it can provide a rapid repayment period in appropriate market sectors, and can often give the company a longer-lasting commercial success than many other types of innovation. For example, though Corning invested substantial sums in designing their range of premium glass cookware, Visions, introduced in 1983, it has now become their best-selling product range, retailing from £10 to £40, and has substantially improved their market share over a five-year period. Black & Decker with stylish cordless DIY drills has managed to penetrate the Japanese market; Vivitar Series 1 lightweight binoculars have substantially increased the market share of Hanimex in the binocular market, neither product offering a substantial performance advantage over the competition. A further facet of design advantage is that the skills can be concentrated in the marketing and product analysis area, and do not have to be necessarily expanded throughout the workforce.

Designs, though they can be protected by registration in many markets, will often be rapidly outmoded, and will require continuous management assessment as to whether the design has dated.

Lego, the Danish toy company, is a major design success story. The company operates in a highly fashion-conscious industry and manufactures products from basic plastic, with a large number of low-cost competitors. The toy industry is also one with a continually changing clientele, as children move on to more sophisticated types of entertainment. Since the early 1970s, the company has concentrated on developing a strong franchise throughout the industrialized world by producing a range of components that can produce a single item or a range of alternatives. The imaginative use of colour and the ease of construction allowed the company to overtake the previous market leader, Meccano, and move into a period of rapid growth. Between 1983 and 1987 sales rose from $150 to $350 million as the company expanded successfully in the majority of world markets (with the notable exception of Japan).

Reformulation

Reformulation involves change in the structure of current product without changing its components. Examples of such change involve the increased *purity* of manufacture. When Pechiney, the main French aluminium smelter increased the purity of its product from 99.7 per cent — the normal commercial level — to 99.999 per cent it was able to raise the per kilo price fifty-fold. Improvements can be made to improve components' *durability* and efficiency. Jaguar started to regain its market position by a rigorous policy of component reassessment by introducing clear and rigid specifications for sub-contractors. This substantially improved the reliability of the Jaguar range and reduced warranty claims by 40 per cent between 1980 and 1986. Though the Sheffield cutlery market largely collapsed under the lower production costs of Far Eastern competitors, Richardson's alone survived and prospered, upgrading components, improving durability and making new knives that never lose their edge, the Laser range. Reducing failure rates by more rigid inspection and higher standards can also be a vital reformulation route through improving the *quality* of the finished products. Wedgwood, the pottery company, reduced product failure by introducing a modified form of quality circles. Margins improved through reduced reject rates and inventories of unsold stock decreased. Similar control approaches enabled AB electronics, a component manufacturer, to penetrate new markets, including some of the most highly competitive Far Eastern sectors. Quality management is therefore a major area of concern for improving the competitive position of many industries. Quality programmes reduce waste, improve relationships with distributors and suppliers, and significantly reduce the level of investment required in inventory.[11] The total range of improvements that emphasis on improved quality can provide are outlined in Table 4.18.

A product's *physical* properties — changing flow, storage, density or some other characteristic — can also play a part in innovation through reformulation. Coffee companies expanded their markets by introducing granules alongside powder products as RHM did with Bisto. The density of Kikkoyan soy sauce was increased for the American market. In agrichemicals, improved solubility and flow properties for automatic equipment are identified as important selling issues by Schering, the German chemical company. Lone Star, a small company in the United States recognized that the setting properties of cement was an important problem for those customers (such as airports) that needed to increase the speed of repair. Introducing a more quickly setting product enabled the company to substantially improve profitability and customer base.

Reformulation policies can also involve the *re-combination* of existing components into new products. This differs from technological reorganization

Table 4.18 The gains from improved quality

Factor	Initial result	Longer-term effect
Improved performance	Improved reputation Higher prices	Greater market share Greater volume Greater economy of scale/ experience curve savings
Reduced component failure	Increased productivity Lower rework and scrap Lower warranty costs	Lower production costs Lower service costs

Source: Adapted from D.A. Gavin, *Sloane Management Review,* Fall 1989

in that it does not involve any importation of product concepts from other sectors, and is based on a reappraisal of the existing material that makes up the current products. Pepsi Cola, Seagrams and IDV, the international alcoholic drinks subsidiary of Grand Metropolitan, have shown how reformulation policies can establish new and profitable products. Pepsi added fruit juice to a soft drink — Slice, which had a 4 per cent market share of the soft drinks market in the United States by 1987. Seagrams mixed fruit juice with white wine in the highly successful 'cooler' concept. Grand Metropolitan by reformulating wine produced one of the most successful 'bland' leaders in the UK wine market, Piat D'Or. The introduction of a new malt whisky for international markets — Singleton, in 1987 — was another example of this innovative approach. A good example of such a policy is the impressive range of innovative products introduced year after year by Kelloggs, the American breakfast food manufacturer, with an estimated four to five new variants of very basic components being tested every year since the mid-1970s. Kelloggs remains one of the most profitable American food companies measured by return on capital employed of between 35 and 50 per cent, by sticking to this policy in what is throughout the world a largely mature industry, with a growing share of grocery retailer private brands. The Kelloggs experience supports the view that there is no such concept as a definitive product or a product sector that is incapable of being changed. Its staff of 400 employed in the development of new products is one of the largest such groups in the food industry; it greatly outnumbers the staff that are employed in its US marketing department, underlining the emphasis that the company places on reformulation.

In conclusion, reformulation policies provide a major opportunity to maintain and improve product performance. For low levels of investment, a company can often substantially improve the return on the initial product. This innovation route will not often provide a substantial competitive edge, but can keep the company ahead of the competition providing it keeps closely in contact with the market and actively plans a reformulation policy, following the identification of consumer dissatisfaction or market opportunities.

The company concentrating on product reformulation has to maintain close liaison between the market and the production staff to ensure that the most viable alterations in the existing product range are introduced and effectively commercialized. To achieve this, rapid and easy flow of information from those closest to the market is essential, as is the ability to monitor the required changes as and when they are introduced. Skills of identification of customer demands and the ability to translate these into specific products are crucial, as is the monitoring of existing products in the marketplace including those of competitors to ensure that market gaps are exploited as they develop.

> In a declining market for super-bikes in the United States, Harley Davidson has, between 1985 and 1990, steadily increased its market share, up from 30 to 40 per cent, revenues from $300 million to $800 million and profits from $10 to $32 million. It has followed a policy of steadily increasing the quality of products and an increase in the numbers of customized variants that it offers, up from 250 to 1053 over the same period. This concentration on reformulation has also made the company the top selling foreign motorcycle firm in Japan.

Service innovation

A 1988 Gallup poll of 615 senior executives in America identified service quality as the key factor for the 1990s — far ahead of issues like productivity, raw material availability and government regulation. Other surveys have shown the deleterious effects of bad service — customers on average complaining to twenty other potential consumers after receiving bad service. A number of studies also suggest that the costs of gaining a customer can be up to seven times that of keeping one. [12]

An improved service edge therefore becomes a vital part of a very competitive scene. Service leadership or service innovation does, however, imply a higher cost for a wide range of benefits. Asked to identify those companies that were predominant in their sectors in providing a higher level of service, polls have shown that companies that emphasize service can grow more rapidly than the average for the industry — good service can generate higher earnings. The main service sectors and their leading companies are in Table 4.19. Many executives,

Table 4.19 Leading service companies and their growth records compared with the industry average

Sector	Company	Five-year growth	Industry growth
Domestic airlines	American	8	7
International airlines	Singapore	7	6
Clothing manufacturers	Liz Clairborne	47	8
Commercial banks	J.P. Morgan	7	8
Computer manufacturers	Amdahl	17	23
Discount brokers	Fidelity	42	25
Drug makers	Merck	7	14
Frozen food manufacturers	Campbell Soup	14	4
Mail order operators	L.L. Bean	16	9
Supermarket operators	Wegmans	16	5
	Average growth	18.8	10.9

Source: Fortune, 12 June 1988

especially in manufacturing, have traditionally ignored exploring the avenue of improving market position by offering a higher or novel type of service, even though improved service provision often offers one of the most cost effective routes for gaining competitive advantage.

Specific service improvement routes will be appropriate in particular company/ market interactions. One often considered too boring and mundane to be thought as innovation is the pioneering and development of overseas markets.[13] Many companies, even the largest multinationals, have still a poor record in developing effectively in some of the major market sectors. The breakdown of turnover by market area for many leading European manufacturers shows that the majority of these large companies are still heavily reliant on the European market for the bulk of turnover (see Table 4.20). The reasons put forward for such a lack of innovation in market distribution include a claimed shortage of interest in Pacific markets, the inability to follow an acquisition route in many markets like the Pacific market to build up market share, and the attractiveness of the United States during the 1980s as a market in which acquisitions could be easily and quickly achieved.

Where organic growth has been concentrated upon, certain companies have

Table 4.20 Geographical distribution of sales of leading European corporations (Percentage of World GDP: Europe (26); US (40); Pacific Asia (18))

Companies	Europe	US	Pacific Asia
	Percentage distribution of sales by region		
Chemical sector			
BASF	65	8.0	6.0
Bayer	58	9.0	9.0
Ciba-Geigy	59	32.0	3.2
Hoechst	57	15.0	9.0
ICI	47	30.0	18.0
Rhone-Poulenc	69	8.0	7.0
Air Liquide	64	23.0	13.0
Automobile sector			
Volkswagen	80	17.0	2.3
Renault	82	4.0	0.5
Rover	85	0.4	1.9
Peugeot	86	2.0	6.0
Electrical			
ASEA	65	13.0	11.7
Siemens	74	18.0	8.0
Philips	52	29.0	6.9
GEC	64	17.0	12.6
CGE	75	6.5	9.5
Consumer products			
Nestlé	32	37.0	13.5
Unilever	55	11.0	11.0
Wella	60	19.0	21.0

Source: J. Labouchere, *Long Range Planning*, August 1988

shown significant successes in achieving an improved world market balance. For example, Nestlé's investment in Japan has gained it market leadership in the instant coffee market, with McDonalds and Kodak also demonstrating the benefits of organic market development policies. Such expansion possibilities even exist for the small or medium-sized company. McIlhenny, the market leaders in Tabasco sauce, achieve an average sale of 6 million bottles a year in Japan by using five companies with access to different parts of the complex Japanese distribution system. With strong local representation the company can maintain an effective physical distribution to the market to ensure that orders are filled on time.

Astute use of the different distribution channels can also supply an innovative edge. Dell Computers, one of the most rapidly growing computer companies, appreciated that it could increase the level of support to customers through direct contact between manufacturer and a customer willing to pay higher prices for better service. Similarly Sinclair Computers in the United Kingdom opened up the home computer market via the use of direct mail for its earliest product, the ZX-1, and successfully used this distribution channel for more sophisticated variants. One of the most successful distribution innovations was the decision by Pepsi Cola to concentrate on the vending industry — a distribution channel which had been ignored by Coca Cola — to establish an initial presence in the market whence it was able to challenge the market leader.

Some companies have used the concept of the CVMS (Corporate Vertical Marketing System or, in plain English, company-owned retail outlets) to penetrate existing markets or become established in new ones. The Tandy Corporation is one example of a company manufacturing and distributing electrical products through its own outlets, and Laura Ashley chose this expansion route opening outlets throughout Europe, America and the Pacific basin to sell its range of English print clothes and household fabrics. The development of franchising as a distribution concept has provided a further avenue for innovative firms to develop new markets. Body Shop, on the crest of a rising demand for cosmetic products based on natural ingredients, has managed to continue to expand its market coverage by franchised outlets both within the United Kingdom and overseas. Benetton, the Italian fashionwear manufacturer, has also followed this route to a European wide coverage and is gearing up to enter the US market in the late 1980s.

Physical distribution and order processing provide another component of improved service provision. Analyses of customers' distribution requirements show that the main demands are for improved *speed, accuracy and reliability*. Large companies that have exploited such customer demands include Caterpillar offering a 24-hour replacement service throughout the world, and Frito-Lay, one of the food divisions of Pepsi Cola guaranteeing a complete product range delivery. Examples of small companies employing such techniques to provide innovative advantage include the Connect electrical chain in the United Kingdom which in 1986 offered customers £10 compensation if the retailer did not deliver on time, make a repair call on time, or finish workshop repairs on time. Such a promotional campaign followed the company's research which showed that 90 per cent of customers considered that accurate delivery and reliable after-sales service were key factors in making a decision on the purchase of an electrical appliance.

Another example of the application of service innovation in a competitive market is the case of the Domino Pizza introducing a computer-based order system, appropriately called POPS (Pizza Ordering Purchasing System). The computer software on a Unisys mainframe can change the speed of calls, route calls to more experienced operators, provide automatic answering facilitites when demand is high, and automatically generate all the required management audit information, such as hourly call rates, disconnect rates, and speed of response. It is claimed that this system has substantially increased the speed of response to customers' orders and reduced the number of lost orders. Such an improved service commitment can significantly improve profitability. Increasing the efficiency of the physical distribution system can lead to a substantial drop in the number of emergency deliveries, the time taken for deliveries and overall productivity. An example of how improving the service can both influence cost areas and improve staff motivation is shown in one study of the beer industry (Table 4.21).

Service innovation can also be achieved by improving staff expertise. Merck, the leading world pharmaceutical company, achieves its high service rating by high-level training of sales representatives who are among some of the most highly regarded sales representatives in the industry. In this context the reorganization of British Airways during the 1980s was one of the most successful exercises of this type. Employees were trained to improve customer contact, to be more receptive to criticism; and flight schedules were altered to meet business customer demands. These changes and a high level of investment in information systems and new aircraft has substantially improved the profitability of the company until it ranks as one of the most profitable in Europe.

Service innovation will provide one attractive option to companies with limited resources as improvements in this area, if successful and well received by the customer, can provide a rapid pay-back in return for relatively low levels of capital investment. In theory, service improvements can only offer a short-term competitive advantage, as other companies can rapidly offer the same type of benefits. In practice, companies that improve service performance are often able to maintain this competitive advantage over long periods.

The identification, establishment and maintenance of innovative and competitive service policies will demand a close and continuing contact with the customer.

Table 4.21 Changes in productivity with improved service in distribution network based on index of 100 in year one

Area	Year 1	Year 2	Year 3
Volume	100	120	130
Manpower	100	102	105
Emergency deliveries	100	75	62
Own vehicle usage	100	125	150

Source: Author

For example, Embassy Suites, voted the best hotel group in the United States, carries out around 350 open-ended interviews with customers every day. The accurate matching of service provision to customer groups will demand planning and control systems to monitor the implementation and continuing achievement of satisfactory levels of performance, and high levels of investment by management in personnel skills and monitoring systems. Information flows must be accurate and rapid. Management must be able to respond effectively to changing patterns of demand within a short period and to monitor the effectiveness of the organization in achieving the desired performance levels. In a competitive environment this will demand an increasingly skilled staff, not only to negotiate with the customer and appreciate the customer's requirements, but also to handle the more and more sophisticated control systems that will be necessary to monitor progress. A by-product of the use of such control systems is that the percentage of routine customer contact is reduced, thereby allowing staff to concentrate in other areas.

The introduction of cash machines (ATMs) in the United States by Citibank is an example of a service innovation that led to a rapid and sustained increase in market share. The system provided 24-hour, seven-days-a-week access to cash withdrawal and account management services, while allowing staff within the banks to concentrate on higher-value, individual customer attention. The introduction of ATMs increased the use of the previously poorly patronized branch network and saw Citibank share of retail banking in New York City increase from around 4 to over 12 per cent.

Packaging innovation

Lord Lever revolutionized consumer goods by the simple introduction of packaged soap; 100 years later this innovation, Lux toilet soap, sells over 100,000 tons worldwide every year and is still the best-selling toilet soap brand. Japanese consumer durables owed much of their worldwide sales growth to the attention paid to packaging, permitting product to travel from the manufacturing point to retail outlet and be ready for immediate use by the customer. Even within established sectors packaging can play a significant role in the success of product performance. The considerable success of Biarritz has already been mentioned (see p. 28) in boosting the brand shares of Cadbury in the boxed-chocolate market. Matchbox, the toy company, managed to establish itself worldwide in another well-established market — plastic model construction kits — by using packages with a transparent window which allowed potential buyers to see inside the pack. Though it is the consumer goods sector that has given the greatest emphasis to innovative packaging, there are many examples in the industrial sector which have enabled firms to considerably expand market shares. One industrial detergents company in the United States altered its packaging to allow automatic dosing of product for particular types of applications.

Changes in packaging can improve product performance in important ways. First, it can open up new markets by changing the amount of product purchased or used at a particular period. A classic example of such a packaging innovation is the introduction by Stowells of the wine box into the UK wine market, which enabled the consumer to buy wine in much larger single quantities. By 1988 it still retained a substantial share of the UK retail wine market. A German manufacturer of specialist nuts and bolts, IMP, found that many contractors and household users were willing to pay a substantial premium for small quantities of product in durable containers that would neither be lost or damaged. Secondly, better packaging can substantially improve the storage qualities of product — Tetrapack containers have revolutionized sales of fruit juice and other liquids. With the increasing demand for prepared meals, many companies are investigating improved ways of preserving such products and new packaging methods which will involve the inclusion of inert 'microatmospheres' within the package are under consideration.

Packaging can also improve product performance and acceptability. Coca Cola and Pepsi Cola pioneered the use of the ring-pull can as they perceived that this could substantially increase their volume of product sold in cans, which previously had to be pierced and poured. One of the most successful new products introduced in the US in 1987 was the squeezable sauce bottle, which enabled Heinz, the market leader to improve its overall market share by several percentage points. A similar introduction by the main toothpaste companies of flip-top tubes was also recognized by the trade as a major product success. Improving attitudes to products through packaging innovation has been crucial in several consumer industries. For example, the development of the chocolate Easter egg market has been largely a history of ever more elaborate and impressive packaging; and a vital part of male and female perfumes is the attention that the manufacturers pay to packaging design.

Among industrial products better packaging can increase safety and ease of handling — important in improving user acceptability. Soilax and Wynadotte in the industrial detergents market have developed containers which reduce the risk of accidental spillage or overdosing. In prepared foods, several companies are now introducing 'doneness' indicators which will inform the consumer when the meal has been adequately cooked. Cost reduction in packaging may also provide important customer benefits. Thus, the introduction of PET plastic bottles substantially reduced transport costs and breakages. Replacement of glass miniatures with plastic is estimated to save an airline using a 747 across the Atlantic around £12,000 per annum.

More important for most manufacturers of both industrial and consumer durable equipment is the role of packaging in reducing damage and product failure, whereby they can also improve the quality of the product reaching the customer. It has been estimated that between 2 and 11 per cent of consumer durables arrive damaged, requiring servicing or replacement; the figures for electronic equipment suppliers suggest that the failure rate, though lower, still produces a high level of customer resistance due to product damage.

Innovative packaging will also have a vital role to play in effectively managing the logistics function. Changes in packaging can increase the speed of production, ease materials management within factory and warehouse, improve load factors by achieving higher packing densities, lower packaging costs, give greater product

Table 4.22 Effect of packaging changes on logistics
criteria

Factor	Old	New
Speed of filling	78	100
Machine breakdown	105	100
Material cost	108	100
Internal stock movement	100	100
Packing density	84	100

Source: Author

security, and allow more rapid transfer within the physical distribution network.
For example, the introduction of a new pack design for a liquid detergent produced
a whole range of logistic benefits which are detailed in Table 4.22.

Packaging innovations pose a number of problems, however. Though it will
often be less expensive to introduce than other forms of product development,
they do not necessarily provide the company with any major long-term advantage
unless the company is able to patent the particular process involved. In addition,
packaging innovations may not be rapidly accepted by the market, and can pose
serious engineering production problems. The introduction of new packaging
concepts will demand a close attention to both the engineering implications of
the change and their acceptance by the marketplace. Management will have to
be able to identify those types of change that are most likely to be required, how
such changes affect the packaging currently utilized, and how best to achieve the
end results.

ICI is one of the world's leading paint manufacturers with its range of Dulux paints.
One of the problems that it has faced, in common with other manufacturers is how
to provide the widest possible range of paints consistent with the demands of the
distribution channels to stock only those paints that provide an adequate return on
the shelf space utilized to stock them. The ICI solution is to add a capsule containing
a particular dye to the paint lid, which is then mixed with a common base to produce
any of eighty-four different paint types. The advantage to the paint stocklist is obvious,
in that it significantly reduces the amount of shelf space that they need to make
available; the advantage to the customer is that they get the exact paint tone they
require. The introduction of this packaging innovation has been to increase further
ICI shares of the paint market.

The discussion in this chapter has concentrated on identifying different types of
change, the types of product benefit that evolve from them and the main demands
that they make upon the organization. The main features of the nine types of
innovation identified are summarized in chart form (see Table 4.23). Innovation
types can be separated by cost, speed of research and speed of production, with
sector-creating innovation having the highest cost and lowest rate of conversion
from concept into commercial products. Innovations can also be separated by
the complexity of demand estimates, with sector-creating innovations again being
the most complex to define and packaging the least.

Table 4.23 Nine types of innovation: a summary

Sector	Sector creating	Performance extension	Tech. reorg.	Process	Branding	Reformulation	Service	Design	Packaging
Cost of research	High	High	Mod	Mod	Low	Low	Low	Low	Low
Speed of research	Low	Mod	Mod	High	High	High	High	High	High
Speed of production	Slow	Fast	Mod	Mod	Slow	High	High	High	High
Demand estimate	Complex	Less complex	Fairly complex	Less complex	Less complex	Less complex	Less complex	Less complex	Less complex
Payback timescale	Long	Mod	Mod	Long	Long	Short	Short	Short	Short
Comp advantage	High	Mod	Mod	High	High	Mod	Low	Low	Low
Value added	High	Mod	Mod	High	High	Mod	Low	Low	Low
Skills emphasis	Pure research	Engineering	Client contact	Engineering	Client contact	Client contact	Client contact	Client contact	Client contact

Source: Author

Notes

1. The implications of various types of innovation are summarized by D.H. Gobelli and D.J. Brown, 'Management Issues and Innovation', *Research Management*, issue 4, vol. 30 (1987), pp. 14–26.
2. Minimum research staffs for effective new product research is discussed in National Economic Development Organisation, *The Chemical Industry*, (London: NEDO, 1987).
3. L. Parker, *Innovation Management*, (Chichester: Wiley, 1987) describes seven crucial elements of a successful research staff: scientists are themselves responsible for project management; they have power and influence; they are secure in their jobs; they have little administrative involvement in their jobs; projects, even in a large research programme are limited in scope and duration; scientists are also active in other areas like teaching; the company can maintain an effective level of motivation.
4. R. Jungk, *Brighter than a Thousand Suns*, (London: Gollancz, 1958) contains an interesting account of the early days of atomic research.
5. T. Margerison and W. Wallace, *The Superpoison*, (London: Macmillan, 1980) recounts the extreme secrecy of Hoffman LaRoche in the Seveso dioxin episode.
6. R.N. Foster, *Innovation, The Attackers' Advantage*, (London: Pan, 1986) discusses S-curves in detail.
7. R. Enrico, *The Other Guy Blinked and Other Despatches from the Cola Wars*, (New York: Bantam, 1986).
8. S.A. Sinclair and K.E. Seward, 'Attitudes Towards Branded Building Products', *Industrial Marketing Management*, 17 (1988), pp. 165–76.
9. R. Jaikumar, 'Post Industrial Manufacturing', *Harvard Business Review*, issue 6, 64 (1986), pp. 112–20.

10. H. Jensen, 'Design for Manufacturing', *Harvard Business Review*, issue 2, 66 (1988), pp. 37—45.
11. D.A. Gavin, 'What Does Product Quality Really Mean?', *The Sloan Management Review*, fall 1989, 30, pp. 19—48.
12. M. Christopher, *The Strategy of Distribution Management*, (London: Heinemann, 1986).
13. J. Labouchere, 'Why Europeans are Weak in Asia', *Long Range Planning*, August 1988, pp. 15—22. A wide range of service innovations and how they have helped competitive advantage are described in B.R. Guile and J.B. Quinn, *Managing Innovation — Cases from the Service Industries*, (New York: National Academy Press, 1988).

5

Defining market attractiveness

Introduction

Profit is the crucial influence on the most appropriate innovation route. This profit can be achieved in a number of ways, ranging from small short-term investments achieved with limited investment to large long-term returns from heavy investment. In order to identify the best route for change firms will need to perform a balancing act that involves considering the interaction of market attractiveness, or the potential financial return from an investment in a particular market sector, and the resources that the company has available to exploit the opportunities available to it.

Ideally, all such investment criteria should be quantifiable and specific. Regrettably, the complexity of the marketplace makes attempts at quantification extremely difficult. Even governments with large departments find quantified forecasting so difficult that the UK Chancellor of the Exchequer stated in 1988 that government was not in the business of providing forecasts. Business planners, lacking the 400 or so staff that are directly or indirectly involved with the UK Treasury model, evaluate markets on a series of qualitative factors, and from these attempt some degree of quantification. This quantification will be most difficult in those markets experiencing extreme and rapid change, which multiplies the problem of forecasting demand. The inevitable result is that each company will develop its own weighting system for identifying attractive market sectors. The following discussion outlines the main issues that preoccupy any planner and some of the current research that supports certain market approaches.

Size of market, current and potential growth

The improved access to major international markets described in Chapter 2 is having a significant influence on companies' perceptions of potential markets for investment. Until fairly recently, companies faced the problem of increasing market segmentation within national boundaries. Rapidly changing segmentation patterns not only made difficult the identification of what exactly constituted the market, but also reduced the potential size of any one particular market for investment. Access to international markets has removed many of these problems — even the smallest segment available across the major trading blocks of Europe, the United States and the Pacific basin can provide an attractive investment target for even the largest company. For example, Glaxo, already identified as one of the most successful pharmaceutical companies has focused activity on anti-ulcerants worldwide and has ceased to rely so heavily on selling general pharmaceutical products in the small UK market (see Table 5.1).

However, rapidly changing market environments, even global ones, produce their own problems. Pentland Industries, the UK conglomerate with a 30 per cent holding in Reebok, the American running-shoe company, reported an overall drop in profitability due to problems encountered in the running-shoe industry. The crucial lack of predictability in the fashion marketplace makes this industry less attractive as an investment opportunity. Where causal relationships exist between demand in certain market sectors and an underlying, continuing trend, the task of the business planner is far easier. For example, certain diseases are closely related to the age of the patient — the greater the average age of the population, the greater the level of demand. Close relationships have been shown between the level of disposable income and the purchase of new cars in the United States and economic growth and trends in air travel.

The relationship between the level of market share held by any company, the rate of market growth and the likely effectiveness of innovation is at best a tenuous one. There is some evidence from the PIMS that returns on research and development expenditure will tend to he highest in mature markets, but this appears to relate mainly to the dominant consumer goods sector in the database. Though the research findings have been heavily criticized in many aspects they remain a useful source of information on likely impacts of particular policies during stages of market growth. The main findings of the study as they relate to market growth are summarized in Table 5.2.[1]

The detailed and wide-ranging scope of this research provides valuable information on the likely attractiveness of particular market growth stages on the level and type of investment that should be considered. The broad conclusion

Table 5.1 Percentage turnover by market sector Glaxo PLC 1977/88

Area	1977	1988
Anti-ulcerants	48.0	—
Respiratory	21.0	14.0
General foods	8.5	31.0
Foods	—	12.0

Source: Glaxo annual accounts

Table 5.2 PIMS database: suggested relationships between R & D expenditure and profit impact

1. High R & D spending depresses ROI when market share is weak.
2. A rapid rate of new product introduction in fast growing markets depresses ROI.
3. R & D is most profitable in mature slow-growth markets.
4. A narrow product line, in early or middle stage of the life cycle, is less profitable than at the late stage.
5. Few new product introductions coupled with low investment intensity generate positive cash flow.

Source: D.F. Abell and A. Hammond, *Marketing Strategy*, 1982

Table 5.3 Impact of market characteristics and purchase type descriptors on three performance dimensions

Factor	Financial performance	Opportunity window	Market share
Market share	ns	ns	ns
Proportion of foreign market share	ns		0.331
Market growth % per annum	ns	0.217	
Customer need	0.313		
Customer satisfaction with competitive products			0.198
Degree of change of customers' product requirements		0.299	
Frequency of new product introductions		0.296	
Typical success level for new products in sector	0.213	0.191	
Newness of purchase task			0.198
Buyer readiness to purchase new products	0.195		
Size of order placed			
Importance of product to the customer		0.240	
Customer familiarity with product	0.205		0.230
Purchase frequency			

Source: A. Cooper *R & D Management*, 2, 1987

is that companies should concentrate their investment at periods at the start of market growth and then, when the market has matured, supply niche products or innovative approaches for a market state which will fragment or segment once maturity has been reached. On the other hand, a different survey of companies in 1987 failed to find any correlation between market size or market growth and successful financial results from investment in innovation, though the higher the rate of market growth and introduction of new products, the greater the opportunity for successful new product introduction — which to an extent supports the findings of the PIMS database and other research (see Table 5.3). Thus it seems that the more innovative the market, the greater the likelihood of success — competition in the market placing a high value on innovative approaches. High rates of new product introduction create both a greater chance of financial success but also create new opportunities in the market for the potential success of new product entrants. The implication for this is very important for the whole range of commercial organizations as they face an increasingly competitive environment, as outlined in Chapter 2.

In conclusion, the trend of the research is to suggest that the stage of market development should not exert an overriding influence on the type of investment policy adopted. It should rather be seen as one of many factors weighed against each other in the final decision. The most important factor for most companies will not necessarily be either the market size or growth rate but the predictability of the environment into which the investment is being made. Unpredictable markets will demand both a more limited time span for the repayment of the investment and perhaps a more cautious overall level of funds commitment.

Substitutes

One pressure on companies is the problem of substitutes which can drastically reduce the potential for long-term investment in particular market sectors. Take, for example, the problem of the company considering investment in the cellular telephone market. Though the current constituents of the market can be identified by market research and some estimate be made of their likely future demands, how will the overall market be affected by the proposed cordless telephone competition and/or change in other types of communication systems? The Prestel viewdata system continues to suffer from substitutes providing more effective service; either in news (teletext services such as Ceefax or Oracle) or market data (specialized database providers such as Datastream or Lexis).

Identification of substitutes and potential entrants will be more acute in areas where there is a high proportion of overlapping products, as in many grocery and consumer durable sectors, where the costs of entering the market are fairly low. The threat will be much smaller in those industrial and consumer markets where costs of entry are substantially greater, and the availability of substitutes is likely to be limited. For example, the very high barriers to entry in the car market make it unlikely that new competitors will become established, or that existing products are likely to be replaced by others — even though the engineering components may vary, the demand for the basic product is likely to continue. By contrast, IBM still dominates in mainframe computers where the costs of establishing an effective competitor are greater than in the mini and personal computer sectors (see Table 5.4), but the changing nature of the microprocessor environment suggests that there will be numerous substitutes by the end of the 1990s. This point is further discussed in Chapter 8.

Where an innovative company can meet unique consumer needs free of the threat of substitutes, market attractiveness will be substantial. One example is Corwin, introduced by ICI in 1988. A development of the beta-blocker concept (one of the discontinuous drug discoveries of the 1960s that propelled ICI into major league status in the pharmaceutical market), Corwin is thought to be the first improvement over digitalis, introduced in 1936, in the effective treatment of congestive heart failure. With a US market of over two million patients and growing markets as populations age in the industrialized world, the lack of

Table 5.4 Market shares by company 1981−87

Company	Micros 1981	Micros 1987	Minis 1981	Minis 1987	Mainframes 1981	Mainframes 1987
IBM	—	36.3	24.5	16.4	74.7	70.4
DEC	—	—	17.3	24.9	—	—
Apple	26.1	16.9	—	—	—	—
HP	—	—	9.5	9.7	—	—
NCR	—	—	9.5	7.7	—	—
Unisys	—	—	—	5.5	—	11.5
Compaq	—	8.6	—	—	—	—
Total market ($bn)	1.5	13.5	11.1	19.4	14.0	23.3

Source: Market research reports, trade estimates, annual reports

Table 5.5 Changing pharmaceutical environment 1962−87

Factor	1962	1972	1981	1983	1985	1987
R & D expenditure in US by US companies ($bn)	—	—	2.0	2.5	3.0	3.5
Effective patent life in US (years)	15	11	8	8	—	—
Number of drugs under development worldwide	—	—	100	120	160	200

Source: Economist, May 1989

substitutes suggests that revenues of £250 million per year may be achievable. However, with the rapid growth in the number of drugs under development by competitors it will be uncertain how long this advantage will last (see Table 5.5). The impact of such substitutes can be seen in the effect on the forecast earnings of Retrovir, the drug produced by Wellcome for the treatment of AIDS, following the introduction of an improved product by Genetech, the Californian biotechnology company.

The existence of such potential substitutes or market entrants is another key component in evaluating the attractiveness of the market and the degree of competitive pressure that is likely to exist. Where the market is stable and there is little problem of likely substitutes or entrants the market will be less uncertain and potentially unstable.

Investment in product change is in such circumstances likely to yield a higher rate of return than in those markets where the chances of substitution or the arrival of market entrants is a real threat. One factor that can aid in the assessment of the likely arrival of market entrants is the stage of technological development.

Stage in technological development

Chapter 4 mentioned the tendency for technological innovations to follow an S-shaped curve relating performance to cumulative investment, with an eventual plateau of performance beyond which the achievement of further improvements of performance will be both minimal and expensive. S-curves therefore provide an indication to the investing company that investment in performance extension is unlikely to provide a sufficient return, and that innovation will need to be sought elsewhere.

The S-curve concept also provides a valuable conceptual framework for evaluating competitive processes in the market. A characteristic of the introduction phase is high development costs and slow market acceptance but with substantial competitive advantage to be gained from pioneering a particular market sector. The vertical phase of the S-curve will have the characteristics of rapid product change and improvement. This will imply that product redundancy will be a major problem; speed to market will be very important.[2]

The dynamics of the market will change as the plateau of performance is reached, with more and more competitors acquiring the technology or familiarity with it. Many companies in an increasing global market follow what has been called an international product life cycle in managing the transfer of technology (shown diagrammatically in Figure 5.1), clearly supporting the view that as technology matures the numbers with access to it will automatically increase. It follows that the market will become less attractive in such circumstances, with well-established companies likely to dominate and thus preventing other companies from entering. The radial tyre market is one such example with a small number of large companies producing a range of products which have shown limited improvements in performance over the last ten years.

There is a second factor that decreases the attractiveness of markets that have reached plateau in terms of technological performance. This is the threat of the

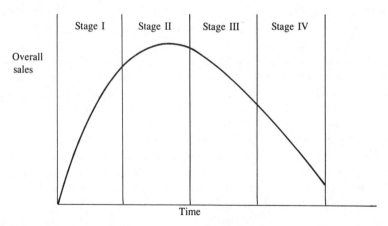

Notes:
Stage I Export from the home manufacturing base to major overseas markets.
Stage II Manufacture in main international markets and exports to all other markets.
Stage III Ceasing manufacture in major markets but manufacture in minor markets established.
Stage IV Worldwide manufacture ceased but licences made available to third parties.

Figure 5.1 The international product life cycle (*Source*: A. West, *Marketing Overseas*, 1987)

arrival of new product concepts which will destroy the existing market, as radial tyres destroyed cross-ply, photocopying destroyed roneo copying, the steamship destroyed the sailing ship, and the electronic circuit destroyed the clockwork mechanism for watches. Companies must consider the stage of technological development as a crucial factor in their evaluation of the attractiveness of the market and as an indication of what type of innovation policy they should be pursuing for that particular strategic business unit. High levels of expenditure on attempts to improve the performance of the product will be inappropriate, but expenditure in other areas will be more cost effective, either by improving the effectiveness of the manufacturing process or extending the consumer franchise.

Diffusion rates

The likely speed of diffusion of the innovation through the target market is another influence on the attractiveness of a particular market sector. But this can vary enormously. One study has identified nine different categories of diffusion with considerable differences at which benchmark penetration (75 per cent of the relevant population) is achieved. This can vary from around three years to the extreme of over twenty-five years. With such extremes, it is essential that the business planner evaluate those factors that are likely to speed or delay the diffusion of innovation in the market. The contribution of economic models does little to explain why diffusion rates of certain innovations are considerably higher in certain countries at broadly the same level of economic development than in others.

Industrial buying research suggests that the speed of diffusion is largely governed by such factors as the level of relative advantage, compatibility with current systems, complexity, divisibility and communicability, though certain other studies suggest that an emotional component is also important.[3] The most important components appear to be the fulfilment of felt needs, compatibility and relative advantage which have been found to be central in a large number of surveys (see Table 5.6). The strongest correlations exist between relative advantage and

Table 5.6 Product attributes and their potential importance in acting as barriers to diffusion

Factor	Ranking
Fulfilment of felt needs	1
Compatibility	2
Relative advantage	3
Observability	4
Immediacy of benefit	5
Availability	6

Source: E.M. Rogers and D.J. Stanfield, in F. Bass (ed.) *Adoption and Diffusion of New Products*, 1967

Table 5.7 Correlations between key aspects of product diffusion

Factor	1	2	3	Correlations 4	5	6	7
1. Relative advantage	1.000						
2. Compatibility	0.529	1.000					
3. Complexity	0.074	−0.020	1.000				
4. Divisibility	0.066	0.039	−0.05	1.000			
5. Communicability	0.175	0.190	−0.342	0.126	1.000		
6. Perceived risk	−0.077	−0.088	−0.375	−0.119	−0.253	1.000	
7. Purchase intention	0.467	0.556	−0.01	0.036	0.161	−0.150	1.000

Source: S.L. Holak and D.R. Lehman, *Journal of Product Innovation Management*, 2, 1990

compatibility (see Table 5.7). It does not appear that the overall cost of the innovation has a major bearing on its acceptance, providing the ratio of benefit to cost remains at the same or higher level. The research gives valuable insight into one of the key criteria of successful innovation — concentrating on the innovation from the customer perspective rather than the producer's internal criteria. In sales jargon, these diffusion studies suggest that companies should concentrate on consumer *benefits* rather than features. This issue will be considered in later chapters. Though the identification of influences on speed of diffusion point to variations in performance among innovative concepts the studies still do not explain why similar innovations offering more or less identical economic advantages should perform so very differently in various national economies.

It appears, however, that a fundamental part is played by the type of individual involved in the buying and how it is carried out. Consumer behaviour research suggests that five types of consumer can be identified for any one specific product — not all individuals occupy the same category for all products. These are innovators, early adopters, early majority, late majority and laggards. Diffusion of an innovation through the population is explained by the speed at which the various groups react and the interrelationships between them. An innovative buyer is more adventurous and risk taking, productive, educated and cosmopolitan, and exposed to a wider range of information sources. Early adopters accept ideas with some care and thought and are generally regarded as opinion leaders, and influence the acceptance of the product by the other groups; they also tend to be the largest consumers of the product. Comparing certain market environments with others shows clearly how some of these factors operate. Information access is obviously crucial, and modifies typical market changes. For example, the French consumer market has not followed its European neighbours in taking rapidly to new alcoholic drinks products, a difference attributed to the ban on alcohol advertising on television in France. Studies of the information sources in large and small companies show clearly that large companies have far greater information sources than small ones which often rely on the sales representative as the main source of information about products. In tandem with the amount of information available is the buyer's sophistication as a decision maker. This will be determined partly by the size of the firm and the type of personnel employed

Table 5.8 Ranking of factors important in the acceptance of innovation

Socio-demographic	Attitudinal
Income	Knowledgeability
Standard of living	Empathy
Education	Positive attitude towards change
Literacy	Motivation towards achievement
Age	Business orientation
	Mental rigidity

Source: E.M. Rogers and D.J. Stanfield, in F. Bass (ed.)
Adoption and Diffusion of New Products, 1967

in buying, because of the clear correlations between socio-demographic characteristics and positive attitudes towards innovation (see Table 5.8).

Large firms tend to employ more sophisticated buyers who use a wide range of techniques to identify new products and take decisions. These include: vendor ranking methods; developing close relationships with suppliers via trade marketing agreements; and using a wide range of information sources. As a result, not only do they receive more quotations, but they also research the market much more deeply than small firms who may only ask for one quotation on a particular buying issue. As a result, of the following three types of possible buying decision:

- straight rebuy — ordering the same product from the same manufacturer;
- modified rebuy — ordering a slightly different product from the same manufacturer; and
- new buy — ordering a new product from a new manufacturer;

new buys make up a very small percentage of the total buying pattern for the small company, which tends to rely more heavily on existing suppliers. It might be expected that as the size of the firm increases, the speed of diffusion will increase too. This has certainly been the case in industries like farming where large firms innovate more rapidly than small. However, when an organization is a monopoly or near monopoly the pressures to innovate tend to be reduced as predicted in several economic models. The decline in the diffusion of new concepts as size increases is also supported by the wheel of retailing concept where organizations that dominate the marketplace are reluctant to innovate, enabling new firms to become established, which in turn grow and ossify as they lead the market.

The level of expertise of buyers employed in industry is another crucially important factor. One of the major differences between the United Kingdom and fast innovation markets overseas is that the UK buying function is a low status one in the company hierarchy, attracting individuals with few skills and little training for the technical role that they are asked to master. This is one of the explanations put forward for the differing rates of diffusion in the United States and Japan. This is further complicated by the fact that UK management has a lower level of formal education than its European competitors. Where technical

Table 5.9 Innovative versus adoptive managers

Adoptive	Innovative
Cost accountants	Financial accountants
Technical engineers	Management engineers
Production management	General managers
	Marketing managers

Source: G.R. Foxall, Technovation, 4, 1986

qualifications for buyers are of recognized importance, selection procedures may recruit unsuitable individuals for the position. Thus, in studies on chemical companies, many of the buyers came from production-related jobs and were unlikely to be highly innovative in their attitudes to new products or processes[4]; a hypothesis supported by research identifying those management types that would be most adaptive (supportive of group decisions) or innovative (see Table 5.9). It is, however, interesting that the United Kingdom has experienced more rapid diffusion of many household durables than comparable EC countries, and this may be a reflection of the sophistication and centralization of durable retail buying in the United Kingdom compared with the rest of Europe.

Increasing segmentation in the majority of markets could have the effect of reducing the speed of new product diffusion as the wide variety of products makes it more difficult for new products to achieve greater relative advantage, considered in some research as one of the key factors in purchase decisions (see Table 5.7). It is clear, however, that increasing sophistication of buyers — inevitable as the base of industrial, consumer and service companies becomes more concentrated — serves to offset this effect of product confusion, with the implication that diffusion rates will be highest in industries where professional buyers exist, and lowest in industries with a large number of small firms, regardless of the number of different segments that exist in each industry.[5]

The French and British yacht building industries illustrate the influence of the various factors on innovation diffusion. The more highly skilled French industry with a small number of medium- to large-sized firms such as Benetteau and Jeanneau has been far more responsive to innovative construction techniques and new types of design, than the British industry which has historically been made up of what are basically craft companies producing small numbers of yachts. Examples of these reveal that markets with slow diffusion rates are likely to be those with large numbers of small firms with conservative buyers, or the other extreme of a market dominated by one or two organizations occupying a monopoly or quasi-monopoly position. Given the role of the home market in providing a platform for many companies in their worldwide expansion, the buyer's contribution in accepting new technology is crucial to the eventual international success of new product introduction. On this basis the market in the United Kingdom for the majority of technical innovations is often likely to be far more hostile than that of other countries, and markets such as that of industrial fasteners, which is highly fragmented throughout the world, are also likely to be less attractive investment opportunities, than markets where diffusion rates can be predicted to be substantially higher.[6]

Cultural barriers may also exist to slow diffusion. These are rarely considered to be important in industrial markets, but are often held up as of considerable importance in many consumer and service sectors. Individual analysis of each particular market sector tends to suggest that such non-tariff barriers are less important in reality. For example, Unilever uses a simple model to determine washing requirements world-wide, an interrelationship of GNP per capita with total consumption providing clear indications as to when the demand for fabric conditioner and liquid detergent is likely to occur in specific markets. The Mercedes Benz has acquired such status in Africa that a Swahili term Wa-Benzi has developed to describe people that own them; Nestlé has developed instant coffee sales throughout the world including Japan; the world's largest McDonald's opened in Moscow in 1990. Examples such as these suggest that cultural barriers where they occur will only be important in a limited range of products, and even these will tend to be reduced over time. Thus the volume of anise products consumed in the French drinks market steadily declines to be replaced by international drinks including Malibu and whisky, and the English beer market is increasingly dominated by lager. As markets become more international it is inevitable that they will become more homogeneous, even though the potential for truly standard products either within national boundaries or across them will be restricted both by increased segmentation and regional variations of demand.

Market access: non-behavioural diffusion barriers

But there are other factors of varying importance that affect the spread of innovation within a market. Often it is government attitudes and market controls that loom largest. They operate in a number of ways. First, specific restrictions on certain activities may limit or direct the market in particular directions. The US ban on the transfer of technology to Eastern Europe has been so vaguely worded that many EC companies using US components in otherwise innovative equipment have been unwilling to risk exports — in contrast, it has been claimed, to many US companies. Bilateral agreements can also restrain overall the ability to exploit fully the market potential. The American and British governments have agreed to limit the total market share for Japanese cars in their respective markets. This has caused certain anomalies; a concentration by the major Japanese manufacturers on four-wheeled vehicles in the US market, for example, which are not covered by the trade agreement, and the move to establish local production inside the EC by both Toyota and Nissan which may have a much more serious impact on the EC car market than the potential loss of market share from direct imports.

Governments can have a major impact on market attractiveness in the whole area of product specification. The EC trade commission has directed its attention at reducing these technical barriers and harmonizing standards on such equipment as central heating radiators — still manufactured to different specifications within various member states. Changing safety regulations can successfully delineate and reduce the attractiveness of the market. One amusing example is the delightful claim of the Japanese authorities that Japanese snow is unique and therefore foreign ski manufacturers (which perhaps not surprisingly dominated that market) no longer met Japanese safety standards. Such safety goalpost moving has a more serious side with a company such as JCB, the world leader in backhoe excavators, deciding not to persevere with the Japanese market.

Government intervention can also affect markets by favouring supply purchase from specific, normally local manufacturers. Such preferences are extremely difficult to prove when, as is normally the case, tenders are confidential. Rare actions against particular authorities such as the Trent Health Authority case brought by Burroughs, the American computer manufacturer, have failed to prove that preference was being shown to the local supplier, in this case, International Computers or ICL. Licensing and restrictions imposed by the government may also mean that only a particular type of outlet is allowed to stock a product, and this will further limit the potential distribution channels. Such restrictions on the access to distribution channels mean that the market will either be totally closed or be far more restricted than might otherwise be the case.

The effective protection of innovation by government is important to a majority of companies' assessments of the attractiveness of a market. Protection for innovation largely relies, in the majority of industrialized countries, on implementation of either the patent or copyright laws. The costs of maintaining the patents throughout the world has to be reviewed constantly as for a marginal patent they will be extremely expensive. One of the reasons put forward by the pharmaceutical companies for the decline in innovation within the industry has been the effect of increasing clearance requirements on the length of time that patents will take to generate high levels of profit. When long clearance procedures reduce the available repayment period the attractiveness of the market is significantly reduced and this, in the view of the pharmaceutical industry, will reduce the attractiveness of the sector as an investment opportunity.[7]

Attempts by the biotechnology industry to use copyright legislation to control effectively a particular genotype (meaning that a particular pattern of genes will remain the property of the company developing them, however many generations the genetic material passes through) may dramatically change the attractiveness of the market environment as an investment. The computer software industry is beset with problems of illegal copying, with worldwide losses estimated at between $250 million and $750 million per annum. This substantially reduces the attractiveness of expensive investment in the development of complex and sophisticated software. None of the current methods of protecting software, either by dedicated discs (that need to be maintained in the computer for the programme to run) or some form of mechanical add-on (or dongle), have been wholly successful. The development of effective protection may again lead to substantial and even more rapid change within this sector of the industry than is currently occurring. The costs and length of time involved in the action brough by Intel against NEC for copyright violations of their 8088 and 8086 chips did little to clarify the position.

It is therefore clear that for companies operating in areas requiring high levels of investment a market's attractiveness is substantially diminished if effective protection is lacking or if the costs of achieving it are too high. This is confirmed by the experience of countries where protection has been limited in specific sectors or across the board; Taiwan, for example, faces a problem of moving from an economy dependent on low labour costs towards one more reliant on innovation. This may be hampered by its historically poor regulation of copyright and patent law. Similarly, the pharmaceutical industry in Italy had been one of Europe's smallest partly because of poor implementation of patent legislation in the Italian market, though there were other structural causes.

Other minor influences on market attractiveness especially relevant to small markets include access to distribution channels and physical distribution restrictions. The distribution of alcoholic drinks in the Gulf is a good example of this. Two companies, Inchcape and African and Eastern, a Unilever subsidiary, have effective control over the distribution of alcohol; supplier companies trying to establish new concepts in the market face the problem of dealing with distributors with already firmly established products. Absence of the necessary physical distribution systems may in certain sectors also reduce the attractiveness of the market. The further processed fresh food market is a case in point. Though the frozen food market has continued to expand once the level of retail freezer cabinets was established, the fresh processed food market has languished in comparison because of the problems of ensuring a rapid movement in specifically designed chilled goods vehicles from the manufacturer to the retail outlet, a transport problem that the frozen market does not face.

Market value added

Historically, the definition of market profitability has relied on the assessment of the likely price elasticity, the way in which price is likely to change with increased supply. This will be a measure of the level of competition and the type of product. In commodity markets such as flour, sugar and oil, the relationship between supply and demand will, all other factors being equal (no cartels, monopolies or government price controls intervening), determine the level of price and hence the level of profitability that can be achieved by the supplier. But many product sectors do not operate with such a clear-cut distinction between supply and demand, and buyer perceptions of intangible factors are often a more important determinant of price.[8] In industrial equipment, for example, product reliability is an important aspect of many purchase decisions, and the perceptions of the buyer about product reliability will be significantly influenced both by prior experience about the company and by promotional information. In many consumer sectors intangible factors such as quality, or perceptions of image are often related to price. Take, for example, the market for trainers or leather accessories. Products such as Nike, Adidas and Puma can demand high prices for products essentially similar to those produced by companies such as Dunlop and Simod. Gucci and Luis Vitton can achieve similar premium positioning in markets where much lower prices are obtainable for standard leather accessories. One can see such distinctions in comparable surveys on the ranking given to certain variables in, first, a typical commodity product where price and other price components (payment terms and delivery are crucial), and secondly, complex industrial equipment such as hydraulic components where non-price factors are far more important (see Tables 5.10 and 5.11).

The results of these and other similar surveys on the purchase of complex equipment and expensive consumer products (see Table 5.12) show that the attractiveness of the market is greater for those manufacturers that can reach and maintain the required quality levels by superior manufacturing expertise. High-value-added market sectors are most likely to be found where high levels of manufacturing expertise are needed. For those companies that can develop and maintain that manufacturing expertise, such markets are likely to be far more attractive as investment opportunities than markets where less rigorous manufacturing standards are required. MITI, the Japanese trade ministry, has

Table 5.10 Ranking of criteria in the purchase of lubricating oil

Factor	Rank
Price	1
Delivery speed	2
Quality	3
Technical service	4
Payment terms	5

Source: Adapted from R.W. Hill and T.J. Hillier, *Organisational Buying Behaviour*, 1984

Table 5.11 Ranking criteria of hydraulic components

Factor	Rank
Product reliability	1
Reliability of manufacturer	2
Reliability of delivery	3
Speed of delivery	4
Price	5
Product capability	6

Source: Adapted from R.W. Hill and T.J. Hillier, *Organisational Buying Behaviour*, 1984

Table 5.12 Ranking criteria for two food processor market segments

	Simple range	Complex
Very important	$49.99 4 quart bowl	Seven speeds use of blender/mixer
Moderately important	two speeds seven blades heavy duty motor pouring spout	$99.99 2 quart bowl cylindrical bowl regular discharge bowl
Minor importance	side discharge	seven blades

Source: A.L. Page and H.F. Rosenblaum, *Journal of Product Innovation Management*, 4, 1987

continued to emphasize investment in such high expertise, value-added areas. The withdrawal of support for such areas as shipbuilding and textiles on which the early Japanese industrial revival was built reflects the declining edge that Japanese manufacturers have over their neighbours such as Korea. Investment in such areas as pharmaceuticals, lasers and fifth-generation computers demonstrate a commitment towards higher value-added sectors. In summary, one can identify the factors that are likely to provide high value-added market sectors as a record of sector profitability, technology restricted to a few companies, and a continuing market demand for high quality and high reliability products.[9]

Relative product life

Sony's advantage over the competition in terms of the decreasing period of time during which they are in sole possession of a particular market sector has already been mentioned. This period of so-called competitive grace is of obvious importance to any company evaluating the potential attractiveness of a particular market sector. Obviously, the protection afforded by patents increases the likelihood of achieving longer periods of competitive grace, but with the confused state of many patent and copyright actions, patents may not necessarily significantly extend the period in which the company has the sole presence in the market with a particular product type, offering similar benefits. The customer, after all, is only interested in the output criteria of a particular product — speed, reliability, and other benefits. How they are provided is largely immaterial. A competitor, therefore, can produce very similar products using a different technical approach.

Attractive markets provide long periods of competitive grace but these, alas, are becoming substantially fewer in number. Companies therefore have to calculate the duration of the three main stages in the product's evolution; competitive grace, market leadership, and product survival, which will differ from sector to sector. The period of market leadership is seen in the past history of many innovations in which, though the company is no longer the sole supplier of a particular product, it is able to hold onto the major part of the market because of its innovative actions. Finally, there will be a varying period of product survival, where the product is under major competitive pressures, either from the introduction of new technology or other competitive actions. In a highly competitive market like semiconductors the altered duration of these three components over five years can be estimated (Table 5.13).

Obviously not all markets are as competitive as semiconductors and different rates will apply elsewhere. Figure 5.2 illustrates a range of product life curves, each with differing attractiveness to the company. Line A is the least attractive — it identifies a very short period of competitive grace, followed by a practically non-existent period of market leadership, with a lengthy period of product survival. Line B suggests a period of competitive grace, followed by a relatively short period of market leadership, followed by a long period of product survival. Line C

Table 5.13 Changes in the length of product life in
microprocessor industry (years)

	1975–79	1988–90
Competitive grace	1.0	0.5
Market leadership	2.0	0.8
Product survival	1.5	0.7
Total life	4.5	2.0

Source: Trade estimates from electronic manufacturers

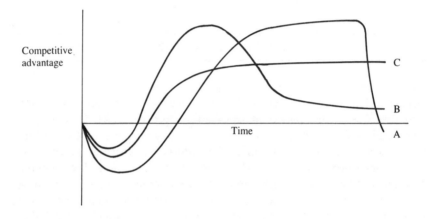

Figure 5.2 Product life curves

illustrates the most attractive pattern, with a long period of competitive grace
followed by a fairly long period of market leadership. The development of
computer technology has made the financial assessment of pay-back periods, rate
of internal return and other investment analyses far easier to complete, and such
issues are outside the scope of this book. However, much of the profitability
analysis that goes into such calculations will depend on a qualitative assessment
of overall product life and price levels maintainable in the market.

Synergy

All studies on profitable innovation support the view that the degree of synergy
or similarity between the current product or service range and the proposed new
introduction is a vital component in success. An established company with
knowledge of a market sector will be more perceptive about opportunities for
profit than a less well-placed competitor. For example Caterpillar or Komatsu
with well-established market positions in the manufacture of construction
equipment would find the market for innovations in construction equipment far
more attractive than a company not established in the market. The level of synergy

achieved will depend on how different the new introduction is in certain key areas. Central to this is the relationship with existing customers. Does the company have to establish a relationship with an entirely new set of customers, or can the product be sold through the current distribution channels? The difference in cost of establishing new customers compared with maintaining the relationship with old has been estimated at around 700 per cent. In other words companies have to be prepared to invest at least seven times the amount in non-synergistic products than they would do with products that can be sold through the same distribution channels. Many companies fail to appreciate the importance of logistics and the cost of setting up alternative systems, which range from separate production points and warehouses to higher levels of stocks, different physical distribution systems and order processing networks. The costs involved are considerable. A 1987 survey of major manufacturing sectors revealed that the average logistics cost in Europe was 21 per cent, with the highest level in beverages and food (see Table 5.14).

Where the company is establishing entirely new product lines there will be additional problems encompassing such issues as separate management, staff and facilities in production, physical distribution, sales, reporting systems, marketing and senior management. One increasingly important component of synergy is information management. In competitive environments where information is crucial for the control of the business, the demands on management time and cost of the information system will often be substantial. For example, General Mills, the large American baking group estimates that database and other information management costs exceed $3 million per annum. A company such as Unilever in the United Kingdom with its centralized consumer goods database accessible by all the operating companies, is ideally placed to explore new fast-moving consumer goods concepts. However, should it hypothetically consider an expansion into ethical pharmaceuticals, an entirely new set of information requirements would exist, and this would lead to the need to invest considerable sums in developing the new information systems necessary for such a venture. One final issue involved in any analysis of synergy is the question of whether the product is taking sales away from the current product range (cannibalism). The assessment of possible cannibalistic effects can often be complex, particularly

Table 5.14 Logistics cost in Europe in selected sectors

Sector	Percentage cost
Aerospace	12.8
Agriculture/construction	13.2
Beverage/food	30.9
Building materials	25.0
Chemicals/petroleum prods	20.6
Clothing/textiles	23.4
Paper/rubber	19.0

Source: A.T. Kearney, company report, 1988

where the company is selling products to market segments that have not been clearly defined. This is a particular problem for many consumer products where the segmentation criteria used are based on life-style assessments where the segment may not — in contrast to long-lasting socio-economic or demographic divisions — be maintained over the life of the product (or, as has been claimed in certain studies, exist at all). In contrast the industrial company is probably able to define far more accurately the positive or negative impact of the product on existing ranges. This problem of possible cannibalism underlines the importance of matching customer benefit to identified and reachable market segments. Where this analysis has been rigorously completed the chances of cannibalism will be substantially reduced.

Summary

Businesses will need to evaluate markets mainly using a series of qualitative criteria to determine whether a particular market is potentially attractive for innovation investment. Though criteria will differ from company to company, the most important elements are likely to be the size and growth of the relevant market, access to markets, the likely speed of diffusion, whether the company can with the expertise at its disposal add sufficient value to the new introduction, and the degree of synergy that the company can achieve with its current business portfolio.

Notes

1. D.F. Abell and A. Hammond, *Marketing Strategy*, (Englewood Cliffs: Prentice Hall, 1982). A. Cooper, 'Success Parameters in New Product Development', *Research and Development Management*, 2 (1987), pp. 13−17.
2. R.N. Foster, *Innovation, The Attackers' Advantage*, (London: Pan, 1986).
3. E.M. Rogers and D.J. Stanfield in F. Bass (ed.), *Adoption and Diffusion of New Products*, (Chichester: Wiley, 1967). S.L. Holak and D.R. Lehman, 'Diffusion of Innovation', *Journal of Product Innovation Management*, issue 2, 7 (1990), pp. 19−27.
4. R.W. Hill and T.J. Hillier, *Organisational Buying Behaviour*, (London: Macmillan, 1984).
5. M. Kamien, *Market Structure and Innovation*, (Cambridge: Cambridge University Press, 1982).
6. V. Mahajan and Y. Wind (eds), *Diffusion Models of New Product Acceptance*, (Cambridge: Cambridge University Press, 1982).
7. R. Coombs, P. Saviotti and V. Walsh, *Economics and Technological Change*, (London: Macmillan, 1987).
8. A.L. Page and H.F. Rosenblaum, 'Consumer Buying Behaviour', *Journal of Product Innovation Management*, issue 4, 4 (1987), pp. 26−37.
9. E. Mansfield, 'The Speed and Cost of Industrial Innovation in Japan and the US', *Management Science*, no 10, 34 (1988), pp. 137−48.

6

National resources for innovation

Introduction

However attractive a market, innovation will only occur if the right resources are available to investigate ideas, develop them and bring them into effective production. Though the final resource environment is more than a sum of the constituent parts it is still important to identify the key components that either promote or reduce innovation.

For even the largest firm, the impact of general and specific government policies is a major influence, improving or reducing the resources that are available for innovation. The role of government in managing change has grown with the greater and greater share of total Gross Domestic Product (GDP) raised by taxes: governments in the majority of industrialized countries take over 40 per cent of total GDP, with the trend upwards rather than downwards. Since the early 1980s commercial organizations in the EC are increasingly influenced by EC policies, so that there are a range of supranational influences on innovation as well, which are summarized in Table 6.1.

Domestic policy

A government has a wide-ranging influence on the resources available to the companies within its sphere of authority. For example, governmental control over interest rates in the majority of markets indirectly influences capital investment levels. It has been suggested that the high interest rates since the late 1970s have been the main cause of the limited capital investment in British manufacturing industry.[1] Inflation, another component of investment, is partially influenced by government action, or by external influences (IMF, raw material cartels), or a mixture of both. Inflation is often identified as the main restriction to increased

Table 6.1 Main macro-environmental issues affecting innovation climate

Domestic economy	Policies aimed at encouraging investment and risk: • Inflation • Bank rates • Legislation directed towards improving the taxation position of investment and research and development • Anti-monopoly legislation • Mergers and industrial management
Support for infrastructure	Policies aimed at enabling businesses to perform better and more efficiently: • transport • communication links • information links
Support for the labour market	Education system provision for innovation needs: • Secondary • Tertiary • Post experience
Enhancement of technology	Research system provision for innovation needs: • Direct investment in specific ventures • Assistance for joint ventures

Source: Author

investment by small to medium-sized companies as illustrated in the findings of Table 6.2. In the case of multinationals operating across national boundaries, governments may have an additional distorting effect on the financial environment by reducing the freedom of financial movements from one subsidiary to another by some form of foreign exchange control. When rigidly exercised in centrally planned economies, exchange control can fundamentally affect the resources available to the organization as a whole and therefore the resource base of operating subsidiaries. Obviously, the taxation and tax allowance environment will also have an impact on the level of resources available. Cash flow back to the organization from an investment will be determined not only by the total revenue generated but also by the level of taxation on those earnings and the ability to depreciate the equipment necessary to manufacture the product.

In contrast, access to external funding is largely determined by the institutional climate while the role of government is rather more restricted even though again

Table 6.2 Factors adversely affecting trading prospects

Factor	Percentage
Economic climate	46
Low prices	30
Manpower problems	11
Technological change	6
Overheads	4

Source: NEDO *Report on the Printing Industry*, 1985

the two will interact. Thus, in the West German and American federal systems, the local structure of finance through the Landbank system on the one hand and the state banks on the other appears more effective in fostering local investment than the United Kingdom's centralized system. It is interesting to note also in this context that Switzerland, with the most highly decentralized form of government, is achieving a very high rate of patent introduction. It is tempting to suggest that local banks, fostered and indeed partially regulated by most federal systems, only survive by developing a local investment programme and are therefore forced by circumstances to accept a higher level of risk than national banks indifferent to the viability of one particular locality. The high failure rate of agricultural banks in the United States highlights the tendency of these local institutions to concentrate their lending within the nearby territory, a factor which is strengthened by legislative restrictions on out-of-state lending. The larger national banks, by contrast, have preferred to lose their money by lending it to Latin America and Africa. However, local funding is not obviously the sole component of the innovation financial resource as can be seen by the success of centralized funding in Sweden and Japan.

Government also has an important role in maintaining a legislative environment that enhances and supports nationally based investment, especially in new product concepts. This may take the form of formal controls over foreign acquisitions, as was the case in Japan until the late 1970s, or may involve the creation of an internal market structure that limits access to foreign involvement by cross shareholdings, the position in Germany. A comparison of the problems of Jaguar and Porsche in the late 1980s is instructive in showing these systems at work. Both Jaguar and Porsche faced a rapid decline in earnings due to the fall in the value of the dollar. Hence the necessity to fund new concepts. The declining share price in the one led to takeover by an American multinational, Ford, in the other to continued independence and control by a German national company.

Anti-monopoly legislation also affects the likely environment for innovation. Reducing monopoly powers and encouraging competition will inevitably influence overall innovative performance in the economy. Where governments encourage monopolies or quasi-monopolies in key sectors of the economy, the competitive pressures that drive change will be substantially reduced. Governments can also direct industrial development by active encouragement of mergers or by the takeover of troubled industrial organizations. MITI, the Japanese trade ministry, has been a particularly good example of how governments can create industrial climates by encouraging developments in particular industrial sectors, but most governments have been involved in such areas (for example the intervention of the Industrial Reorganisation Board in 1968/69 in the United Kingdom created a single large ball-bearing supplier RHP from a number of independent companies). Government intervention through financial support or public ownership — important features of the modern industrialized country — can significantly affect the pattern of innovation in a particular nation. Thus, the acquisition of Rolls-Royce aero engines under one UK administration helped support a continuing significant presence in that area of international research activity; whereas the lack of support for Inmos, a semiconductor venture under another, meant that a possible major role for the economy in that sector was ended.

Support for infrastructure

Of all the resource factors influenced by national governments, physical infrastructure problems have historically been the least likely to be limiting, certainly through the bulk of the industrialized world. Stated simply, the majority of firms are not physically prevented from bringing goods to market by lack of power, water or transport facilities. For less-developed countries (LDCs) and newly industrializing countries (NICs) infrastructure limitation may be a far more important component of the resources environment, and a crucial one in limiting innovation. As economies become more sophisticated and value-added in their manufacturing policies, the type of infrastructure requirement is likely to change.

Earlier chapters have concentrated on the concept of knowledge competition, and this has implications for future government infrastructure provisions. Investment by the Federal government in the United States in the development of high-speed data transmission lines providing high-quality error-free information transfer is one such example of the possible new infrastructure demands of the knowledge culture in the twenty-first century. Singapore, too, has developed sophisticated data bases in a number of key business areas, supported by advanced supercomputers and accessible by both commercial and research organizations. The importance of government investment in this area is magnified by the rapid growth in the amount of technical information entering the public domain. It has been estimated that the number of books in print doubles every fifteen years; the numbers of journals every sixteen. Various researchers claim that the declining investment in physical infrastructure by the UK government will substantially reduce the ability of technically advanced companies to operate in the market, by failing to create an environment in which businesses can either operate efficient logistics systems, travel with ease or communicate rapidly.[2] Similar suggestions have been advanced for the development of an advanced components industry.

Government support for the labour market

How a government invests in the organization and development of the labour pool is a key influence on innovation.

The first, most obvious, way in which the government intervenes is the level of investment in secondary, tertiary, and postgraduate education, and where this investment is directed. One analysis of influences on economic growth in the United States underlines the importance of this investment. In this study the author identified a large number of possible factors including capital, the total size of

Table 6.3 Main causes of US economic growth 1929–62

Increased employment	34
Increased education	23
Advancement of knowledge	20
Increased capital	15
Economies of scale	9

Source: E.F. Denison, *Why Growth Rates Differ*, 1967

the labour force, hours of employment, and education. It concluded that economic growth could be ascribed to five main factors. These are detailed in order of importance in Table 6.3. Since the 1960s when this survey was completed the importance of the knowledge base has been further extended in the majority of industrialized countries as the labour force ages, and the working week has been generally reduced by legislation and corporate/union agreement.

The many comparisons between the UK, West German and Japanese systems, reveal substantial differences between the countries in the acquisition of different skills, especially in the areas of mathematics and science-based subjects.[3] The investment in the education system can be separated for convenience into the acquisition of theoretical engineering knowledge, theoretical management expertise and technical skills. Each industrialized country differs in how these knowledge and skills components are developed and integrated into the industrial infrastructure. Though straightforward comparisons of the number of engineers per head of population is fairly similar between the industrialized countries (see Table 6.4) the type of engineers and how they are used are more important resource components. The Japanese system produces a far higher proportion of engineers specializing in process and electronic areas than the British system, with up to seven times more process engineers graduating in 1987 on a per capita basis; thus, in addition to quantitative differences there are large variations in the quality or type of graduates generated. Overall figures on the use of engineering and other graduates suggest that as a percentage of the total graduates the number employed in British manufacturing are equal to or better than other industrialized countries.

Table 6.4 Comparisons of total numbers of engineers per 10,000 of the population

Country	1965	1977	1984
France	21.0	29.9	35.0
West Germany	22.6	40.5	44.0
UK	21.4	30.0	32.0
Japan	25.0	48.0	54.0
US	64.0	57.0	54.0

Source: Department of Education and Science (UK)

Table 6.5 Employment of qualified engineers in metal manufacturing as a percentage of overall workforce 1977 in various industrialized countries

Country	Percentage employed
Sweden	6.6
West Germany	5.7
France	5.3
UK	1.8

Source: A. Albu in K. Pavitt (ed.), *Technical Innovation and British Economic Performance*, 1980

Table 6.6 Percentage of age group in degree level education, 1987

Country	Percentage
US	27
Japan	27
Netherlands	12
Italy	25
France	22
UK	10
West Germany	18

Source: Department of Education and Science (UK)

Here again, analysis of employment patterns in specific sectors of the economy where a high engineering component is essential, suggests that qualitative rather than quantitative assessments are important. Thus, for example, a survey of metal manufacturing industries showed that in 1977, Sweden employed nearly four times the number of engineers per head of the workforce than the United Kingdom (see Table 6.5). Though the percentage of university graduates in the United Kingdom is lower than in other industrialized countries, a comparison of middle management in West Germany and the United Kingdom reveals a further qualitative gap between the two systems, with a higher proportion of graduates entering management positions than in the population as a whole compared with the United Kingdom (see Tables 6.6, 6.7).

There are also qualitative differences in how management skills are developed in the major industrialized economies. In France, for example, the managerial elites pass through the Ecole Nationale d'Administration or the Ecole Poly-technique, which emphasize specific administrative skills (an approach similar to that of the United States, with 70,000 graduate MBAs produced per year, where specific graduate skills in management are now practically obligatory in acquiring a management post). By contrast the emphasis of German, and to an extent Italian education is on the development of technical skills with government support without the acquisition of overall management skills — which is learnt on the

Table 6.7 Comparison of middle management education West Germany/UK

Type of qualification	West Germany	UK
Degree	26	12
Professional institution	18	6
HNC/A level	7	5
Degree ratio[1]	150	120

Note: [1] The number of graduate managers in proportion to the number of graduates in the population as a whole

Source: NEDO, 1987

job during in-house training. This emphasis is broadly similar to the development of skills within the Japanese management system. The UK system largely falls outside these two broad approaches. It neither emphasizes the acquisition of technical skills within the management grade nor the development of administrative skills, either within tertiary education or in additional part-time educational oppportunities. All the comparative studies indicate that the many UK corporations still perceive a role for the 'gifted amateur'.

In the area of technical skills, there are also major quantitative and qualitative differences between various systems. The West German education system is concerned very much with the development of technical skills within a clearly defined framework, leading to the acquisition of specific qualifications. The comparison between the United Kingdom and Japan — which has approximately double the UK population — shows a considerable gap in the output of the two education systems, especially in students involved in mechanical engineering (see Table 6.8). A study of the changes in the French education system revealed a rapid shift towards the acquisition of formal skills in the late 1980s.

Governments have acknowledged the importance of investment in the nurturing of new skills and the revitalization of old ones within the labour force. To understand the crucial component of training it is necessary to consider the effect of the changes in the knowledge base on the working population. The reason why this is so important is the effects of the rapid rate of change in the knowledge base. In the nineteenth century working practices changed slowly, and over the working life of an industrial worker skills acquisition could proceed at a fairly leisurely pace, and skills, once learnt, would remain effective for many years. The pattern of the late twentieth century places entirely new demands upon both nation and corporation. This can be demonstrated by a fairly simple equation:

$$LR = (S - F)N$$

S = The total knowledge base possessed by the individual (the knowledge 'stock').

F = The fraction that is forgotten every year.

N = The annual growth rate in the new knowledge component.

R = The time necessary to acquire the new knowledge.

L = The learning rate (based on thirty-week academic year, i.e. 450 teaching days).

Table 6.8 Vocational schooling Japan/UK 1982−84

Area	Japan 1982	UK 1983−4
Mechanical engineers	50,400	16,900
Electrical/electronic	41,000	17,330
Business studies	175,000	13,900

Source: National Institute for Economic and Social Research

Assuming that the learning rate remains constant to the rate in higher education (again a questionable assumption to those that are involved in training), and that the annual growth rate equals the loss rate of around say 3 per cent per year (which is consistent with the doubling of the information base every fifteen years), the required level of training each year can easily be calculated. Changing either the rate of knowledge loss or the information growth will substantially alter the pattern of the table. Use of this equation shows that a workforce member would have to receive a substantial level of training, around thirty working days in the first year (about 15 per cent of the working year) to maintain the equivalent position to that reached by the time of graduation from tertiary education. Obviously, this is just to maintain the status quo; higher levels of skill acquisition would require greater training. A table can be created from such an equation which identifies the cumulative effects of skills shortage (see Table 6.9).

Someone who has worked in a technical field without additional educational training would therefore require an entire year's training at the end of the sixth year. If the rate of knowledge increase is greater or the rate of loss more extreme, the greater the required training input. Personnel working in data processing for example would need substantially higher levels of knowledge acquisition merely to stand still in a rapidly changing environment. It is interesting that as a rule of thumb the old academic concept of the sabbatical granted during the seventh year to improve understanding and knowledge is very much a reflection of this 'knowledge' table.

The resource implications for the innovating company are clear; the higher the knowledge component at the start the lower the additional training cost. The rapid

Table 6.9 Movements over the years of original knowledge (stock), new advances in knowledge (new stock), new existing level of knowledge at year end (new level) and required training input to maintain existing knowledge level (cumulative days training) based on knowledge loss of three per cent per year, knowledge increase of four per cent per year and similar learning rate to original training.

Year	Stock	New stock	New level	Cumulative days training
1	97	5	104	31
2	94	4	108	63
3	91	4	112	94
4	88	5	117	130
5	85	5	122	166
6	82	5	127	202
7	79	5	132	238
8	76	5	137	274
9	73	6	143	315
10	70	6	149	355
11	67	6	155	396
12	64	6	161	436
13	61	6	167	477
14	58	7	174	522
15	55	7	181	567
16	52	7	188	612

Source: Author

growth in knowledge puts a premium on the quality of the initial knowledge input. Compare an educational system that delivers entirely up-to-date information and knowledge, at an index of 100, and one that is ten years out of date, with an index of 50. Assuming the cost of training at around £200 per day (at 1989 prices) for in-house development and average industrial wages in 1988 plus overheads plus training costs, the additional costs to the company would be of the region of £45,000 to raise the knowledge component from the lower to the higher level. Any analysis of the resources available for effective innovation will be increasingly dependent on the *quality* of the education system rather than the *quantity* generated. Education systems that emphasize cost analysis in the production of technical or management skills will often be failing to provide an attractive and productive resource base for innovation.

Where the government takes an active role in supporting vocational and additional training, or provides improved access to information for individuals and firms, the resources for innovation will be correspondingly improved. The example of the German educational system in supporting technical education is a case in point: this inevitably lowers the cost to the firm and improves the resources environment available to the firm. The shift towards educational proposition A rather than B (see Table 6.10) is an important part of the support that the government can provide.

With the steadily increasing information base, the role of government in sifting and analysing potentially valuable commercial information will become more and more important. Here the impact of MITI within the Japanese environment has perhaps been crucial in the successful implementation of innovation, with the emphasis on the identification and support of areas of interest. The database maintained by MITI — the Japanese Trade and Industry Ministry — to support industry is one of the most impressive governmental resources that commercial firms can call upon. Governments can also improve the resource base of the firm by improving the access to overseas markets, investing in the development of effective overseas support. Thus Japan not only has over a dozen offices of JETRO (Japanese External Trade Organization) in the EC, but many of the 300 or so diplomats are involved specifically in trade development. In comparison the UK and other EC representation in Japan is far less extensive and, on anecdotal evidence, much less effective also.

How a government supports and develops research is another key element in the creation of resources for effective commercial innovation. Often this is in

Table 6.10 Different educational propositions

Proposition A	Proposition B
Education is straightforward (reading, writing, arithmetic)	Education is complex
Takes place over limited time period	For life
Takes place at school	Relevant everywhere

Source: Author

Table 6.11 Some investment failures of MITI, the Japanese trade ministry and reasons for those failures

Item	Cost ($m.)	Reason for failure
Remote-controlled oil drilling rig	36	No improvement in cost or operating efficiency
Electric car	46	Battery problems
Nuclear powered blast furnace	110	Resistance to application of nuclear systems
Petrochemicals from coal	84	Fall in oil prices
Weatherproof integrated circuits	11	Total lack of industrial interest

Source: Fortune, 13 February 1989

the form of direct funding of government research organizations for particular types of investigative activity. Thus the UK Atomic Energy Authority was a government institution receiving large grants for atomic energy research. In addition to specific funds directed to single bodies, government can provide additional resources by supporting sector-wide research projects. Japan's MITI again provides a classic example of co-operative funding supplying support in such areas as the development of the so-called fifth generation computers to enable Japan to enter a market currently dominated by the Americans. Governmental support is vital in such ventures because of the huge scale of the potential losses should an ambitious project fail. Japanese successes make it easy to consider failure as the preserve of European and North American administrations but Table 6.11 indicates that fortune is not necessarily on the side of the brave.

Government funding of research at universities and other partially independent institutions provides an additional resource in the support of innovation by analysing technological advances and providing 'digest' material via governmental or quasi-autonomous governmental organizations (quangos). The rising costs of such research support caused many countries to reappraise the role of such funding, and have led to calls in many industrialized countries for universities and research institutes to become more integrated with the business world. Though certain of the US universities have been adept at increasing their revenue from patent activity, overall net reduction in government grants has been negligible, with patent revenue rising over the last ten years from $10 to $50 million, though for some institutions the returns have been more satisfactory than others. Though the revenue generation from such ventures is considerable it rarely exceeds 10 per cent of total university income (Table 6.12).

The role of universities in supporting innovation is obviously a complex one as it may involve the following activities: pure research related to the development of a general understanding of particular issues; applied research to solve specific problems; the provision of a knowledge resource for the entire community, public, government and industry; and the site of training for future technical experts and general administrators. One option explored by government to increase the speed and value of the technology transfer from education to the business sector involved the attempted integration of universities with small entrepreneurial organizations, the 'science park' concept. Many of these ventures have been unsuccessful. Studies

Table 6.12 Number of patents issued to
American universities in 1988

Institution	Number
MIT	66
University of California	60
Stanford University	56
University of Minnesota	26
University of Florida	24

Source: Economist, June 1989

of the United States suggest that four components are essential to the success of areas like Silicon Valley and the area around Massachusetts. They are as follows:

1. A large and expert research base.
2. A large pool of local skilled labour.
3. Availability of local management with good business skills.
4. Sufficient locally available venture capital.[4]

The absence of one or more of these key components is a likely forerunner of failure. The conclusion from such studies is that the number of successful centres for such marrying of tertiary education and industry will be limited in any country. Within the United Kingdom there are very few research environments that have sufficient depth of expertise and knowledge to support such programmes, and this coupled with the shortage of management with good business skills will tend to mitigate effective return on investment in many of the thirty-eight units currently in operation within the United Kingdom.

This concept of a required 'critical mass' to support such developments was severely weakened by the growth of higher education in the 1960s which tended to dilute the concentration of technical expertise within the university community, creating UK institutions with limited depth in any one particular field. It is perhaps no surprise in consequence that the most thriving science park within the United Kingdom is concentrated around Cambridge, which retained much of the existing leadership in the development of natural sciences in the United Kingdom and retained a high staff density within a limited geographical area. Similarly, the progress of such American parks has been most apparent on the West and East Coasts, paralleling the concentration of research centres, further strengthening the argument for the need for concentration in the provision of government support to speed industrial innovation.

The conflicting issues in tertiary education suggest that though the university sector may be able to provide some potential support in certain areas, the uptake within the business community will vary from market sector to market sector and from country to country. Regardless of how it is handled, it appears that the role of tertiary education in providing a major direct source of support for innovation will be fairly limited, and can only be effectively channelled if the government provides centralized access to the information provided. This is one of the major problems in maximizing the effectiveness of all types of central government funded research in influencing innovation.

National investment in research and development

Direct investment by governments in specific areas of innovation is a further resource base available to help the commercial organization improve its competitive position in the international environment. The first factor in assessing this improved resource environment available to national companies is to consider overall expenditure by national governments as a proportion of GDP. This gives some idea as to the general climate in which companies operate. Statistics on total R & D expenditure show that between the mid-1960s and the mid-1980s the combined major trading blocks have increased spending (see Table 6.13). As might be expected the overall shares by trading block of world research and development expenditure have changed as a result of this altering pattern of expenditure and the relationship of world economies. Thus, the substantial increase in the Japanese share of total world research expenditure is clearly shown from the mid-1960s to the mid-1980s (see Table 6.14).

Much of the downturn in research and development expenditure in certain of the major OECD countries can be explained by a decline in either military-related expenditure or fundamental research on atomic power. Examples of the withdrawal of the UK government include a reduction in the commitment to the space

Table 6.13 R & D as a proportion of economic resources

		US	Japan	Europe
Total R & D as % of GDP	1967	3.07	1.58	1.78
	1975	2.38	2.01	1.81
	1983	2.73	2.67	2.08

Source: P. Patel and K. Pavitt, Research Policy, 1, 1987

Table 6.14 Percentage share of world R & D expenditure in five leading industrialized countries

Country	1965	1985
US	70	55
Japan	7	20
West Germany	6	11
UK	11	5
France	4	9
Total	100	100

Source: OECD

Table 6.15 Comparison of UK government expenditure 1979/80 and 1987/88 at 1979/80 prices (£m)

Sector	1979/80	1987/88
Regional assistance	509	159
Support for industry	142	240
Specific sector — aerospace/shipbuilding/steel/cars	338	80
Support for international trade	28	26

Source: Department of Trade and Industry (UK)

programme, the HOTOL jet project, and reduced commitments to the continuation of the atomic fusion project, JET. The balance of UK governmental expenditure has changed even within an overall decline. Thus, when one compares 1987 expenditure levels with those of 1979, substantial reductions have occurred in regional assistance and grants to the aerospace, shipbuilding, steel and car manufacturing sectors (see Table 6.15). In specific terms, UK government investment in support of innovation is small and, in relation to total government expenditure of over £190 billion (1991 estimates), minute, (see Table 6.16).

Superficially it seems that the resource base for innovation has improved internationally. However, it is obviously more important when considering national investment to identify specific areas of expenditure concentration, and how this has either helped or hindered national innovation policies. Whereas most of the Japanese research and development budget has been directed towards commercial innovation, much of the US and UK national research budgets have large military research components, and this is reflected in global research expenditure figures which identify the preponderance of spending in military-related research (see Table 6.17). The impact of such direction of government expenditure has been subject to comment at a national level and in relation to particular industries.[5] These studies make clear the considerable long-term impact of the emphasis of government expenditure on the success or otherwise of particular industrial sectors, even though certain studies find the relationship a weak one. How national

Table 6.16 UK Government grants to industry 1987/88 (estimates in current money)

Sector	£m.
Regional development grants	95
Regional selective assistance	93
Support for advanced manufacturing	15
Support for microelectronics	16
Major projects	11
Aerospace	86
Steel/shipbuilding	48
Space investment	64
Aircraft research and development	26
General investment in innovation	241

Source: Department of Trade and Industry (UK)

Table 6.17 Global research and development budget, 1979

	Percentage
Military related:	
Military	24
Space	8
Energy (mostly fusion/fission)	8
Social related:	
Health	7
Pollution control	3
Industry related:	
Transportation	5
Agriculture	3
Information processing	5
Basic research	15

Source: L. Brown, *Building a Sustainable Society*, 1981

governments direct their expenditure also influences the effectiveness of national investment policies. Each of the three major trading blocks has evolved fairly distinct approaches to channelling governmental support for research and development, with different focal points for investment, methods of support for the development and diffusion of knowledge, and ways for encouraging and improving the climate for innovation (see Table 6.18).

Large-scale programmes like NASA and SDI are good illustrations of how American governments stimulated innovation. Europe's concentration on key industries has led to research funding for projects such as RACE (digital networks for communications) and ESPRIT (advanced microelectronics, software technology, advanced information processing, office systems, and computer-aided manufacturing). In contrast the support given by MITI in Japan is closely associated with the development of specific projects, by no means always successful but often yielding considerable commercial results.[6] Some of the more important in the microelectronics sector are included in Table 6.19. The combination of overall expenditure, the type of industrial concentration, and method of organization go some of the way to explaining differences in the national resources for innovation and the consequent industrial performance of each market. These differences help to explain the changing pattern of national competitive development.[7]

Table 6.18 National differences in innovation management

Area	US	Europe	Japan
Focal points	Government programmes	Key industries	National vision
Knowledge diffusion	Research integration	Research stimulus	Mass education
Innovation climate	Fiscal incentives	Financial support	Industrial co-operation

Source: OECD

Table 6.19 Some MITI projects in information technology

Item	Years
High capacity IBM-style computers	1962−66
Superperformance IBM-style computers	1962−67
Mainframe IBM-style computers	1972−76
Fourth generation peripherals	1972−80
Fourth generation operating systems	1979−83
Supercomputers	1981−88
VLSI components	1976−79
Optical measurement	1979−86
Automatic software	1976−81
Inter-operative database development	1985−90
SIGMA	1985−90

Source: E. Arnold and K. Guy, *Parallel Convergence*, 1986

The historical wisdom on the UK economy is that there has been a continuing inability to convert ideas into effective commercial products, and that though there is a large reservoir of talent and ideas they are generally brought into production elsewhere. However, the lack of competitiveness ranges across all industrial sectors, from the most mature to the highly innovative. Thus, comparisons of basic industries in West Germany and the United Kingdom (until unification, remarkably similar in population and land mass) show a similar lack of competitiveness (see Tables 6.20 and 6.21). The problems in certain sectors are

Table 6.20 Annual output of UK and West Germany 1948−87

Product	1948		1987	
	UK	W. Germany	UK	W. Germany
Coal (m. tonnes)	213.00	119.00	104.00	115.00
Crude steel (m. tonnes)	15.00	6.80	17.00	36.00
Cement (m. tonnes)	8.65	5.74	13.41	25.32
Cotton yarns (000 tonnes)	409.00	119.00	50.00	222.00
Man made fibres (000 tonnes)	106.00	70.00	267.00	982.00
Motor vehicles (000)	347	30	1143	4340

Source: UK and West German trade estimates

Table 6.21 Production volumes of electrical engineering and transport equipment 1986 (1980=100)

Country	Electrical engineering	Transport equipment
Belgium	98	129
Denmark	137	109
West Germany	126	125
France	113	92
Italy	113	110
USA	127	129
Japan	221	105
UK	117	89

Source: EUROSTAT, 1977−86

Table 6.22 Production levels in electronic equipment by country 1982–86 as a share of world production (percentages)

Country	Consumer equipment 1982	1986	Industrial electronics 1982	1986	Components 1982	1986
US	20	18	64	58	55	46
Japan	60	70	11	21	27	41
West Germany	10	6	9	8	8	6
France	6	3	7	6	4	4
UK	4	2	8	7	4	4

Source: OECD

even more acute. Thus, an assessment of the share of world production of consumer electronic equipment, industrial electronic equipment, and electronic components demonstrates an even more worrying picture, with the loss of world market share in all but electronic components, where UK market share has been maintained (see Table 6.22). The overall share of world sales of high-technology products also shows a similar decline (see Table 6.23). As industry becomes more specialized and dependent on suppliers to provide high-quality components, a continuing decline in national technology leadership affects the ability of the existing innovators to bring products to market. A company such as Molins, one of the United Kingdom's leading innovators, has found increasing difficulty in maintaining technological leadership as suppliers prove incapable of meeting more and more demanding specifications. Because of this and other reasons Philips, the sole mass manufacturer of semiconductors in Europe, says it has withdrawn from this market sector. The argument of poor local component supply is also often put forward for low local component percentages in UK manufactured products of Japanese companies.

The implication of this is that there will be a symbiotic relationship between groups of innovative companies and institutions within a national economy. It is likely that those countries with the highest level of technical expertise will continue to support such interlocking groups and will go on giving the strongest national resource base for innovation. The relationship between the level of patent activity and sales gives one initial measure of the potential resource base in each market. Using patent performance in this way suggests that by the mid-1980s

Table 6.23 Percentage market shares of technology intensive products by year

Country	1965	1980	1984
US	27.5	22.9	25.2
Japan	7.3	14.3	20.2
West Germany	17.0	16.0	14.5
France	7.3	8.5	7.7
UK	12.0	11.0	8.5

Source: DRI Technology Survey, 1987

Table 6.24 National patent performance 1986

Country	Total number of patents	Number per 100,000 population	Index[1]
Top gear			
Switzerland	28,416	435	221
Japan	346,425	289	197
Sweden	19,092	229	153
West Germany	126,624	208	153
Third gear			
UK	57,395	101	115
Netherlands	15,732	109	100
Austria	8,498	112	100
Australia	14,521	92	100
Finland	6,101	124	85
Denmark	5,336	104	75
France	48,985	89	75
Second gear			
US	213,573	89	64
Belgium	5,956	60	54
Ireland	1,309	37	50
Norway	3,191	77	42
Italy	18,747	33	33
First gear			
Canada	8,521	34	27
Greece	1,293	13	25
Spain	4,051	10	13

Note: [1]The index is calculated by dividing the total share of OECD patenting by share of OECD GDP

Source: OECD

four groups within the OECD countries could be clearly identified. Using the analogy of a four-speed gearbox, countries can be designated top gear, third, second and bottom (see Table 6.24).

Though the analysis of patent activity gives a pointer to the likely overall measure of resources available to support innovation in specific markets, it will naturally be modified by historical strengths and weaknesses in particular market sectors. Thus, the problems of Philips in semiconductor manufacture could be considered to flow from the continuing weaknesses of the European trading block to maintain a viable semiconductor sector. This is in contrast to other market sectors where countries such as West Germany have strong world market shares, some of which are summarized in Table 6.25.

The maintenance of a resource base for innovation

For those countries that rely on international trade for most of their affluence, maintaining and increasing a technological edge is the main method by which

Table 6.25 Relative sector strengths in US, Japan, W. Germany, France and UK

Sector	US	Japan	W. Germany	France	UK
Aircraft	***		*	*	*
Chemicals	**		**	*	*
Cars	***	***	**	*	
Drugs	***	*	**	*	*
Engines	***	**	**	*	
Instruments	*	***	*		
Communication equipment	**	***			
TV		***			
Household electrical	**	**	**		
Commercial electrical	**	*	**		
Transport equipment		*	**	**	
Machine tools		**	**		
Robots	*	***	**		
Semiconductors	***	***			
Software	***		*	*	*
Plastics	*	*	**	*	
Composite metals	**	*	***	**	

Sources: Author from DRI Tabulations, OECD, EC, company reports

labour forces can move from a low value-added economy, paying low wages to a knowledge or high value-added economy. Much of the economic growth of the Pacific basin has been the effective management of low value added, or assembly systems to provide positive cash flows. Countries such as Taiwan continue to prosper following such manufacturing patterns — by 1988 it had the second largest positive balance of trade in the world after Japan. The problem that all these developing countries face as affluence increases is to pay for the higher wages with higher value-added activities. Germany clearly demonstrates that higher value-added manufacturing can offset a steadily rising exchange rate against most other currencies with continuing export growth in capital goods (up from 350 billion Deutschmarks in 1980 to around 550 billion in 1988), and can increase the share of world markets even in some of the most basic commodities.

Japan has successfully achieved the transition from an assembly culture, and the results are shown in the patterns of world trade in high-technology goods and its position in the leading echelon of world technical innovation. It has moved progressively from the position of an economy based primarily on the cost-effective application of labour to one based on the effective application of knowledge. With steadily increasing world competition, greater sophistication and productivity of manufacturing systems, capital and resource-based economic competition is slowly being replaced by competition in the way firms and national economies apply knowledge. The end of the twentieth century and the twenty-first century can be perhaps perceived as seeing the start of an international *knowledge war* with national administrations engaged in supporting firms competing on how they acquire and use knowledge.

It might be thought that those countries with an established knowledge culture — the industrialized world of the nineteenth and early twentieth century — will continue to maintain a favourable position with their tradition of applying knowledge to economic progress. However, the lesson of the last fifteen years is that corporate and economic performance is only as good as the last product or service provided. Old glories will die quickly in the 1990s. It is inevitable that the management of knowledge will become more and more important for the company operating in the 1990s. Companies, and national governments as the other main channel of reallocating resources, must make choices about the correct innovation route and the level of resources essential to ensure that targets, once set, are achieved. Accurate assessment of both these factors will enable both corporate and national units to generate higher levels of value-added products and services to achieve higher wages, greater corporate prosperity and enhanced national wealth.

Notes

1. W. Keegan, *Britain Without Oil*, (London: Penguin, 1988). National Economic Development Organisation, *Report on the Printing Industry*, (London: NEDO, 1985). National Economic Development Organisation, *The Making of Managers*, (London: NEDO, 1987). E.F. Denison, *Why Growth Rates Differ?*, (Washington DC: Brookings Institution, 1967).
2. K. Pavitt (ed.), *Technical Innovation and British Economic Performance*, (London: Macmillan, 1980).
3. For a discussion of Japanese investment and support of commercial development see E. Wilkinson, *Misunderstanding — Europe vs Japan* (Tokyo: Chuokoron-Sha, 1981).
4. A. Shanklin, *Marketing High Technology*, (Lexington: Lexington Books, 1984).
5. The impact of high levels of military spending and its effects on national prosperity are discussed in P. Kennedy, *The Rise and Fall of the Great Powers*, (London: Unwin Hyman, 1988). G. DiFilippo, *Military Spending and Industrial Decline*, (New York: Greenwood Press, 1986). L. Brown, *Building a Sustainable Society*, (New York: Norton, 1981).
6. E. Arnold and K. Guy, *Parallel Convergence*, (London: Frances Pinter, 1986).
7. M.E. Porter, *Competitive Advantage of Nations*, (New York: The Free Press, 1990). H.H. Glismann and E.J. Horn, 'Comparative Invention Performance in Major Industrial Countries', *Management Science*, issue 10, 34 (1988), pp. 117–29. R. Ballance and S. Sinclair, *Collapse and Survival*, (London: Allen & Unwin, 1983).

7

Corporate resources for innovation

Earlier discussion of the resource environment necessary for effective innovation was partly concerned with the issue of non-financial resources. Understanding the interrelationship between personnel policy, company infrastructure, market and manufacturing expertise is crucial to the management of effective change. Without appropriate resources in all these areas no organization can effectively innovate, whatever the attractiveness of the market, the level of government support, financial resource and market position. The key areas of personnel and other internal resources are summarized in Table 7.1.

Structure

Innovation studies frequently emphasize the interrelationship between company structure and the ability to either encourage or resist innovation. In the traditional business, a department established to perform specific tasks is given direct responsibility and authority to implement them. For a large company, examples of such functional divisions involve a subdivision of the organization into a large number of distinct areas as illustrated in the example in Figure 7.1. The impact of this subdivision of responsibility and authority is far-ranging especially when one considers a specific department such as sales. The department is set specific budgets with workloads split between various individuals. Sales representative A or sales manager B is judged on how effectively these specific targets are achieved. In this department an innovative policy is likely to introduce a whole series of conflicts and it is worthwhile examining some of them. First, salesforce involvement in generating ideas may be perceived as secondary to the main task of achieving sales. Secondly, the salesforce may have strong views about particular strengths and weaknesses of any new direction, and its managers will be correspondingly wary of supporting change. Thirdly, new products mean devoting

Table 7.1 The main internal resource issues

Factor	Key components
Personnel	
Strategy	Planning and allocation of resources.
Structure	The development of the appropriate lines of authority to cope with the strategy.
Subject	The translation of strategy into the identification of the appropriate tasks.
Support	The provision of adequate technology to make the performance of the task more efficient, including information transfer.
Skills	The development of appropriate expertise to carry out the tasks required.
Systems	Recruitment, appraisal, compensation.
Style	Management control of staff interrelationships.
Staff	Total numbers of individuals required for particular tasks.
Shared values	Perceptions of goals and objectives within the organization.
Market expertise	
Market position	
Manufacturing expertise	
Production history	

Source: Author

a considerable amount of time and effort to getting them accepted in the market, inevitably causing conflict with established targets. Fourthly, new products demand new knowledge, new customers, new working practices all of which will be at odds with the current operating budgets and targets. It is clear from this one department that whereas the traditional scalar or pyramidical organization is ideal

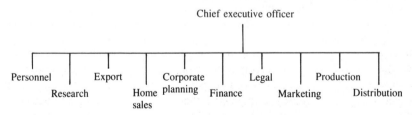

Notes:
A personnel department responsible for recruitment, personnel monitoring, remuneration and motivation.
A research and development department responsible for the identification of new concepts.
An export department, responsible for markets outside the home country.
A sales department with sole responsibility for sales performance.
A corporate planning department responsible for long-term planning.
A finance department responsible for controlling budgets, payments and receipts.
A legal department, responsible for a whole range of activities including patents and product liability.
A marketing department for control of budgets and development of advertising and promotional activity.
A production department, responsible for the change of raw materials into finished goods.
A distribution or despatch department, responsible for the storage and despatch of finished goods to their final destination, and the receipt of raw materials.

Figure 7.1 Functional divisions in a large company

for the completion of specific tasks in an unchanging world it will experience severe stress if rapid change is required, which is all too often what is needed in today's world. The innovation process demands a concentration on change which is at odds with the basic functioning of this type of organization. At its worst, the characteristics of this type of departmental organization which are most likely to scuttle effective innovation are rigidity, decreased management/customer interaction, inadequate staff development, poor communication, and ineffective approaches to problem solving.

Rigidity

Hard and fast departmental boundaries encourage hostility, conservatism and duplication of effort. Management find that within the firm power structures evolve which hinge on the interrelationships of departments and which can range from coolness to open war. The old cavalry colonel dictum 'First feed the horses, then the men, then yourself' has been reworked by one managing director, faced with internecine warfare between departments, into 'Stop the memos, then stop the meetings, then you may have time for the customers'. This is often known as Greshams' Law which states that programmed activity will drive out non-programmed.

Interdepartmental rivalry often means that far more energy and enthusiasm is put into the furtherance of departmental goals than in developing new products or providing the customers with service. The effects on new product development of such attitudes are serious. Because innovation is a high-risk process and one demanding high levels of commitment from the management team for success, department rivalry will mean that departments will be unwilling to risk their current position by supporting a change that might be a failure, and also that where intradepartmental co-operation is necessary it will be grudgingly given, if at all.[1]

Secondly, when the organization is rigidly structured, departments will often be extremely conservative about concepts originating from the outside. This is the NIH (Not Invented Here) syndrome, where there is positive resistance to such ideas.[2] For example, a research department with responsibility for new product development may receive ideas from the salesforce for product improvement, but downgrade the suggestion as being beyond the scope of salesforce duties. The main implication for the innovation process is demotivation throughout the organization as individuals find that their suggestions are blocked or ignored. The clear delineation of responsibilities makes individuals concentrate on mechanical tasks rather than overall contributions to company development. Thus, the marketing department will concentrate on developing sales promotions and advertising material rather than thinking and contributing towards longer-term corporate positioning; the sales representatives take no interest in a particular customer's problem which might lead to a new product concept, but concentrate solely on achieving the sale of the current product range.

The more rigid the organization the greater the tendency for individuals and departments to narrow their horizons and concentrate on technical task performance. Such limited horizons extend to the planning process with serious consequences for the development of new products. A departmental plan developed in isolation will show little understanding of where actions taken fit into the broad developmental policy of the company. For effective innovation it is essential that each part of the company sees how the specific operational and action plan developed fits into overall business policy, and how individual actions support the development of strategy. Such integration of planning also has a valuable motivational input but is difficult to achieve where there is rigid departmentalization.

Thirdly, departmentalism encourages duplication as studies of large organizations show. For example, the UK government not only has a government department called the Central Office of Information, but each major ministry has its own information section as well. In areas such as information gathering and dissemination, which are vital for innovation, such duplication of effort makes the entire transfer process extremely inefficient and limited. Any manager working in industry will be aware of occasions when a report laboriously completed is criticized because it has failed to take into account work already completed (often several years before!) in a different part of the organization. Organizations facing the demands for rapid change are of necessity facing the need to reappraise the issue of structure to reduce interdepartmental rigidity; to speed progress and increase the chances of a coherent approach to a particular problem.

Decreased management–customer interaction

As organizations grow there is a tendency to increase the number of layers of authority. This may take the extreme form in government service where fourteen management tiers exist, whereas in large firms there may be only eight! Decisions must therefore be passed up the chain of command and then down another, as senior managers will often wish to retain authority. One study of the flow of paperwork within a large organization found that major proposals generated at the base of the management pyramid often took four months to reach the top and be passed back down.

With the speed of innovation steadily increasing throughout the industrialized world, such lengthy clearance procedures often mean that the firm is unable to respond as quickly as better-organized competitors. Another study suggested that doubling the number of managers involved in a particular project effectively quadrupled the amount of internal communication required, thereby substantially increasing the time taken to bring new products to the market. In a large commercial firm, such as TI, this delay has substantially reduced their competitiveness as other firms with different structures can introduce products far more rapidly. In addition, each management tier may consider (and this will occur in succession, with one flea having a lesser flea to bite them) that a particular proposal cannot be allowed to proceed without its own imprint: some minor or major modification. It is often said that a camel is a horse designed by a committee, and the attentions of many management layers can have a similar effect on new product proposals.

The changes may make the concept more complex — a phenomenon which is often seen in military equipment which acquires a steadily greater number of roles and sophistication the more departments it passes through until it cannot be handled without some form of postgraduate degree; or make it less distinctive, and closer to the current competitive products.

As the layers of management increase, there is a tendency for more senior staff to become more and more divorced from the reality of the marketplace, as they give their time to supervision and internal meetings. As a result, the decisions will often be taken on inadequate understanding of what is currently occurring in an often rapidly changing demand pattern. One favourite anecdote concerns the managing director who was convinced that no competition to a particular product existed whereas a cursory visit to a neighbouring wholesaler identified no less than five well-established competitors. Siemens the German electronics giant recognized this in its 1988 reorganization, cutting the number of management tiers from eight to three, and decentralizing the previous seven operating units into around twenty market-led subsidiaries.

The multilayered management structure can also lead to the pursuit of status rather than achievement. In other words the management team will be more interested in how a particular proposal might affect their status within the firm, rather than the effect of the proposal on the wellbeing of the organization. This means that any entrepreneurial direction will tend to be squashed rather than fostered because of the high level of risk that new directions entail and the damage that this can cause for the status of the individual.[3]

Increasing numbers of non-line management

There is a tendency for the number of staff employed in advisory functions (staff rather than line management) to steadily increase. This feature of pyramidical organizations also reduces the ability to respond to change in a number of ways. Staff members, as they are often given responsibility for new product development, may effectively isolate the executive management from new product development until major decisions need to be taken. The result of this is that the executive management will often be unwilling to take such decisions as they have not been involved in the preliminary stages. Such isolation will be compounded should the organization have a large number of management layers — staff managers will tend to provide senior executives with an additional barrier against contact with the marketplace.[4] One study suggested that differences between the typical German manufacturing firm and the United Kingdom could be perceived mainly as a difference in departmental organization (see Table 7.2). Because staff managers have an advisory role, where they are involved in new product development they may often concentrate on research rather than action. New product development managers with staff-related backgrounds will dedicate themselves to collecting all the relevant facts before a particular line of action can be recommended. As a result, emphasis will be given to detailed research and analysis delaying action instead of acceptance that decisions need to be taken

Table 7.2 Differences between West German and UK manufacturers

---

Fewer hierarchical levels
Less distinction between functional divisions
Far fewer staff employees as percentage of workforce
Greater involvement of majority of workforce in production
More insistence on formal qualifications as measure of functional competence
More institutionalization of training
Longer and more detailed training

Source: G. Burkvalt, *Werkschafft in Deutschland*, 1988

often on inadequate information to meet particular customer needs or competitive action. The predictive value of market research is fairly limited in forecasting the performance of new goods and services, especially where the product is providing an entirely novel set of benefits. Furthermore, research is often used as a substitute for decision making rather than as something that contributes to the final action. Ensuring that the market research actually will provide objective answers is a final major problem as inevitably many research programmes will be aimed towards producing the desired result rather than unbiased data on which to take decisions.

Communication

Departmentalization has a significant effect on the movement of information in an organization. A rigid bureaucracy perceives the control of information as essential to its power, reducing information flows by either formal (instructions or laws) or informal methods. Many UK organizations operate on the so-called mushroom principle — to keep employees in the dark for as long as possible while occasionally opening the door and piling in manure. A survey, conducted by the author, of technical staff involved in sandwich training underlines this point. They were asked to comment on what knowledge they had of their employer company after an average of three years in the organization (see Table 7.3).

Information regarded as 'sensitive' and needing security covers various areas, but the normal list would include: the profitability of particular products — this information is often unavailable to the line managers responsible for those

Table 7.3 Level of knowledge of company activities (percentage)

Factor	Clear understanding	Vague understanding	No knowledge
Company strategy	5	40	55
Main competitors	18	26	56
Main profit lines	8	21	71
Current importance of particular projects	3	15	82

Source: Author

Table 7.4 Changing perceptions of internal communication (percentage)

Factor	1976	1985
We hear about things before management tell us	72	71
Top management are in contact with what is going on	65	48

Source: Mori

products' day-to-day administration; the profitability of the operating unit; long-term plans for individuals and units within the organization; and pay and conditions of everyone within the company. Many surveys have suggested that internal communication tended to get worse rather than better throughout the 1970s and 1980s; an example is given in Table 7.4.

Information flow is vital because it improves control of complex and rapidly moving events. Various studies highlight the advantages of good communication. A study of seventy-five companies using regression techniques showed that approximately 65 per cent of the changes in financial performance could be explained by particular aspects of the company personnel policy, including how information is shared, the degree of confidence shared between management grades and the amount of consensus achieved in management decisions.[5] Distrust arising from poor communication was identified as the main area of dissatisfaction in another analysis and it became more acute the longer the employee remained in the organization (see Table 7.5). This perception of the importance of communication is supported in another survey of the British knitting industry — greater productivity, better management of change, greater employee commitment, a lower turnover of labour, reduced absenteeism, and much better standards of recruitment.[6] Improving internal communication is therefore one of the major components in an effective motivational strategy. Barriers to communication may also affect the quality of decisions taken. Because of the complexity of new product development poor communication may have particularly deleterious effects, especially if senior management are either unable or unwilling to maintain contacts within the organization (often defined as networking). For example, failing to inform project teams about conflicting objectives within the organization limits their usefulness; cost and profit information is essential for accurate identification of profitable markets and assessments of returns on capital employed. There are

Table 7.5 Perceptions of management information

Years of service	Trustworthy	Untrustworthy
Under 1	40	59
1–2	33	66
3–4	31	69
5–9	27	73
10–19	27	73

Source: Financial Times, 8 March 1989

Table 7.6 Reasons for lack of R & D involvement in different stages

Need	Focus	Evaluation	Make/buy	Negotiate
No experience with similar projects	Resource lack	Lack of R & D credibility	Lack of R & D credibility	Lack of interest
Too removed from marketing/ production	Perceived lack of expertise	No structure to involve R & D	Lack of formal structure	Lack of formal structure
Main focus on new products		Engineering in control of pilot plant		

Receive	Construct	Start up	Improve	Retool
Few trained people in R & D for this function	No engineering skills in R & D	Lack of influence	Lack of influence	Not considered involvement necessary

Source: F. Sen and A.H. Rubenstein, *Journal of Product Innovation Management,* 6, 1989

a large number of areas in which the research department for example will not be involved due to poor communication (see Table 7.6).[7]

Good communication improves morale by reducing the distrust which often breeds group suspicions that events are occurring which will significantly affect their position and authority. Suspicion is an inevitable component of change; the more rapid the change, the greater the likelihood that employees will feel threatened — especially in an era where change has tended to reduce job security. Quality circles are thought to be important in increasing involvement and lowering resistance to change in Japanese industry.[8] Furthermore, improving communication can significantly speed the rate at which individuals become effective, either within the organization or the new product development team. Good communication improves the so-called learning curve, employees can become effective more rapidly by contrast with a secretive organization where the acquisition of essential information occurs informally over a long period of time. Where management sets innovation policies that expect employees to acquire new knowledge and skills over a fairly limited period of time, information transfer policies are an important component of success. Finally, the development of rapid and complete communication transfer within the company considerably expands the capacity of the organization to meet changing conditions as staff are able to adapt more readily because they are aware of the general problems of their company.

Single corporate attitude to problem solving

Departmentalization and bureaucracy often nurture specific management attitudes, favouring particular skills and backgrounds for promotion and ending up with all senior management being drawn from a particular promotion path. The result is a company dominated by a single corporate philosophy, either technical, financial or sales. Often these attitudes accompany a period of success over a number of years and so become enshrined within the organization as the single appropriate method to solve all the problems. One author describes such executives as having 'an almost trained incapacity' to appreciate long-term strategic problems and to understand specific requirements of different market sectors. It is interesting that a comparison of managers made redundant during large company reorganizations with those that stayed found that the remaining staff were far less individualistic and innovative than those that had been discarded.[9]

There are notable examples of this blinkered philosophy causing major problems: the collapse of Rolls-Royce followed a complete concentration on the engineering aspects of the jet-engine, the Rolls-Razor empire of John Bloom failed through concentration on sales at practically any price. Companies with such single-minded concentration on one particular approach will inevitably fail in the attempt to innovate; change which does not accord with what is historically 'correct' will be resisted at all costs. Should the company then run into serious problems it will have to look outside for its salvation — it is interesting to note in this context that the number of chief executive officers of major American corporations recruited from outside the company has risen from around 10 per cent in the 1960s to over 25 per cent in the mid-1980s.

Continued success will also often lead to complacency, with the result that a company fails to explore all the possible avenues of innovation and becomes vulnerable to competitive action. Even the most sophisticated marketing companies may face such problems. Procter & Gamble in its development of the disposable nappy market reached almost total brand dominance with Pampers in the United States in the late 1970s, holding 75 per cent of the market. Kimberley Clark introduced a competitive product in 1979, Huggies, which provided a closer fit. Procter & Gamble, ignoring the competition saw market share drop towards 50 per cent, until in 1985 it decided to totally re-equip its ten factories at a cost of $500 million.

Limited management spans of control

The span of control is the number of individuals reporting to a particular manager or supervisor. In hierarchical management structures the tendency is for management spans to be limited. In the British civil service for example the span of control varies between three and five. The rationale for close management supervision is, of course, that it will ensure that staff complete tasks on time and to specification. This conflicts with the development of expertise and individual responsibility within the skilled company environment of the 1990s and also with the need for organizations to become less management 'rich'. Both these factors suggest that with the changing employee base, management spans of control should be expanded to increase individual responsibility and involvement in company development, and this is likely to improve the company personnel resource for innovation. This view is supported by a comparison of German and UK factory structure which identifies the span of management control as being one of the key differences that make the German system more able to handle change.

Structural reorganizations for innovation

Large companies can obviously improve the structural resource by decentralization so that the operating units resemble small companies, with group decision making, good communication, limited management tiers and a lack of internal rigidity. This concept has been well developed by one of the most successful innovators, 3M, and is fundamental to the success of companies such as Grand Metropolitan and Unilever with a multinational base of independent subsidiaries. A product such as Baileys Irish Cream may be developed in one part of the world, locally tested and then spread to other subsidiaries. Calcite rather than silica-based scourers were first developed by the French Unilever subsidiary before appearing on the UK market as Jif. The international telecommunications company Erickson is one of those that uses the concept of the World Trade mandate in encouraging individual subsidiaries to act in an entrepreneurial fashion, by allowing them to exploit particular innovations throughout the world rather than by taking over the concept and passing it to other parts of the group.

There are, however, limitations to this concept which prevent its being universally applicable. A company existing in a technical environment such as Thorn EMI, having over one hundred subsidiaries, has found it difficult to innovate, with two major factors operating against excessive decentralization. The first is the need in high-technology operations for shared access to production and design facilities. There are large investments involved in sterile manufacturing environments for microprocessors and such central manufacturing facilities act as a natural brake on the ability of a company such as Motorola to decentralize. Centralized operations under such circumstances appear to be potentially more profitable.[10] Secondly, there is a minimum number of skilled personnel necessary to generate innovative concepts and bring them into production. This number will vary from industry to industry but will be largest in sectors requiring fundamental research, and high levels of production skill. Thus, Intel and Motorola have found it important to maintain a close relationship between research and production to ensure that rapid progress can be maintained in semiconductor development and manufacture. Such constraints mean that these companies must maintain large central cores of staff, even though manufacturing bases may be spread throughout the world. Even in less demanding environments the number of development staff employed may be a major force towards concentration: Kelloggs, relying on innovation from reformulation, employs over 400 individuals working on product development.

A partial solution to the problem of managing innovation in conjunction with a large company organization is to externalize the search for new concepts by funding small companies with particular technical expertise — a route favoured by British Petroleum, for example. These venture capital approaches are valuable in adding valuable knowledge about particular types of development, but they are to an extent putting off the major problem that the company faces: ensuring that change can take place. A logical extension of the venture capital approach is for firms to establish what are effectively internal venture operations for particular types of project, entirely responsible for the development and commercialization of a particular product. These can range from the small development subsidiary to the very large — the Saturn Corporation set up by General Motors to organize the introduction of new manufacturing methods and to develop the new small car ranges for the company, and IBM creating a new division to develop, manufacture and distribute the new personal computer.

These internal venture companies are highly appropriate for projects where the problems and end result are clearly defined. Where the benefits are less clear, the structural solutions to achieving internal innovation in organizations that have to be large for capital investment and quality control reasons are less simple. One solution is to provide a central focus for all research activity within the organization, allowing it to sell concepts externally if no departmental interest is shown. The Saab group has followed this policy by setting up an independent subsidiary, Combitech, to develop and sell technology within the group. An early development from this company has been a series of applications within space technology. DuPont has also established its research and development unit as a separate profit centre.

The last approach to decentralization is to create a 'sponsor' system within the organization whereby a senior manager can lead an internal group towards a particular developmental task. The problem of using a senior manager in this way is that he or she will often have departmental responsibilities which are far more important than the high risks and often unrewardingly large amount of time that can be consumed in new product development proposals. Companies such as Ford overcome the problems of such concentration by appointing managers close to retirement as 'uncles' for such projects. This makes available senior management with good internal contacts, sufficient time to devote to project development and with few conflicting career goals. The problem is that such managers are unlikely either to promote the proposal actively, or to be considered seriously by the internal power structure within the firm because their position is essentially that of a consultant.

Regardless of the route chosen, the large centralized company still has the problem of creating a new authority and responsibility base for the completion of the project. This will involve the recruitment and monitoring of a new multidisciplinary team to take charge of the complex and detailed activities involved in the introduction of new products. Each project will demand a different type of team, with substantial variations in the numbers employed, skills and responsibilities. Not only will the structural demands vary overall from product to product, but each individual stage within the project will demand changing levels of input from specific areas within the company. The exact constituent of the team is one of the major contributions that the chief executive officer can make in the effective management of innovation.[11]

Subject

Translating strategic goals into specific tasks is obviously one of the most important aspects of innovation personnel management. The effectiveness of this process of strategy implementation substantially affects the ability of the entire company to realize its goals. It would otherwise be impossible to define the skills and staffing levels required to manage particular types of change. Evidence supports the view that there is a greater likelihood of success when there is a close relationship between the innovation task and knowledge of what the current organizational structure is capable of achieving. This supports the perception of synergistic markets discussed in Chapter 5 — where a company fully understands the resource requirements — as being potentially the most attractive for innovation investment (see Table 7.7).[12] It is also important that strategy translates into specific achievable goals and targets. Management must be able to define in detail the various stages of particular projects and what the performance characteristics of each step will be. An example of the detailed planning that is necessary during the technical development process is in Table 7.8. Because the translation of strategy into specific tasks and goals is a complex one it has an inevitable effect on the type of skills required in the management of innovation.

Support

The interdependence between manufacturing industry and technology has been clear since the beginning of the Industrial Revolution — the replacement of hand spinning by power looms and manual forging by steam hammers being but two examples. Their modern day equivalents, the development of robotics and flexible manufacturing systems, further eliminated the manual component from increasingly sophisticated production processes.

Table 7.7 Impact of synergy on three dimensions of performance (correlation coefficients)

Fit with	Financial performance	Opportunity window	Market share
Company/distributor salesforce	0.301	ns	ns
R & D personnel resources	0.387		
Engineering resources	0.329		
Production resources	0.237		
Advertising resources	0.231		
Marketing research resources	0.322		
Customer service resources	0.256		
Management resources	0.466		
Financial resources	ns		

Source: R.G. Cooper and E.J. Kleinschmidt, *R & D Management*, 17, 1987

Innovation strategy

Table 7.8 The detailed components of the technical planning process

Stage	Characteristics	Testing	Documentation	Market research	End result
Concept	Scaled model, non-functioning		Functional description, rough operating specifications	Benefits Market size	Go/No go
Model development	Rough working, inexpensive	Test plan	Detailed drawings, production design, production cost	Revised market size Customer acceptance	Concept proved?
Engineering prototype	Durable for testing	Meets specifications? In-house testing	Operating procedures	Engineering meets market demands?	Complete product package
Production prototype	Designed for assembly	Meets market demands? Independent test	Production implications	Consumer reactions, pricing benefits	Verify product package
Product qualification	Check production equipment	Regulatory problems?	Complete plan for production/ finance	Refine/test acceptance	Check earlier stages

Source: A. Hise *et al.*, *Journal of Product Innovation Management*, 6, 1989

What is really new and is having a more fundamental impact on how companies handle innovation is the involvement of technology in the way in which companies assimilate, organize and use information or knowledge. As earlier chapters have mentioned, access to the technology of knowledge is becoming — and is likely to be — one of the key resources for innovation in the future. Research is increasingly suggesting that such technical support is central to effective innovation.[13] This revolution in technological support is so important that it is worth examining the components and advantages of knowledge management. The first and most obvious is the ever-expanding capacity of data processing equipment to store large amounts of information. Originally, such databases were merely convenient filing cabinets which reduced the physical volume of information into a more easily storable form. By the 1980s the potential value of linking information within the data store was realizable and the directional database to explore linkages between information grew steadily in importance, replacing the old concept of the relational database, where information could only be searched along single pre-determined pathways. The importance of database provision in improving company performance has been highlighted by one survey of the major constraints to improvements in company integration (see Table 7.9).

Some companies used this new technology to gain a considerable competitive edge simply because it helped them to understand their customers and organize their business far more efficiently. Here, then, is the concept of database marketing. The advantages claimed for it are improved segmentation of customers (a key component of the marketing exercise in relating products to customer types), better recording of responses to particular types of marketing initiative, far greater

Table 7.9 Constraints to improving integration

Factor	Percentage[1]
Inadequate information systems support	53
Lack of adequate database	48
Lack of control over external events	44
Functional/organisational boundaries	40
Flexibility of labour	29
Lack of management awareness	26
Lack of management commitment	24
Lack of appreciation of benefits	22

Note: [1]Percentage of companies reporting

Source: A.T. Kearney

co-ordination of effort, and a possible automatic identification of potential market threats. An example of the power potential of databases is the EPOS systems used by many retailers. These systems allow retailers to reduce stocks overall, to tailor product ranges more precisely, where properly applied, to local conditions, and to identify successful promotional campaigns far in advance of the supplier. EPOS provides daily information on product progress, in contrast to competitive information available to the manufacturer from such research companies as Nielsen, which are produced on a monthly or bi-monthly basis. Such information systems are also a central part of the idea generation phase in certain types of innovation policy.

More and more data within the system requires a far greater effort among physically separated staff to obtain essential information in organizations using traditional communication systems. This, combined with the decreased costs of processing, generated demand for networked processing systems — units that could work alone yet be part of the overall business knowledge environment. Networking supports companies in different ways. Firstly, it speeds communications and can cut costs, thereby substantially improving productivity. Indeed, one report claimed that the likely increase in productivity for the introduction of network systems was around 25 per cent. Secondly, networking substantially improves the ability of the company to harness all its managers in particular areas, wherever they are physically situated, to resolve problems. One company that has effectively used this bulletin board approach to corporate development is Digital, with units throughout the world communicating on specific problems faced by individuals. For example, a manager in Australia is able to ask the worldwide network of staff facing similar problems for their proposed solution, and so substantially improving overall group responsiveness and speeding up the introduction of new ideas. Such a network supports research findings that information transfer between research and marketing are vital for effective new product introduction.[14]

Centralization of information is the key: for staff able to feed the centre with new ideas for product development; and for the centre able to keep the periphery informed of changes in the environment that might supply new opportunities. The information flow in most UK organizations is particularly poor in this respect,

Table 7.10 Applications of computers
in R & D

Category	Percentage[1]
Data analysis	21.4
Lab automation	19.7
Data base	16.1
Modelling	14.6
CAD	5.9

Note: [1] Percentage of firms reporting the
use of information technology in particular
categories in 1985

Source: E. Sanderstrom and B.M.
Winchell, *Research Management*, 29,
1986

with one poll of middle managers finding that over half were unaware of where
they should take a new product concept or idea for progress. Similarly, a majority
of managers were ignorant of both the range of information available to their
firm and about its whereabouts. Centralized data bases go some of the way in
helping to resolve these problems by giving valuable support in a crucial area
of new product development. They can also substantially improve the available
resources to bring product concepts rapidly from the idea stage into the screening
process. However, the diffusion of such advanced information technology is fairly
limited, as Table 7.10 indicates.[15]

Parallel with the access to individual items of information, software development
is enabling staff to model and integrate data in increasingly sophisticated ways.
Already, off-the-shelf systems give help with problems such as budgeting, project
management, ideas generation, forecasting, market modelling and design.
Advances in the area of design are among the most startling. Drug companies
can view the likely three-dimensional structure of drugs; aircraft companies and
motor manufacturers can see wind flows over surfaces; engineering companies
can visualize likely metal fatigue areas, and so on. The Sensor Frame announced
in 1989 will allow direct manipulation of designs on screen (rather than by
keyboard input or mouse), and the complexity of such design systems will increase
as will their ability to improve design. But tailor-made approaches are often even
better at improving efficiency and control, and this enters the realm of expert
systems and artificial intelligence. What the expert system does is to attempt to
parallel the organizational and thought processes applied to problem solving by
experienced and skilled individuals in specific fields. Many of the companies
developing such systems — Great Universal Stores, Schlumberger, and DuPont
— claim a number of benefits, mostly in the quality, speed and consistency of
decision making. A major problem for Great Universal Stores (GUS), the leading
mail-order company in the United Kingdom, is in deciding who qualifies for credit
and who should receive its increasingly expensive catalogue. By applying a mixture
of knowledge and statistical relationship between customer types and risk, GUS

managed to further reduce the costs to the organization. Digital Computers improves the consistency of customer service by using expert systems to determine the appropriate type of configuration — this has the added benefit of speeding orders through the system.[16] Another likely impact of expert systems is in training. For example, sales representatives using expert systems to develop quotations and proposals learn more quickly about what type of approaches are likely to be successful. With the rapid growth in knowledge requirements such expert systems are likely to become increasingly important in ensuring that the firm can train its staff in a cost-effective and comprehensive fashion.

Staff

Effective innovation then is possible only if the firm has the right number and type of staff. A minimum number of staff is important for certain types of innovation; reference has already been made (see p. 48) to the estimate of thirty research staff to provide the minimum critical mass in electronics, another investigation of the chemical industry produced a viable minimum of three research units with around fifty-five to sixty active research scientists. At 1988 prices this would cost around £3 million to finance in direct costs, with an additional £9 million in project work generated from this research base.

The exact number of staff required will obviously depend on their level of expertise and the amount of technical support that the company provides. The more expert the staff, and the greater the provision of sophisticated equipment, the lower the total staffing requirements. With the reductions in the numbers of school leavers entering employment in the 1990s throughout the industrialized world, employers must invest in support systems to cope with the effects of having fewer 'bodies'. Health services in continental Europe have already moved in this direction with the replacement of staff by far higher levels of expenditure on equipment; combined numbers of doctors and nurses per thousand of population in West Germany and France are 65 per cent of that in the United Kingdom. The greater staff expertise, and the more sophisticated the support provided, the lower the staff limits for effective innovation will be. Developing a new diesel engine might involve over one hundred draughtsmen in the 1950s for a company such as Perkins; with the advent of computer-aided design, the numbers required are far fewer.

Anecdotal evidence suggests that the requirements of effective innovation in other areas are lower; the 3M structure suggests that technological reorganization innovation can be achieved with a technical staff of less than twenty; successful companies in knitwear manufacture will be employing fewer than ten in the design department. Small companies face most staffing constraints in terms of numbers that can be brought together for particular types of innovative activity — a factor of particular concern to those companies that evolve through management buy-outs from the parent company when a management team moves from a theoretically richer staff environment to one more poorly resourced.

Effective new product development obviously needs more than just numbers;

it also requires an interplay of expertise and attitude. This can often increase staff numbers beyond the minimum necessary for normal levels of manufacturing demand in those companies where one type of skill is predominant — engineering or marketing perhaps. Indeed, many organizations fail to implement innovation because of an overreliance on the role of the creative innovator, failing to appreciate that within each team there will have to be additional types of staff, performing different and mutually beneficial functions. The rise and fall of Sinclair Research illustrates this point. The company, after a number of false starts, produced a series of successful home computers, the ZX-1 followed by the Spectrum range. Problems with these machines, however, continued and multiplied with the advanced Spectrum 128. This machine was so beset with technical problems that the lead that the group had established was rapidly lost and the company was eventually taken over by Amstrad. The failure of Sinclair illustrates a crucial personnel resource factor. This is, that while any company needs creativity in the specific area in which it is concentrating, it will also have to ensure that the correct balance of staff is available to handle the considerable demands of new product development. In the case of Sinclair this would have involved a greater preponderance of production engineers and marketing co-ordination.

The evaluation of the staff types available to manage innovation is of primary importance in any project assessment; a secondary issue is how to organize them into effective groups.[17] Research on effective group behaviour and the management of change in organizations points to the approaches that are more likely to succeed. First, the bias of the group will need to reflect the importance of the various components of the task. So, for innovations requiring a large engineering component, the co-ordinator or group leader should be an individual with engineering skills, whereas an innovative design or change in packaging will require an individual with marketing skills. Some studies suggest that the commercialization of products by Japan, West Germany and Switzerland is more effective because of the emphasis given within those management cultures to detailed planning and integration, rather than the less structured and more amorphous approach in the United Kingdom.[18] The experience of companies with quality circles as part of their production management is that they have focused attention on the minutiae of product improvement and innovation.

Secondly, it is clear that the group needs to have a considerable diversity of skills and talents to achieve the desired result, though the exact mix will be determined by the nature of the project. Many studies identify at least five, and often more, distinct innovation tasks, each requiring different staff types. Those identified are: the ideas individual, providing the creative impetus for the group and also problem solving; an overall co-ordinator responsible for fine detail and control of the project; individual(s) with technical skills essential to the project; individual(s) acting to promote the concept internally; and one senior sponsor who has the authority to represent the project at the highest level. Table 7.11 summarizes the role of these key personnel. Exact group requirements will depend on the complexity of the task involved and on how a company's structure promotes

Table 7.11 Main staff types required for effective innovation team

Description	Background	Influence
Ideas individual	Any	Problem solving
Technical co-ordinator or manager	Graduate/technical/ management skill	Budgetary/timing
Technical or market analyst	Graduate/management skill	Financial
Salesman	Any	Internal support
Senior sponsor	Any	Prioritization

Source: Author

or limits innovation. The range of expertise and attitude is, however, crucial in all the successful innovation teams studied — the lack of one particular component is likely to cause the project to founder. Naturally, as might be expected the team leader has a crucial role to play as a communicator, climate setter, and planner.

The size of the group is also a limiting factor. Much of the research on the effectiveness of groups demonstrates that although one with diverse talents is much more likely to reach effective decisions (provided, of course, that they have access to the same amount of information), this 'group effect' is achieved with small numbers, with maximum effectiveness with five to seven individuals. Once this upper limit is passed, certain members of the group will no longer fully contribute. The way teams are developed for innovation will have to concentrate on integrating the lowest number of people necessary to achieve the task — with obviously the more highly skilled teams being able to operate with fewer people. Other likely failure points for innovative team performance include the lack of clear goals/requirements, low motivation, little team involvement, and limited top-management commitment to the project.

Skills

A comparison of skills requirement in the 1960s with the 1980s suggests that more and more organizations require the greater proportion of their work staff to be in the categories proficient or above, to understand the implications of particular policies, and the likely impact of change in the environment (see Table 7.12). One detailed case study on the implementation of change in the retail sector showed how important the level of skills in the company was in achieving the desired level of change.[19] Companies operating in technical environments will need to change the skill profile of their employees from a normal pyramid (with a large base of novice or advanced beginners), towards an inverted pyramid with the majority of staff in the expert sector of the skills universe. The specific skills required depends on the innovation route chosen; high levels of academic expertise for discontinuous innovation, or high levels of technical skill such as process engineering for performance extension and technological reorganization. Such technical skills will be even more important at senior levels within the organization so that the resource implications for particular development routes are fully

Table 7.12 Skills analysis

Novice   Lacks any clear understanding of overall task. Can only judge performance by reference to rules. For example, a machine operator will learn that a lathe can change its rate of operation by the operation of a gear, but not how this is achieved.

Advanced beginner   Begins to be able to identify best solutions to problems from previous experience, but still lacks overview of total task. The advanced beginner will know what type of output is achieved from the lathe by changing the gearing.

Competent   The competent performer is able to identify possible reference points for evaluating the performance levels in the task and to define job requirements in this context. For example, the lathe operator will know from previous experience what type of job requires a particular type of lathe operation, but is not able to predict likely outcomes in new operations.

Proficient   The proficient individual is one that is able to predict either intuitively or analytically what type of performance will be required in new situations. For example, the lathe operator will be able to determine what type of action will be required for a range of work outside previous expertise.

Expert   The expert is able to understand not only the implications of the particular job in which he or she is involved but also the implications on other areas of the business. For example, the lathe operator would appreciate the implications of maintenance, raw material and finished goods movements for a particular type of task.

Source: M. Cooley, *Architect or Bee: The Human Price of Technology*, 1987

appreciated. The requirement of full technical understanding of chief executive officers in technical companies is, as might be expected, supported by research on successful and unsuccessful companies in these areas.

Part of the resource analysis for innovation must evaluate employee skills and how to improve them in order to handle new products and concepts. From such an analysis the company must consider whether to acquire the necessary skills from recruitment or internal development. The resource problem posed by recruitment has already been identified as to whether the organization is able to hire sufficient quality of knowledge and skill for a particular task. External recruitment has one other disadvantage — it has serious demotivating effects on staff already within the organization that see potential routes for advancement disappear above them. The other route is to develop the necessary skills internally via a programme of training. High levels of expenditure on training are positively associated with the successful management of change. A 1985 survey of major British employers found that those that had shown earnings growth over the past five years had increased their training expenditure by 25 per cent, whereas less successful companies had increased by a lower 15 per cent, and the unsuccessful companies in the sample had reduced their investment in training by 20 per cent. Overall this survey suggested that the percentage of turnover directed towards training was of the order of 0.15 per cent of turnover or £4 per week, which provided on average 2.1 days off-the-job training per annum. A 1988 survey suggested that training investment was considerably higher at £809 per employee; this survey is at odds with anecdotal evidence from a wide range of sources which indicates that UK training expenditure lags behind other industrialized markets. This is supported by any measurement of specific skills acquisition. Thus the number of individuals entering particular craft areas can be shown to have

Table 7.13 First-year craft technical registrations/construction equipment

Year	Craftsmen registration	Technician registration
1975/76	345	34
1976/77	326	56
1977/78	338	51
1978/79	285	58
1979/80	227	54
1980/81	197	37
1981/82	120	24
1982/83	89	14
1983/84	58	15

Source: NEDO, *Design from Corporate Culture*, 1987

consistently fallen since the mid-1970s (one example is given in Table 7.13). The specificity of the training is another key component in improving the personnel resource for innovation. Much of the investment made by companies in the United Kingdom is not directed towards the acquisition of particular skills. This is underlined by a comparison with the output of the West German training system, with its practically identical population (see Table 7.14). Research evidence also supports the importance of identifying specific training requirements and tailoring individual programmes to meet requirements identified via appraisal as a major force in retaining skilled staff. Companies that follow such specific and individual training programmes such as IBM and Johnson & Johnson are far more likely to build up the required skills in the workforce effectively and quickly, and, once it has been achieved, to maintain this level of skill within the organization.

Systems

The systems resource refers to how a company recruits, appraises, and motivates personnel. Change and competition demand the replacement of inappropriate, old approaches to personnel in order to build, maintain, and use effectively the knowledge within the firm. The importance of recruitment quality in many

Table 7.14 Training standards in occupations in Britain and West Germany: numbers of individuals passing final exams

Area	UK	W. Germany
Mechanical craftsmen	16,058	50,678
Electrical trades	12,482	33,198
Building craftsmen	11,183	58,084

Source: National Institute for Science and Economic Research

environments to reduce the training load has been mentioned (see p. 136), and since personnel costs are rising all the time the entire process will require more care and time. The use of selection panels, detailed analysis of candidates' strengths and weaknesses, the identification of particular skills, and personnel aptitudes for the company plan all play a part in developing an effective resource base for innovation policies.[20] Many companies are also using psychological methods such as aptitude tests and even graphology to identify suitable candidates, with very mixed results. The research shows that it is the taking of time and trouble over selection that is likely to find the people who will fit into the organization. Therefore it is those companies with detailed and comprehensive recruitment procedures that are likely to achieve much greater base personnel resources than those that do not have them. Companies will want to maximize the efficiency of new recruits as quickly as possible. Here, a structured induction programme geared to individual requirements is more valuable than the old approach of large organizations to learning about information sources, project details, and personnel structures at the desk.

Though recruitment techniques may be improving, the underlying problem of maintaining a productive and involved workforce continues to be a major problem and one that fundamentally affects the resource base of the company attempting to achieve effective innovation. First is the issue of effective appraisal. Appraisal systems in many large organizations are directed towards the completion of set forms instead of the identification of individual problems and opportunities for personnel development. The mere existence of an appraisal system does not necessarily improve the resources available for innovation. It may, perversely, make it worse as employees resent the inability of the system to provide what it is supposed to. With the steadily rising costs of recruitment and training in many sectors (see Table 7.15) the ability of company systems not only to keep skilled and knowledgeable employees but also to maximize their commitment and involvement will become more and more vital. An effective and acceptable appraisal system can be considered as an important resource for product innovation where traditional working methods must often be abandoned and problems can only be rapidly and successfully overcome if the organization has staff dedicated to the project's long-term success.

Table 7.15 Recruitment and training costs of selected employees in the UK

Staff type	Cost (£s)
Administrative staff — local authority	5,000
Bank staff	8/10,000
Nursing staff	12,000
Engineering staff	18,000
Technical export staff	25,000

Source: UK manufacturing and service employers' estimates, 1989

Table 7.16 Main reasons for either leaving or staying in
an industrial sales environment (percentage response[1])

Factor	Stayed	Left
Sales manager	28.6	25.6
Senior management	26.5	22.5
Pay/benefits	10.8	9.5
Work	23.7	21.1
Customers	26.2	26.4
Promotion	13.5	10.5
Co-workers	24.5	23.4

Note: [1]Figures add up to more than 100 due to multiple
responses from certain individuals

Source: G.F. Fern, *Industrial Marketing Management*,
18, 1989

Furthermore, a company must be able to respond to the individual needs of
staff in order to keep them productive and effective. Historically, the simple
solution to motivation was to ladle out increases in pay or some other form of
compensation. Though this attitude persists, all post-war research reveals that
pay as a motivating factor is fairly low on the overall ranking of factors considered
important by individuals established in their jobs.[21] Indeed, one survey showed
a negative correlation between pay and performance amongst the chief executive
officers of major corporations in the United States, concluding that paying golden
peanuts produced golden monkeys! Other surveys agree with this conclusion,
finding few, if any, significant correlations between pay and performance, and
pay is not often mentioned as a reason for staying in or leaving a particular job
(see Table 7.16).

More important than pay in maintaining high levels of performance and interest
in the firm are aspects of group involvement (including the accuracy of company
communication), group recognition, and opportunities for advancement, either
as promotion or in the form of new challenges.

Senior management must therefore concentrate rather more on individual rather
than blanket approaches to motivation. One manager may, for example, find the
creation of new products intensely stimulating whereas another will enjoy customer
contact and find the detailed planning of new product development unstimulating.
The most effective motivation in both cases may be to provide the freedom for
both managers or staff to do more of what they like best, rather than force them
into some preconceived organizational mould. In other words, the development
of a motivational system that is directly linked to individual requirements will
provide the most positive resource environment for effective innovation, and those
that apply overall or blanket approaches will be less likely to be effective.

Where compensation is directly linked to performance in some way, the
effectiveness of the organization in handling change will generally be substantially
enhanced. Thus, in retailing, the John Lewis Partnership, with its substantial profit-
sharing schemes for employees, higher overall wages and a greater proportion

Table 7.17 Performance-related payment schemes: main advantages and disadvantages

Scheme	Requirements for effective operation	Advantages	Disadvantages
Profit sharing	• Employees must be able to influence outcome	• Easy to install and understand • Develops shared values • Sharing only when profit has been reached	• Difficult to use unless profit centres exist
Gain sharing	• Objectives must be clearly stated • Staff must trust management to set realistic objectives	• Company can target non-profit activities	• Patchy overall performance
Lump sum bonus	• How bonus is awarded must be clearly defined	• Can reduce fixed costs • Can be directive	• Inequalities in bonus payments cause friction
Skills payments	• Targets clearly identified • Step by step progression	• Highly directive	• Adds substantially to wages bill/not profit related

Source: Adapted from *Fortune*, 19 December 1988

of full-time staff, (65 per cent in 1987 compared with 35 per cent in Marks & Spencer and 40 per cent in Sainsburys) continues to achieve one of the highest levels of value added per employee and outperforms its main competitors in this respect. The best type of performance bonus depends on the size and homogeneity of the organization as each of the main alternatives have certain advantages and disadvantages (see Table 7.17). For a performance-related pay structure to work it must be integrated with overall company strategy, and must clearly identify profit centres and relevant targets.

Finally, the organization must be able to develop some form of effective appeals and disciplinary procedure, especially where the organization is split into small quasi-autonomous units with branch management inevitably in the position to affect seriously the career prospects and job involvement of staff reporting to them. In organizations where the appeals procedure is perceived as over-favouring the executive (it will inevitably always favour the executive), it is likely that levels of conflict will rise to the detriment of the effective management of change.[22]

In conclusion, an effective resource environment for innovation requires the creation of systems far more demanding than the old. A company has to appreciate that personnel management in an innovative organization needs an individual approach which will require time and attention. The comparison between the classic systems approach and the new systems approach necessary for the 1990s is summarized in Table 7.18.[23]

Table 7.18 Systems comparison between the old organization and the new

Factor	Old	New
Underlying philosophy	People are costs that must be minimized	Never get enough good people. People key component of success
Recruitment	Milkround approach. Most people will do	Detailed screening. Time taken to identify right people
Induction	Feet under the desk. Learn on the job	Time taken to make recruit productive
Training	Hire/fire to get right skills. Structured programmes often unrelated to specific requirements	Emphasis on retraining. Minimal involvement of personnel dept. Training related to individual requirements
Development	Single track to progression. 'Dead men's shoes' promotion	Rotation through function. Rotation through areas. Internal career growth
Appraisal	Technical skills = promotion. Common salary levels. Annual step increases	Complex appraisal. Individual setting of objectives. Individual rewards
Motivation	Pay	Performance recognition. Individual development

Source: Adapted from NEDO, *Design from Corporate Culture*, 1987

Style

Much of the literature on innovation has concentrated on the issue of leadership and its influence on corporate achievement.[24] Though leadership is essential in overcoming the problems of change, the central resource question should be whether the type of leadership is appropriate for the innovation task. Some of the important components for sector-creating innovation have been mentioned elsewhere in the text (see pp. 123–5) — openness and free exchange of information. Certain types of leader create organizational climates that mitigate against this, others generate poor attitudes towards business ethics, aggressive personal attitudes and so on.[25] General leadership style is also influenced by general attitudes prevailing within national boundaries. Thus, American executives tend to be more direct and task orientated than their Dutch counterparts, for example.[26]

Company executives will have to be honest about the prevailing management climate within the corporation and whether it either encourages or discourages innovation. The management style in place should obviously approximate to the demands of the innovation process, and if there is a serious mismatch the likelihood of a firm being able to carry through a particular programme of innovation is seriously reduced. However, it may still be able to operate successfully in other areas. This problem of management styles will often be most acute where the company is changing its area of concentration from one type of innovation policy to another. Management styles vary along a continuum from what can be broadly described as democratic/participative to directive/task-related, which may be

Table 7.19 Characteristics of management styles in democratic vs directive organizations

Democratic:

* Organizations often undirected in the way in which they approach tasks and communicate with other members of the team.
* Have a continuous revision and reappraisal of products and processes.
* Have open channels of communication.
* Accept diversity of opinion and the involvement of non-specialists in problem solving.

Directive:

* Highly directed and well-defined task definition and communication systems.
* Structure tasks in a sequential rather than a parallel fashion.
* Restrict free-ranging discussion and evaluation, and concentrate heavily on engineering problem solving rather than analysis of all possible concepts.

Source: H.I. Ansoff and J.M. Stewart in R.R. Rothberg, *Corporate Strategy and Product Innovation*, 1981

applicable to individual managers or whole organizations (see Table 7.19). Within these extremes there are many intermediate positions.[27] One of the most widely quoted is the analysis by Reddin, separating individuals along three dimensions: their degree of interest in completion of the job, or *task* effectiveness; their involvement with individuals, or *relationship* effectiveness; and their ability to achieve high levels of *productivity*. From these three components, eight fairly distinct management styles are noted and summarized in Table 7.20.[28]

Management styles, both organizational and individual, must be appropriate to the type of policy that the company is following. Democratic management styles are most appropriate for those companies involved in the introduction of fundamental research or those that are heavily dependent on the market for innovative concepts (these are the 'common room' and 'coffee shop' organizational concepts referred to in Chapter 8); whereas the directive management style is essential for the achievement of manufacturing targets and reaching markets on time (the 'rugby scrum' organizational concept referred to in Chapter 8). Those styles that are essentially based on non-involvement will be poor resources for

Table 7.20 Management styles and their characteristics

	Conflict	Personnel problems	Attitudes towards Change	Decision making	Motivation
Deserter	Avoids	Avoids	Resists	Avoids	Avoids
Missionary	Avoids	Involved	Goes with crowd	Avoids	Laissez-faire
Autocrat	Initiates	No interest	Resists	Single-minded	Hire/fire
Compromiser	Vacillates	Avoids	Vacillates	Avoids	Follows rules
Bureaucrat	Follows procedure	No interest	Follows procedure	Avoids	Avoids
Developer	Resolves	Involved	Involved	Avoids	Interested
Benevolent Autocrat	Resolves	Involved	Involved	Single-minded	Laissez-faire
Executive	Resolves	Involved	Involved	Democratic	Interested

Source: Adapted from W.J. Reddin, *Managerial Effectiveness*, 1970

Table 7.21 Employee survey on factors either encouraging or discouraging innovations

Factor	Greatest strength	Greatest weakness
Communication	7	7
Organization	18	26
Education	8	1
Management	12	22
Policy	6	8
Environment	24	16

Source: S. Baran, *Research Management*, 29, 1986

innovation management of any type. Senior management in particular will need to be involved and committed at all stages of the process, as the majority of innovation studies reveal this as being crucial in creating the right climate for change. A good example is an employee survey which identified the environment as the most important factor in encouraging innovation (see Table 7.21).

Shared values

The pervasiveness of shared values or common goals within a particular company is of crucial importance in coping effectively with change. Change introduces enormous strains into organizations, and however good the communication systems are within the enterprise, they substantially reduce efficiency unless the staff are aware of, and share a common perception about, the task involved and the individual sacrifices or commitment necessary to achieve it. Many surveys identify positive 'internal attitudes' as one of the main necessary internal building blocks to achieve rapid and successful change, and often the most important (see Table 7.22).[29] High levels of shared values are often considered one of the main reasons why large Japanese industrial companies are able to switch from one area of activity to another so smoothly. One example in the mid-1980s was Mitsubishi's intention to retrain some of the shipbuilding workforce to act as ski instructors in a new leisure venture. It is worth considering the likely response of autoworkers in Detroit, Dagenham or Düsseldorf to a similar proposal. These shared values

Table 7.22 Factors most favourably affecting trading environment

Factor	Percentage
Attitudes	35
Better plant	26
Better marketing	14
Customer attention	11
Better pricing	8
Company structure	6

Source: NEDO, *Report on the Printing Industry*, 1985

Table 7.23 Shared values in Japanese and US companies; main differences in attitudes

Japan	US
Work designed around co-operative teamwork	Work largely individually based
Generalist orientation	Specific job description
Harmony and stability emphasized	Creativity and aggression more important
Considerable job mobility	Limited mobility
Worker involved as equal; kept informed of prices, targets, competition	Worker treated as subordinate
	Rarely informed of business targets
Suggestions welcomed. Training to improve quality of suggestions, high implementation rate	Suggestions rarely welcomed
	Poor systems to collect ideas, with low implementation rate
'Work smarter, not harder' philosophy	'Work harder' philosophy

Source: Adapted from O.L. Crocker, S.L. Charney and J.S.L. Chiu, *Quality Circles: A Guide to Participation and Productivity*, 1984

are part of a far greater involvement of the labour force at all levels within the organization in the majority of Japanese organizations when compared with US and most Western companies. The main points of difference are summarized in Table 7.23.[30]

In conclusion, the importance of the personnel resource in producing an environment in which successful innovation can proceed cannot be understated.

Table 7.24 The successful innovator

Factor	Old product development	New product development
Strategy	Development of explicit plans and budgets	Broad objectives communicated throughout the organization Long-term clear target creation Emphasis on organic development
Subject	Clear understanding of the needs of the strategy in terms of personnel resource	
Support	Updates technology for improved performance	Acquires appropriate technology
Structure	Decentralized decision making Thin organization	New forms selected as appropriate to investment level
Skills	Uses as sophisticated planning systems as possible	Expertise perceived as essential knowledge-based workforce
Style	Top management available and interested Openness to new ideas	Top management closely involved No 'them and us' syndrome
Staff	Existing line managers given responsibility	Senior management identify and appoint appropriate teams Understanding of critical mass requirements for specific development
Shared values	Encouragement for development Closeness to customer	Enthusiasm for innovation 'Can do' rather than 'can't do' environment
Systems	Close attention to recruitment, appraisal, motivation. Information systems designed to keep organization closely integrated	

Source: Adapted from A. Johne and P. Snelson, *R & D Management*, 18, 1988

Table 7.25 The unsuccessful or less successful innovator

Factor	Old product development	New product development
Strategy	Responsibility delegated No clear planning procedure, plans or budgets	Concentration on acquisition throughout the organization
Subject	Very limited understanding of the demands of the strategy in terms of personnel resource	
Support	Technology not updated	Appropriate technology slowly, if ever, introduced
Skills	Limited use of skilled staff	Traditional work methods Training limited and routine
Style	Top management not interested	Top management operate at a distance
Staff	Direction from the top	Single approaches to new product management
Structure	Centralized decision making Pyramidical structure	Departmental structure still used
Shared values	Few attempts to develop shared goals for either old products or new developments	
Systems	Rigid system associated with the implementation of clearly defined grading systems	

Source: Adapted from A. Johne and P. Snelson, *R & D Management*, 18, 1988

Table 7.24 summarizes the likely characteristics of the company that is likely to manage innovation successfully. In contrast, the unsuccessful or less successful innovation company has a quite different profile summarized for comparison in Table 7.25.

Core competence

The discussion in this chapter has concentrated on the demands of innovation and personnel policies. The personnel resource cannot be isolated from the history of the company and its previous ability to meet the demands of particular market sectors. Personnel skills and staff numbers will therefore be dependent to an extent on the position that the organization occupies in the market, and the length of time that it has been established. Many analysts of market structure define either five or six possible positions that a company can occupy: market leadership, market challenger, market follower, market specialist, commodity supplier and market entrant. Each of these categories has a particular relationship with the market in respect of price, distribution channels, position on the so-called experience or learning curve,[31] promotional policy and the like, the most important of which are summarized in Table 7.26.

It is evident that the market leader will have lower production costs and generally greater financial and personnel resources than the commodity supplier, and will have a product range that is widely accepted in the market as superior to many

Table 7.26 Functional differences in market status

Functional factors	Market leader	Market follower	Specialist	Commodity producer	Market entrant
Distribution	Very wide	Wide	Narrow	Small	None
Price	Good	Fair	Good	Poor	Very poor
Order size	Large	Fair	Fair	Large	Small
Selling effort	Small	Fair	Fair	Small	High
Quality perception	Good	Fair	Excellent	Poor	None
Cumulative volume	Large	High	Small	High	None
Cumulative research	High	Moderate	Small	Small	None
Product quality	Meets market needs	Meets market needs	High	Low	Must be higher

Source: Author

other companies in that market. It will probably have lower production costs than the market entrant — it will almost inevitably achieve better prices and have greater control over the distribution channels.

The question facing firms in whatever category is whether the combination of financial, product, production and personnel resources match the demands of the market place, a combination termed the core competence. What is the overall position of the firm in comparison to the competition, given this specific range of factors, and what can it achieve? It has always been apparent that though a firm may be a market leader or have a strong financial position, it will nevertheless lack the overall core competence that will provide it with a dominant business position. In order to arrive at a final judgement as to the position of the firm in the market it will be necessary to compare competitive core competences, comparing personnel, production, product and financial strengths. In markets where it is difficult to establish core competences such as the pharmaceutical sector the barriers to entry will be large and the position of the potential market entrant weak, whereas in those markets where investment can yield effective core competence, the potential threat of market entrants will be considerable. This further underlines the fact that competitive advantage is not immutably on the side of the big battalions — companies by the appropriate policies of matching resource to market can establish core competence that eventually will oust existing major forces in the industry.

Some examples can illustrate the point that financial resources and market position do not alone define the effectiveness of an organization in achieving effective change. IBM during the late 1980s has come under increasing pressure in a rapidly altering computer environment from competitors with lower growth and profitability. With the rapid decline in hardware cost, the tendency towards emphasizing peripheral rather than centralized data manipulation continued to develop. As the hardware became faster, the trend towards a wider variety, flexibility, and ease of use of the operating systems and software became more important than further increases in processing speed which was already entirely satisfactory for the majority of applications. The problem for IBM is that the core competence of the company is in the development of large centralized computing systems, with the emphasis on power and speed of the individual machines rather than flexibility and ease of use. The core competence is entirely suited to large-scale investment in sector creating innovations such as the possible breakthrough in room temperature superconducting materials, but not suited to meet less resource intensive market-led change such as that demonstrated by Compaq (see p. 53).

It is argued that the result of this core competence has been a continuation of company policy to emphasize their existing product resource and major area of expertise, even though both the hardware and software systems were increasingly inappropriate for the marketplace. This has led IBM to miss major opportunities such as the work station and the growing market for multimedia systems in the late 1980s. Should the company be able to redirect its resources — personnel, production and financial — into new areas by creating *a new core competence*, the company will again be one of the major forces in the computer market. Until this occurs the company will suffer as it continues to lose competitive advantage, dropping from the position of universal pre-eminence in the computer industry of the late 1970s and early 1980s into market-follower positions in many sectors.

Similarly, the problems that GEC of the United Kingdom face also relate to a long-term weakness of core competence in the main areas in which the company operates: power generation, defence electronics, telecommunications and consumer electronics. In many of these areas, the weakness of core competence extends across many of the important areas, including personnel, production and product, even though the company maintains a strong financial position. By contrast, GE of the United States has continued to concentrate on building core competence in its main areas of operation, with strong products, personnel and production facilities combining to strengthen its existing competitive position.

The problems that General Motors has faced in the motor car market have also stemmed from a mismatch of core competence and market demands, with further complications caused by the dilution of investment that should have been directed into re-establishing the correct core competence into other areas such as aerospace (Hughes) and data management (EDS).

In a market environment dominated by knowledge wars the maintenance and redirection of the firm's core competence will be of increasing importance, and the method of assessment of business units will need to move away from the traditional concentration on product-based divisions towards an analysis based more on knowledge as well as existing products and market position. The main differences in emphasis between the two approaches, one based on the concept of the strategic business unit and the other on the concept of core competence, are in Table 7.27. The implications for the corporation as it assesses its overall resource position for change in the 1990s are clear; market position and production expertise will no longer be sufficient to ensure that the company can effectively maintain its competitive advantage. The company will need to concentrate on

Table 7.27 Comparisons of analysis based on the historic strategic business unit (SBU) concept and core competence

Factor	SBU	Core competence
Corporate structure	Product-based	Knowledge-based
Key feature	Product development	Knowledge development
Investment criteria	Profit	Competitive advantage
Role of senior management	Allocate capital	Identify knowledge requirements and allocate overall resources (inc. staff) to meet competitive advantage requirements

Source: Author

developing and maintaining core competence in the market sectors where it is most likely to achieve competitive advantage. The following chapter will consider the investment issues involved; given a particular type of market/resource interaction, where the firm should consider concentrating to build competitive advantage and the likely organizational implications of such decisions.

Mosaic management

In such an environment where the need to build competitive advantage is paramount the problem faced by the vast majority of resource-limited corporations is how to move effectively from a position of relative weakness to a position of relative strength in a consistent and coherent fashion. A technique employed by many of the successful Japanese and German concerns is to concentrate on building competitive advantage via the development of core competence in specific high-value-added activities and steadily to increase the range and effectiveness of such core competences.

This can be defined as mosaic management — choosing particular areas for concentration and eventually creating an overall business operation that is able to out-compete the current market leaders. JVC has followed a very successful policy of concentrating in developing expertise in particular aspects of component manufacture, thereby creating a company that would eventually be able to outcompete such established organizations as Philips and Sony in many areas of their operations. Many of the Korean companies such as Samsung and Goldstar have followed this particular line of development initially by selling components to OEM (original equipment manufacturers) and thus gaining experience and expertise which can then be transferred successfully into full-scale manufacture of fully competitive OEM products.

Notes

1. For some classic descriptions of large organizations' resistance to change see L. Chapman, *Your Disobedient Servant*, (London: Chatto and Windus, 1978). L. Chapman, *Waste Away*, (London: Chatto and Windus, 1978). For a discussion of Gresham's Law see H.A. Simon, *The New Science of Management Decision*, (Englewood Cliffs, NJ: Prentice Hall, 1977).

2. See T. Peters, *Thriving on Chaos*, (London: Macmillan, 1988) for a discussion of barriers to innovation.

3. A. Jay, *Management and Machiavelli*, (London: Penguin, 1978) and A. Jay, *Corporation Man*, (London: Penguin, 1980). Both books consider the political aspects of company life in detail.

4. P. Townsend, *Further Up the Organisation*, (London: Pan, 1987) gives a clear view of the problems that non-line managers cause. G. Burkvalt, *Werkschafft in Deutschland*, (Springer Verlag, 1988).

5. R. Lickert, 'A New Twist to People Accounting', *Business Week*, (October 1972).

6. National Economic Development Organisation, *Report on the British Knitting Industry*, (London: NEDO, 1987).

7. F. Sen and A.H. Rubenstein, 'Aspects of Research and Development Management', *Journal of Product Innovation Management*, issue 6, 6 (1989), pp. 19–36.

8. O.L. Crocker, S. Charney and J. Sik Leung Chiu, *Quality Circles: A Guide to Participation and Productivity*, (New York: New American Library, 1984).

9. *The Financial Times*, (8 March 1989). P. Drucker, *The Practice of Management*, (London: Heinemann, 1955).

10. C.W. Hill, 'Corporate Control and Financial Performance', *Journal of Management Studies*, 25 (1988) pp. 141–53.

11. A. Pinchot, *Intrapreneuring*, (London: Harper & Row, 1987).

12. R.G. Cooper and E.J. Kleinschmidt, 'Synergy and Financial Performance', *R & D Management*, 17, (1987), pp. 51–64.

13. A.R. Weiss and P.H. Burnbain, 'Technological Infrastructure Strategies', *Management Science*, No. 8, 35 (1989), pp. 127–39. L.C. Rhyne, 'Control Planning Systems in High, Medium and Low Performance Companies', *Journal of Management Studies*, 24 (1987), pp. 17–23.

14. R.K. Moenaert and W.E. Sonder, 'Information Transfer and Innovation', *Journal of Product Innovation Management*, issue 2, 7, (1990) pp. 43–58.

15. E. Sonderstom and B.M. Winchell, 'Information Technology in Innovation', *Research Management*, 29 (1986), pp. 3–18.

16. D. Leonard Barton and J.J. Sviokla, 'Putting Expert Systems to Work', *Harvard Business Review*, issue 2, 66, (1988) pp. 81–97.

17. There is a considerable body of literature on human groups. For example, W.J.H. Sprott, *Human Groups* (London: Penguin, 1964).

18. R. Oakley, R. Rothwell and S. Cooper, *The Management of Innovation in High Technology Small Firms: Innovation and Regional Development in Britain and the United States*, (London: Frances Pinter, 1988).

19. G.J. Bamber and R.D. Lansbury, 'Management Strategy and New Technology in Retail Distribution: A Comparative Case Study', *Journal of Management Studies*, 25, (1988), 3–27. M. Cooley, *Architect or Bee: The Human Price of Technology*, (Glasgow: Hogarth Press, 1987).

20. C. Goodworth, *Effective Interviewing for Employment Selection*, (London: Business Books, 1979).

21. For example, H. Mintzberg, *The Nature of Managerial Work*, (New York: Harper & Row, 1979). J.E. Muckley, 'Dear Shareholder', *Harvard Business Review*, issue 2, 62, (1984) p. 46.

22. W. Brown, *Exploration in Management*, (London: Heinemann, 1968) is a good case study of changing disciplinary environments giving a working model for restructuring disciplinary procedures.

23. National Economic Development Organisation, *Design from Corporate Culture*, (London: NEDO, 1987).

24. W. Bennis and B. Namus, *Leaders* (New York: Harper & Row, 1985). R. Michel, *The Strategic CEO, How Visionary Executives Build Organisations*, (Quorum, NY: Quorum Books, (1988). J. Bandtowski, *Corporate Innovation Plus Five Steps to Translating Innovative Strategies into Action*, (New York: The Free Press, 1990). J.M. Burns, *Leadership*, (New York: Harper & Row, 1978).

25. L. Heilbroner (ed.), *In The Name of Profit*, (New York: Doubleday, 1972) contains fascinating insights into organizational culture. Of particular interest is the contribution by Kermit Vandivier, 'Why Should My Conscience Bother Me?' which is about the development of a new braking assembly for an American airforce plane. A.P. Sethi, *Up Against the Corporate Wall*, (Englewood Cliffs, NJ: Prentice Hall, 1982).

26. J. Hunt *et al.*, *Leaders and Managers: International Perspectives on Management Behaviour and Leadership*, (Oxford: Pergamon Press, 1984). R.M. Hodgetts, *Management Theory, Process and Practice*, 3rd edn, (Los Angeles: CBS Publishing Company, 1982). H.G. Hicks and C.R. Gullet, *Management* (London: McGraw-Hill, 1981). H. Harding, *Management Appreciation*, (London: Pitman, 1987).

27. H. Ansoff and J.M. Stewart in R.R. Rothberg (ed.) *Corporate Strategy and Product Innovation*, (New York: The Free Press, 1981).

28. W.J. Reddin, *Managerial Effectiveness*, (London: McGraw-Hill, 1970).

29. National Economic Development Organisation, *Report on the Printing Industry*, (London: NEDO, 1985).

30. O.L. Crocker, S. Charney and J. Sik Leung Chiu (1984).

31. G.S. Day and D.E. Montgomery, 'Diagnosing the Experience Curve', *Journal of Marketing*, 2 (1983) pp. 14–27.

8

Matching resources to market

Introduction: the role of strategic models

Innovation does not exist in a vacuum and cannot therefore be considered the sole component of any business plan — obviously a company must generate positive revenues from one part of its business in order to invest in the development of new concepts. But innovation involves a change of direction and hence an altered investment policy, so it is essential from the beginning for the business planner to be clear about such areas as the current state of the product 'portfolio', balancing current products with possible policies for future development and their likely implications in terms of cash flow, market share, return on capital employed and other key components of company objectives. Businesses are resource limited and must determine where and in what way resources should be allocated to achieve the objectives that have been set. Increasingly, as the previous chapter has indicated, these objectives must concentrate on building core competence (see pp. 145–8), and from that, competitive advantage.

In the changing competitive environment the contribution of models that aid in the assessment of strategy need to be reviewed in order to identify the specific assistance that such models provide in the definition of appropriate policies for change. An initial simplistic division can be made into two categories: 'what' models, providing a picture of the company at the moment of analysis; and 'which' models, suggesting alternative action paths for the company to take. While each of these models has specific strengths and weaknesses, they provide information which can be used to build a more complete picture of events within the business and the options for future development. However, few businesses make much use of them to further their understanding of the current environment or the most viable future actions. This is shown by surveys of middle management by the author (see Table 8.1) even though long-term studies continue to show the value of strategic planning. For example, one investigation of small firms in the Southern

Table 8.1 Percentage of middle managers using business planning models

Number of models used	Percentage of managers
None	35
1 or 2	47
3 to 5	15
More than 5	3

Source: Author

United States showed that the planners are far more likely to survive than non-planners. Strategic planning, though not a universal road to riches, at least seemed to minimize the risks of failure.

Another study of the planning process in several hundred firms clearly showed how few UK companies were producing complete plans (including environmental analysis, macro-factors, competitive issues, internal resources, long- medium- and short-term objectives, relevant assumptions, and a fully detailed implementation including budgets, personnel planning and fall-back positions) (see Table 8.2). It is clear from surveys like this, and anecdotal information, that often it is not the planning concept that is at fault but the inability of the companies to use effectively the planning systems they had. On the other hand, it could, regrettably, be argued that companies do not use strategic planning models because they do not offer what the customer wants. A model may be inadequate because its analysis of the relationship between company resources and markets, results in advice about overall investment decisions rather than about the specifics of *how* to manage the alternatives in the market/business relationship — because there are always alternatives — in order to gain the maximum competitive advantage. Nor do the majority of models provide any concrete suggestions as to what type of change should be considered. With the management of change becoming such an important aspect of business in the 1990s, it is worth reviewing the contributions that the various models can make to the innovation process. The two categories are detailed in Table 8.3 and the remainder of this chapter

Table 8.2 Sample of companies in different surveys producing 'complete plans'

Survey	Percentage
1	14
2	25
3	12
4	14
5	10
6	20

Source: G.E. Greenley, *Quarterly Review of Marketing*, 2, 1985

Table 8.3 Models for strategic direction

What models	Which models
BCG	PLC
GE	Product viability
Porter	Market growth/business position
Market growth/business position	Ansoff
Ansoff matrix	Technology change/market change
Development risk/opportunity cost	

Source: Author

will review what the various portfolio analyses can provide in the way of specific advice for the investment planner geared toward gaining competitive advantage.

BCG

The BCG or the Boston Consulting Group portfolio analysis identifies four main subdivisions of products (or profit centres/SBUs) based on relative market shares and market growth (Figure 8.1). The position of the product group or SBU in the matrix broadly determines the type of investment strategy to be followed. The broad alternatives suggested are: product abandonment/harvesting — that is, the removal of the SBU from the portfolio within a short period of time or accepting its eventual retirement after providing substantial positive cash flows to the organization; product consolidation/maintenance — holding the SBU position in the market by a steady level of investment, and continuing to generate positive cash flows; or product investment — using cash flows from consolidation and harvesting areas to produce new concepts and products to generate future revenue growth.

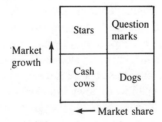

Notes:
Cash cows: products generating cash which have high relative market shares and are established in slowly growing markets.
Dogs: products unlikely to be generating substantial positive cash flows due to the fact that they are in slowly growing markets with low relative market shares.
Stars: products generally with negative cash flows but with high relative market shares in rapidly growing markets.
Question marks: products also with generally negative cash flows but with low relative market shares in growing markets.

Figure 8.1 BCG matrix

Dogs, in this assessment, are the most suitable candidates for product abandonment; cash cows are to be consolidated and their position maintained within the market by limited investment; stars are components of the portfolio which should receive continuing high levels of investment to ensure their continuing progress; and question marks, by their very description, require careful consideration and do not easily fall into a single action framework — the decision as to whether they should receive additional investment or should be abandoned, will depend on the individual circumstances of the firm at a particular stage in their development. The BCG matrix, though helpful for strategic investment in broad terms, does not assist the planner in identifying a single product development proposal for further progress from a number of alternatives; nor, in an era of much more slowly growing markets, is it of use in many product sectors, where stars and question marks are more difficult to find. The assumption that products in the dog category should be discontinued may also dissuade management from exploring low-cost innovative approaches which could significantly improve profitability or market share.

The use of the BCG matrix to develop specific proposals is therefore limited, especially as it concentrates on product rather than core competence, issues that were discussed in the previous chapter (see pp. 145−8). Nevertheless, the information from the BCG matrix provides valuable information, as to the likely future cash flows from within the organization, that can be used to evaluate which of the possible innovation routes can be achieved.

Porter

The strategic model developed by Michael Porter concentrates on the application of experience curves and economies of scale to identify two key components of business policy, cost and differentiation.[1] Depending on where the company is positioned, generic strategies could be developed which relied on either cost or differentiation. Companies could either concentrate on developing cost leadership by establishing economies of scale and benefiting from the learning curve by producing higher volumes than the competition, or could concentrate on producing new products either for the entire market or for small niche sectors.

The problem with the generic strategies concept is that a rapidly changing market environment may decrease the viability of any particular policy. Thus, in a study of the UK cutlery market, the company attempting to gain cost leadership by high levels of investment in capital equipment, Viners, went into effective liquidation, whereas Westall Richardson, following a flexible and responsive policy, managed to improve profitability continually throughout the entire period.[2] The overemphasis on cost domination via a concentration on investment in improving manufacturing systems can create a perception that efficiencies of scale will be the sole viable route under most conditions, and ignores the potential impact of substitutes or new entrants as performance plateaux are reached. The concept of generic strategies also does not give guidance on the type of differentiation policies that should be followed — suggesting a limited range of options that may be open to gain competitive advantage.

GE

The General Electric portfolio defines products along the axes of market attractiveness and business position on a nine-grid basis (see Figure 8.2), with the two elements being defined by a certain range of components. The model concentrates on return on capital employed in contrast to the BCG model which provides information on cash flow. Products or SBUs with strong business positions in attractive markets will yield high returns on capital employed. Those with medium positions will yield average returns and those with poor positions in relatively unattractive markets will give a poor yield. The nine positions on the grid suggest three broad investment strategies: business units in the top left-hand quadrant should receive high levels of investment to build their market position; business units in the central sector should be maintained by continuous medium levels of investment; business units in the lower right-hand sector should either be harvested or abandoned. These broad recommendations have been narrowed in further developments of the GE matrix, to suggest a series of specific actions (see Table 8.4).

Much of the relevance of the GE portfolio depends on how the firm rates the various market and business position factors as the portfolio grid depends on a subjective weighting of the various components. This shortcoming does not exist

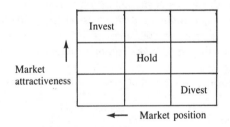

Notes:
Components of the GE portfolio

Market attractiveness:	Business position:
Market size	Business size
Market growth	Market share
Number of market subdivisions	Price position
Competitive intensity	Product quality
Profitability	Technical superiority
Inflation trends	Market knowledge
Technical requirements	Profitability
Social components	
Legal issues	

Figure 8.2 The GE matrix

Table 8.4 Product policy suggestions based on the GE matrix

Market attractiveness	Strong	Business position Medium	Weak
High	All-out struggle to maintain position	Selective growth	Test market opportunism
Moderate	Maintain superiority	Selective expansion	Limited expansion
Low	Limited harvesting	Total harvesting	Loss reduction

Source: Author

in the BCG matrix which relies on absolute measures of market growth and relative market shares. A technically-based company will for example often place far more importance on technical advantages, whereas a fashion-based company will place more emphasis on its market expertise when it comes to the assessment of the relative resource availability. The GE matrix also fails to identify the type of innovation likely to yield the greatest return at each stage of market growth and maturity. Consideration of the stages of market growth and their particular demands led to the development of additional portfolio techniques to consider investment strategies at each stage of the market evolution.

Market growth/business position

This model uses the same concept of the business position as the GE matrix, divided into five separate levels — dominant, strong, favourable, tenable and weak — and relates this to the stages of market development — embryonic, growing, mature, and ageing — to produce a series of strategic guidelines for company development. The main recommendations of the resulting matrix are in Table 8.5.[3] The market growth/competitive position provides valuable guidance about

Table 8.5 Strategic guidelines as a function of industry maturity and competitive position

Business position	Embryonic	Market position Growing	Mature	Ageing
Dominant	All-out push for share Hold position	Hold position Hold share	Hold position Grow with industry	Hold position
Strong	Attempt to improve position	Attempt to improve position	Hold	Hold
Favourable	Selective or all-out push for share	Selective push for market share	Find niche and protect	Harvest
Tenable	Selectively push for position	Find niche and protect	Find niche and hang on	Phased withdrawal
Weak	Up or out	Turnround or abandon	Turnround or phased withdrawal	Abandon

Source: W.G. Glueck, *Business Policy and Strategic Management*, 1980

broad policies, replacing the concept of market attractiveness in the GE matrix with stages of market growth, considering embryonic and growing markets as more attractive than mature or ageing. This model does not differentiate between the rate of market growth and the overall attractiveness of the market. Next in the discussion is one analytical approach that does. It separates markets into slow growth or rapid growth, in a similar approach to the Boston Consulting Group, but concentrates on the concept of business position rather than market share.

Market growth/speed/business position

This model, in common with the BCG approach identifies four potential quadrants of market growth and business position, each associated with a number of appropriate strategies. The main options (most attractive listed first in each case, and the least attractive last) are in Table 8.6.[4] The action standards proposed by the model are mainly concerned with corporate restructuring, and do little to analyse the investment options should the organization decide to change its products or markets. It does not consider the level of investment necessary to gain competitive advantage, the problems posed by rapid changes in technology, or what specific types of investment should be considered. Another portfolio model was developed to provide conceptual support on the issue of investment intensity; the 'competitive advantage versus investment intensity' matrix.

Competitive advantage versus investment intensity

This matrix divides the product portfolio by *ease of gaining competitive advantage* and the *investment requirements of the industry*, with four subdivisions. The

Table 8.6 Market growth speed/business position

Group I Policies	Rapid market growth, strong business position:
	Concentration
	Vertical integration
	Concentric diversification
Group II Policies	Slow market growth, strong business position:
	Concentric diversification
	Conglomerate diversification
	Joint ventures into new areas
Group III Policies	Rapid market growth, weak business position:
	Reformulation of concentric strategy
	Horizontal integration or merger
	Divestiture
	Liquidation
Group IV Policies	Slow market growth, weak business position:
	Retrenchment
	Diversification
	Divestiture
	Liquidation

Source: Adapted from A.A. Thompson and A.J. Strickland, *Strategic Management, Concepts and Cases*, 1984

Table 8.7 The quadrants of the competitive advantage versus investment intensity matrix

1. Stalemate or commodity sectors where the investment requirements are low and there are few ways to gain competitive advantage.
2. Volume markets where the investment requirements are high but there are few ways of gaining competitive advantage.
3. Fragmented markets where both the ease of gaining competitive advantage and the necessary investment are low.
4. Specialized markets where the investment requirements are high and the ease of achieving competitive advantage is also increased.

Source: Adapted from APA

components of the four quadrants are in Table 8.7. The competitive advantage versus investment intensity model is valuable in giving some indications as to the likely effectiveness of investment in particular market sectors. It is suggested that stalemate or commodity sectors pose the most difficulty for effective innovation, with fragmented markets presenting the lowest barriers. Again, this model fails to produce specific investment recommendations on what types of innovation strategy should be followed to take advantage of what opportunities may exist in specific markets.

These 'what' models all use historic information about where the business has been and what type of broad options exist for future investment. They do little to suggest specific types of investment policies under certain types of market condition or product sales pattern. 'Which' models, on the other hand are designed to provide specific recommendations for action relating to particular sales or market conditions.

PLC

Similar broad conceptual frameworks for planning are provided by applications of the product life cycle (PLC). This states that a model of introduction, growth, maturity and decline can provide valuable insight into the likely future investment demands of the product at stages, as summarized in Table 8.8[5] Though the PLC provides some guidelines about marketing-mix issues, it gives little information on likely innovation policies. It suggests, however, that specific changes in product policy should be followed after the initial product introduction. A major problem is that few products follow 'typical' PLC curves. This implies that the organization evaluates the likely progress of each facet of the product's performance over the ensuing timescale to identify particular areas where investment should be concentrated, without a clear indication as to whether that product will follow the predicted path of the PLC. The result is often a self-fulfilling prophecy, whereby the organization takes actions that lead to the decline and eventual withdrawal of the product without clear evidence that this decline is already occurring. The use of the PLC for defining investment is risky; and it does not identify specific changes in product policy. A most useful method of attempting to anticipate real changes in the environment, and thereby to narrow the likely areas for investment, is the product viability analysis.

Table 8.8 Investment issues in the product life cycle

	Introduction	Growth	Maturity	Decline
Sales	Low	Increasing	Slower	Dropping
Profits	Minus	Maximum	Dropping	Low
Buyers	Innovators	Early adopters	Majority	Laggards
Competition	Few	Increasing	Many	Fewer
Price	Low	Higher	Highest	Reduced
Product range	Basic	Improved	Extended	Reduced
Ad. spend (%)	High	Lower	Lowest	Low
Promotion	Awareness	Preference	Loyalty	Various
Distribution	Limited	Expanded	Maximum	Reduced

Source: A. West, *Understanding Marketing*, 1987

Product viability analysis

The product viability model is based on a forecast of the likely changes in the product over the planning horizon. It evaluates possible pressures upon the product or product sector and helps the planner decide on possible effective courses of action. The concept can be used to provide a qualitative assessment of any of the main factors that may or may not adversely affect the product over the planning cycle (see Table 8.9). This model can give indicators about where specific investments should be made to maintain the product in the marketplace — it emphasizes the issues of changing technology, packaging and formulation as areas where a company can take specific action. It is, as a result, more action specific than the PLC. However, it does not attempt to assess the implication of company resource on the actions that the firm can realistically take in the marketplace. The impact of technology and market change is the subject of another action-oriented portfolio analysis developed by the marketing consultants, Booz Allen, the 'market newness/technological change' matrix.

Market newness/technological change

This model proposes that action decisions can be taken on product change

Table 8.9 Product viability analysis

Factor	Short-term	Medium-term	Long-term
Economic	/	//	///
Technology	///	///	///
Price	/	/	//
Competition pressure	/	/	/
Packaging	///	///	///
Formulation	/	//	///
Product range	/	/	/

Note: / = viability not severely affected; /// = viability severely affected

Source: A. West, *Understanding Marketing*, 1987

Table 8.10 Market newness/technological change matrix

Market change	None	Technological change Improved technology	New technology
None	No action	Reformulation	Replacement
Changing market	Remerchandise	Improved product	Product line extension
New market	New use	Market extension	Diversification

Source: Booz, Allen and Hamilton, Company report, 1957

according to the relationship between the rate of change in technology and how rapidly the market is developing. Nine potential market segments, are identified with particular types of action potential (see Table 8.10). The specific actions proposed in the various sectors of the grid are as follows:

- *Reformulation*   To maintain an optimum balance of cost quality and availability in the formulae of present company products;
- *Replacement*   To seek new and better ingredients or formulation for present company products in technology not now employed in the company;
- *Remerchandising*   To increase sales to consumers of types now served by the company;
- *Improved product*   To improve present products for greater utility and merchandisability to consumers;
- *Product line extension*   To broaden the line of products offered to present consumers through new technology;
- *New use*   To find new uses for present company products;
- *Market extension*   To reach new classes of consumers by modifying present products;
- *Diversification*   To add to the classes of consumers served by developing new technical knowledge.

Though this grid suggests specific types of action it fails to relate the company resources to the market opportunities available. Moreover, changing technology is only one factor contributing to investment uncertainty and should not be considered the sole issue for the development of company policy. One further development of this matrix is to consider technology positions in relation to pre-market (R & D phases) and post-market trends of either rapid or slow growth.

Technology position/market growth matrix

Companies are placed in one of a number of categories depending on whether they are technological leaders, followers, and developers or those that do not compete via technological development. The position of the company within the matrix suggests a number of alternative strategies (see Figure 8.3). The identification by this matrix of the important components of developmental speed and non-technological concentration, as means of entering particular markets,

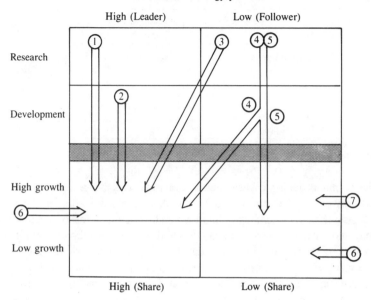

Relative technology position

Notes:
1. Technological leader: first to market
2. Technological acquirer: first to market
3. Research follower, strong developer: first to market
4. Technological follower: strong marketing thrust
5. Technological follower: weak marketing thrust
6. Minimal technology: acquire leadership position early
7. Minimal technology: acquire follower position early
8. Minimal technology: acquire follower position late

Figure 8.3 Technology position/market growth matrix (Source: N. Capon and R. Glazer, *Journal of Marketing* 51, 3, 1987)

is significantly different to other approaches that concentrate purely on technology as the key component, and is, as a result, much closer to the realities of the market environment. However, it does little to consider what particular route a company should follow given a particular set of market circumstances and resource position. One such matrix concentrates on the issue of opportunity cost and development risk.

Opportunity cost/development risk

The McKinsey group developed the concept of looking at the relationship of opportunity cost versus development risk. High development-risk routes coupled with high opportunity costs should only be considered in relation to joint venture and acquisition. The main viable development routes vary from the top left-hand quandrant to the bottom right, with strategies ranging from crash programmes

Table 8.11 Opportunity cost/development risk matrix

Opportunity cost	Low	Development risk Moderate	High
High	Crash program	Acquisition	Exit/Leap frog
	Hybrid step		Joint venture
Moderate		Step by step	
		product line	
		Outside niche	
Low	Quantum leap		
	Parallel programs		100% right

Source: McKinsey & Co. Inc

for the company facing a very low development risk but a high potential lost opportunity cost — for example, IBM in the development of the microcomputer — to the right-hand bottom quadrant in which low potential lost opportunity costs are matched with high development costs and where it will be essential that the product is correctly defined and developed. Examples would include the development of anti-Aids drugs such as Retrovir by Wellcome (see Table 8.11). The McKinsey matrix concentrates most heavily on technological components of product development and the strategic implications of the various options. It does little to consider the other, non-technological options open to the company for long- or medium-term innovative development.

The Ansoff matrix

The Ansoff approach identifies broad options open to the company considering change. The model considers that companies can either grow by changing their relationships with customers or products giving four main options for action, in addition to maintaining the product at its current level of activity, or market consolidation (see Table 8.12). The options identified are: to expand the sale of current products or services within the current customer environment — a market penetration policy; to sell the current product or service range to new customers — a market development policy; to investigate the possibilities of selling new products or services to the current customer base — a product development policy; or to sell entirely new products or services to new customers — a diversification policy. As a planning tool, the Ansoff matrix is useful in that it clearly states

Table 8.12 The Ansoff matrix

Products	Customers Old	New
Old	Market penetration	Market development
New	Product development	Diversification

Source: Ansoff

that change does not have to rely solely on alterations in the physical components of the products, and that other changes in company policy may be just as, or more, effective and just as appropriate under certain circumstances. However, it does not attempt to consider the level of investment involved for each type of product development policy, the likely benefits, and where each policy will be most appropriate.

The innovation matrix

The portfolio and competitive analysis approaches focus attention on broad options of investment. They do not, however, attempt to define what type of innovation policy will be appropriate under what conditions of resource availability and market dynamics. This is a major shortfall in the appraisal material available to management; how to translate portfolio techniques into specific market activity. By carefully defining the likely market attractiveness *for innovation* and the resource environment *for innovation*, the management can identify the specific types of innovation appropriate for particular business units.

The interrelationship between the attractiveness of the market and the resources available within the organization obviously yield one approach to the definition of what type of innovation strategy is appropriate. The key components of the market and the resource environments have been outlined in Chapters 5−7 and are summarized in Table 8.13. Earlier discussion emphasized that market attractiveness and business resource are largely determined by qualified assessments of the various components rather than specific quantification. The most important components of market attractiveness are likely to be degree of synergy,

Table 8.13 Innovation matrix components

Market attractiveness	Resource environment
Market size and growth	Government economic policy
Barriers to diffusion	Government research policy
Value-added component	Government skills policy
Synergy	Personnel: structure
Technological stage (S-curve)	subject
Market access	skills
Relative product life	staff
Substitutes	support
	shared values
	systems
	Market expertise:
	product
	promotion
	distribution
	Financial strength
	Production expertise

Source: Author

Table 8.14 The innovation matrix

Market attractiveness	High	Resource position Medium	Low
High	Sector creating	Performance extension	Reformulation
Medium	Process	Technological reorganization	Design
Low	Branding	Service	Packaging
Broad category	Resource-intensive[1]	Resource-directed[2]	Competitive advantage[3]

Notes:
[1]Resource-intensive: large investments need to be made with a slow expected pay-back rate, but with high levels of improvement in long-term profitability. These resource intensive categories will include sector creating or discontinuous innovations, process and branding.
[2]Resource-directed: moderate investments need to be made with a faster rate of return, providing lower levels of improvement in profitability. This section will include performance extension, and technological reorganization.
[3]Competitive advantage: relatively low levels of investment need to be made with the fastest rate of return, but with the lowest potential increase in profitability. This group includes reformulation, design and packaging.

Source: Author

market size, barriers to diffusion, the expected product life and the stage of technological development. The most important resource components are likely to be market position and personnel resource which combine to yield a definition of the company core competence.

Establishing an effective weighting scheme will enable the analyst to create a three-by-three grid of market attractiveness versus resource environment (see Table 8.14) which will provide a measure of the likely ability of the organization to carry out particular types of innovation and the eventual profitability of the proposed innovation policies. Three broad investment categories can be identified, each relevant to particular company/market interactions.

Applying the innovation matrix

Like many of the other portfolio models, the assessment of the various components that make up either market attractiveness or determine the resource environment will be subjective (often more grandly termed as 'heuristic'). The most effective approach of the business planner is to score each of the various factors, relating them at all times to competitive positions of nations, industries and competitive companies. Thus, the resources made available by government economic policy would vary between a very low score (for example, a country with very high inflation) to those that are considered to be the most effective for stimulating investment. Such ranking systems for economic performance are already in existence and can be applied without difficulty to the innovation matrix. Similar ranking processes can be used to compare industry attractiveness: from those that have, for example, high diffusion rates — such as consumer electronics — to those with historically low rates of diffusion, such as the pottery industry. Companies can also make competitive comparisons of resource bases, identifying other organizations that have been most effective at a particular type of product development, and comparing their level of resource availability and core competence for particular types of innovation. This process of comparison can also yield valuable lessons to the firm through assessing the effectiveness of others in achieving greater results with either fewer or identical resources. The final overall assessment will provide a measure of the realistic resource base. Thus, a small drug company would have limited research facilities compared with some of the giants of industry but might have a significantly better resource base in terms of closeness to the market. In other words, its core competence would be based on an ability to respond rapidly and effectively to particular demands in the marketplace for minor changes in the product offering.

Concentrating the evaluation on a *competitive* analysis of national economy, industrial sector and company position in that sector focuses the minds of the business planners on the investment realities that the organization must face; on what can realistically be achieved within a particular set of circumstances and where the organisation should attempt to build and maintain competitive advantage.

For a well-resourced company in an attractive market, the market leader route — concentration on high levels of research to establish new markets and maximize the return from the existing technology — is an obvious strategic option promising a high level of added value from the knowledge that the company can develop. An alternative, to maintain market leadership in high volume but less attractive markets, is to invest heavily in process developments, so that company productivity is maintained at a higher level than that of competitors — added value via production improvements is still high. Less apparent, but no less of an innovation for that, is the use of the market position to innovate through branding — to use high levels of resource to build up a long-term flexible position in the mature or less attractive markets.

For the market challenger or market follower, the key to successful competitive activity is more effective use of the resources available to improve profitability through the increased added-value route so that the market leader can eventually be challenged. Concentration on the implementation of performance extension, technological reorganization and service improvements all require lower resources than those available to the market leader, provide a more rapid payback, and strengthen the market challenger's position.

Market specialists, with fewer resources than either the market follower or the market leader, should concentrate on innovation policies that provide differentiation at low cost — and potentially high return, concentrating on design, reformulation, and packaging to provide added-value products in specific market sectors, using the developed technology of the market challengers and market followers. As the market position changes, new innovation policies become more appropriate, with market specialists looking to develop into areas of technological reorganization, performance extension and service improvement. A company such as Jaguar, for example, successfully reformulated its product range by improving quality, and was able to use the resulting gain in market position and profitability to introduce new products based on technological reorganization innovation policies.

The options open to the market entrant depend on its resource base and on the level of acceptable risk. Building knowledge and market position via internal developments requires initial concentration on reformulation, design and packaging innovations. The acquisition of technological advances from other companies is another possible route, but this has its own problems, as discussed later in this section. Companies able to afford the high investment and long paybacks of sector creating innovations are rare — the estimate of ICI for a 23-year payback for a company considering commencing investment in pharmaceuticals has to be coupled with a requirement of over $1.5 billion.

Integrating innovation components with other models

These innovation components fit into many of the other strategic models. The most useful addition is to the Ansoff matrix with the additional component of market consolidation. Companies considering the five available options can broaden their implementation policies by considering possible innovation routes outlined in Table 8.15.

Companies considering market penetration policies can identify options depending on business position, such as branding, service, design or packaging, in which to develop competitive advantage. Opportunities within product development to gain competitive advantage include reformulation, technological reorganization, and performance extension. For the company considering diversification the most effective option would be to concentrate on sector creating innovations in closely allied industries. This would create substantial competitive advantage, build core competences in new areas and provide the firm with an effective platform on which to build future developments. This supports research that suggests the most effective diversifications will be in closely allied industries and ideally in those that reduce overall seasonality, and is only appropriate for those companies with a substantial existing core competence and resource base.

Another useful integration is to consider the interaction of the innovation matrix with the market-growth/business position portfolio (see Table 8.16). Here the

Table 8.15 Ansoff alternatives and innovation

Development option	Innovation route
Consolidation	Process innovation
Market penetration	Service, branding, design, packaging
Market development	Service
Product development	Reformulation, technological reorganization
	Performance extension
Diversification	Sector creating/discontinuous innovation

Source: Author

Table 8.16 Market growth/business position and innovation issues

Business position	Establishment	Introduction	Market growth Growth	Maturity	Decline
Strong	Sector creation	Process	Process Branding	Process Branding	Branding
Moderate		Performance extension	Performance extension Tech. reorg.	Tech. reorg. Reform	Reform
Weak		Service	Service Design	Reform Design Packaging	

Source: Author

position of the strong business unit is clear. The initial advantage will be established by the creation of a unique concept which will provide the initial competitive edge. Should the company then not be involved in competition in the growth phase of the market the emphasis on process innovation will enable the company not only to service growing demand, but also to improve the level of overall return. Finally, maintaining added value by a process of branding in a mature market is most likely to maximize long-term revenues. However, in most markets the introduction phase is likely to be one in which the business position is weakened by the arrival of other competition. In such markets the original market leader will have to invest in performance extension to maintain competitive advantage, while reverting to process investment and branding as the market develops further.

For the company in a moderate business position, adding value through the stages of market growth will involve concentration on performance extension, technological reorganization and reformulation policies, and will provide the most effective route to gain competitive advantage. In certain market conditions it is clear that no single route will be ideal and a combination of innovation policies will have to be chosen. Where the market position is weak concentration on mainly non-technical aspects, such as service or design, will create a competitive advantage with limited investment.

The integration of innovation concepts with other portfolio techniques yields similar suggestions for action, and underlines the fact that no product or strategic business unit should be discarded before all potential avenues have been explored. Earlier discussion emphasizes the contribution that innovation can make towards improving significantly the position of the most problematic product or product sector, but indicates that the innovative routes chosen will probably be directed towards limited investment for potentially high return in areas such as design, packaging or reformulation.

Integrating the innovation matrix with other strategic models reveals that no market or product should be considered at the end of its viable existence before all possible avenues have been explored; low-cost changes in product performance or associated factors may provide substantial long-term benefits in profitability.

Organizational implications

Once a company has selected a particular innovation route it must ensure that the right organizational infrastructure is in place to identify and manage effectively the policy chosen. The implementation of an innovation strategy must concentrate initially on organization since the argument throughout this book has been that personnel resources are at the heart of a continuing effective innovation policy. It is also clear that in a demanding competitive environment these organizational implications are long term.

The most important factor in sector creating innovation is the concentration on academic and theoretical concept development, which demands a specific organizational framework. This contrasts both with the rapid developmental demands of performance extension, technological reorganization and process innovations, and with the need for close contact with the market required by other types of innovation. As a result, three broad types of organizational patterns can be described as appropriate for the components of the innovation matrix and can be given loose descriptions as follows:

1. Common room.
2. Rugby scrum.
3. Coffee shop.

Common room approaches are most appropriate for the development of sector creating innovations; rugby scrum approaches are best for the management of performance extension, technological reorganization and process innovations; and those innovations that require a close and continuing contact with the marketplace for effective control, reformulation, service, branding, design, and packaging are most suited to coffee shop management styles (see Table 8.17).

Common room

The common room approach must concentrate on the development of unique products and the maintenance of a knowledge base superior to the competition's. The investment emphasis is on the recruitment and motivation of talented and highly skilled individuals who can work within a team to produce novel and effective ideas. To maximize their efficiency and productivity, such groups must be encouraged to develop concepts individualistically within a broad framework

Table 8.17 Organizational implications for innovation types

Market attractiveness	Business Position High	Medium	Low
High	Common room	Rugby scrum	Coffee shop
Medium	Rugby scrum	Rugby scrum	Coffee shop
Low	Coffee shop	Coffee shop	Coffee shop

Source: Author

Table 8.18 Comparison of traditional and current approaches to sector-creating innovation

Issue	Old attitude	New attitude
Freedom	Limited	Wide
Internal communication	Restricted	Encouraged
Publication	Discouraged	Encouraged
External links	Discouraged	Encouraged
Academic excellence	Unimportant	Vital

Source: Author

keeping up contacts inside and outside the company. The high investment in research and development demanded by such approaches implies that senior representation of the research teams is vital, and requires that the board of directors fully understands the personnel policies that encourage effective innovation (see Table 8.18).

Many of the companies that are involved in such types of innovation have already been discussed (see Chapter 4). They include the majority of the high-technology companies such as those operating in the pharmaceutical, biotechnology, chemical and electronics industries. By their very nature common room organizational structures will be associated with large resource-intensive innovation routes, and will reflect the company's willingness to invest long term in complex and demanding development, that will often not yield effective commercial results but will have the overall effect of building overall core competence. Risk reduction will be achieved largely by setting clear goals for performance and achieving the maximum performance from the group.

Rugby scrum
Where a particular type of innovation emphasizes speed of development, more leisured structures and interdepartmental liaison must give way to a streamlined management. In the traditional management of new product development, different sections of the business would be involved at each stage. Thus, the early agenda would be set by departmental heads; search teams operating at often low levels in the organizations produce ideas for review by normally independent screening panels which pass the better ideas to internal development or sponsor groups. In the 1990s environment, such stately dances are no longer possible in many innovation fields. Companies have to ensure that ideas once generated are rapidly acted upon. Most of the ball passing (to carry on the analogy of a rugby scrum) between sections of the firm must be eliminated and decisions to proceed must be taken on the highest authority.

Once taken, decisions are progressed by a single small team acting in concert at the heart of the entire operation, with particular problems handled by particular specialists within the team. The team will rely heavily on the use of appropriate technology to develop concepts and consider the engineering implications of the proposals. Where problems arise these teams can call upon the resources of the

Table 8.19 Traditional new product development patterns

Phase of new product evolution	Interdepartmental responsibility
1. Overall company and product objectives	Departmental heads
2. Exploration	Search teams and idea men
3. Screening	Screening panels
4. Proposal	Sponsor groups
5. Development	Sponsor groups
6. Testing	Product committees
7. Commercialization	Departmental heads

Source: Author

individual departments. This integrated team approach cuts through many of the organizational tiers that were previously involved in the development of new projects and ensures that there is a clear path through from initial concept to final commercialization (see Tables 8.19 and 8.20). Many of the Japanese companies which dominate the world in particular market sectors — especially in machine tools, cars and consumer electronics — specialize in translating market requirements rapidly into specific market offerings.

This new approach emphasizes the role of the chief executive officer at three stages of the development process. First, in the setting of clear organizational objectives which are understood throughout the organization. Secondly, in the identification of viable projects, and allocating the resources necessary to develop them. Finally, in personnel selection — choosing the head of the relevant team and being jointly involved in the selection of other team members will be crucial tasks to ensure that the correct avenues are identified and the task completed on time, to specification and within budget.

Rugby scrum organizational structures will be associated with detailed and demanding schedules which will be resource demanding and will require the concentration of the organization in achieving specific targets. Risk reduction will be part of the planning process, with the exact definition of the target market, the product specification (or protocol) — discussed in the following chapter — timescale and budget crucial to meeting the requirements of the company within the market conditions.

Table 8.20 New format for product development

Phase of new product evolution	Interdepartmental responsibility
1. Overall company and product objectives	Chief executive officer
2. Exploration	All relevant personnel
3. Screening	Senior development executive/CEO
4. Proposal	Development group
5. Development	Development group
6. Testing	Development group
7. Commercialization	Departmental heads

Source: Author

Coffee shop

The primarily market-led innovations require a thin management structure and skills of product analysis and testing, close co-operation between all departments, a labour force closely involved in the production process, and the maintenance of an extensive database. Management styles that encourage close co-operation and rapid formation of small groups to solve individual problems are an essential feature of the coffee shop innovation route. The style of the chief executive officer is essential to this approach, with an emphasis on close contacts with both staff and customers. This attitude can be summarized as management by walking about (MWA) rather than management by memo (MM). A comparison between traditional structures and the coffee shop innovative approach is given in Table 8.21.

Coffee shop organizational systems are ideally suited to small starts and evaluation of concepts and ideas, as the resources involved will be significantly lower than those involved in either common room or rugby scrum organizational systems. Risk reduction in such companies will involve the effective use of testing discussed in Chapter 10 to ensure that the final project will meet customer requirements and yield a satisfactory rate of return on capital invested. The early stages of such coffee shop development are generally not resource intensive and therefore do not require the same level of risk evaluation as the other two approaches. Indeed, certain companies such as 3M insist on staff spending a proportion of their time (normally 15 per cent for 3M) on projects that are of the individual's own creation.

Evaluating routes for knowledge acquisition

Once a company has formulated an innovation policy it must evaluate whether to acquire the expertise from outside the organization (acquisition), to borrow it (licensing), to develop it with a partner with some specific expertise in this area (joint venture), or to concentrate on developing the knowledge internally. By studying how knowledge has been acquired and the problems associated with each route, it is possible to come to some general conclusions about the best method overall for developing competitive advantage in the 1990s and beyond.

Table 8.21 Coffee shop organizational features

Factor	Old	New
Information	Limited	Extensive
Information sharing	Restricted	Shared
Management style	Authoritarian	Democratic
Organization	Centralized	Decentralized
Working method	Departmental	Loose groups

Source: Author

Licensing

Licensing, though not strictly innovative — because it involves the use of other companies' intellectual property — has a number of advantages in building up expertise to improve the skills resource for future innovation. The reverse — that of leasing out existing technology to rival companies — is, however, a major source of potential competition, as a number of studies have shown. The role of licensing is clear — it enables the firm to build competitive advantage by understanding the problems of particular industries or technologies without major investments. It will help the organization that licenses such products or processes to build core competences in a shorter time and at lower cost than would be the case if the company had initiated the development itself. As a means of reducing risk in acquiring core competence the licensing route is very attractive, as all the time-consuming and expensive existing problems with either process or product have been removed.

Much has been written about the progress of Japanese industry since the 1950s and the reliance of Japanese companies on licence arrangements with mainly American companies. These Japanese firms could now develop new core competences enabling them to out-compete the Americans in the late 1970s and early 1980s. The overall cost to the American economy has been estimated at trillions of dollars, and to the Japanese, a mere ten billion in fees. Commentators have long wondered why many firms license particular items of technology that are central parts of their core competences — the advantages to the competitors are clear, but the advantages to the licensee are less obvious, as revenues from licences are for the most part limited.

Acquisition

Acquisition has been the most popular route whereby UK companies have sought access to new technology, with over 30 per cent of new businesses being developed in this way and with a minority of companies using internal development as the preferred route (see Table 8.22). Though acquisition policies have a part to play in instances where fundamental restructuring is occurring (for example, the redirection of ICI in the 1980s) and in eliminating competition (the Amstrad

Table 8.22 Business entry decisions for 150 major European companies 1985/89 (percentages)

Type	1985	1989
Acquisition	32	43
Licensing	15	11
External venture management	35	27
Internal development	20	17

Source: Company annual reports

acquisition of Sinclair, Boots of Underwoods, British Airways of British Caledonian), their role in company innovation strategy is far less obvious.

Japanese expansion into Europe and North America in the 1960s and 1970s avoided the acquisition trail entirely. The strength of the yen in the mid-1980s witnessed the start of acquisitions, but these have been largely directed at eliminating competition (for example, the Bridgestone acquisition of Firestone, the Hitachi purchase of Fairchild) or at gaining particular assets (CBS Records for Sony), rather than at acquiring new business concepts. Only a minimal amount of the Japanese investment in the United Kingdom has been in the form of acquisitions, in contrast to the type of investments made by British firms in the United States. This avoidance of acquisition has even been in the favoured area for this strategic route, the so called 'mature' market. Kao, the Japanese detergent company has, for example, begun manufacturing in the United States without following the perceived wisdom of acquiring an established business in that country as a base; the US detergents market being considered one of the most 'mature' consumer markets in that or any other industrialized country. The company is so sure of its ability to produce new products that it has set up its main manufacturing plant next door to one of the largest plants of its main competitor, Procter & Gamble.

It is interesting that the contribution of acquisition to overall growth in the thirty-six companies identified by Peters and Waterman has been small and mostly defensive in origin. Though many of these companies have encountered problems since the completion of this text in 1982 the choice of these companies still provides an interesting analysis of the strategic routes followed by some of the leading, and entrepreneurial corporations in the United States (see Table 8.23).[6] The exceptions have tended to prove the rule that successful development of innovations is rarely compatible with a policy of acquisition. IBM, for example, has sold its interest in the chip maker, Rohm; Schlumberger sold its venture into semiconductors, Fairchild, at bargain basement prices to Hitachi after notching up several years of heavy losses. The past history of acquisitions supports the

Table 8.23 The top 36 1982

Amdahl	Amoco	Avon
Boeing	Bristol-Myers	Caterpillar Tractor
Cheeseborough-Ponds	Dana Corporation	Data Corporation
Data General	Delta Airlines	Digital Equipment
Disney Productions	Dow Chemical	Du Pont
Eastman Kodak	Emerson Electric	Fluor
Hewlett Packard	Intel	IBM
Johnson & Johnson	K-Mart	Levi-Strauss
Marriot	McDonalds	Maytag
Merck	3M	National Semiconductor
Procter & Gamble	Raychem	Revlon
Schlumberger	Texas Instruments	Wal-Mart
Wang Labs		

Source: T.J. Peters and R.H. Waterman, *In Search of Excellence*, 1982

Table 8.24 Acquisition rules

---

1. Acquiring company must consider what it can contribute to the acquisition, not vice versa.
2. Acquisitions must have a common core of either technology, markets or common management approaches.
3. The acquirer must respect the work of the acquired company in the markets/customers/ products.
4. Company must integrate management of acquired with parent company
5. Company must develop the common values of the parent company within the acquired company.

Source: P. Drucker, *Wall Street Journal*, 15 October 1987

view that using that route as the main method of developing new business concepts is very problematic. Acquisitions are most likely to be effective where there is a close match between the acquirer's and acquired's markets, products, management style and geography, and the acquirer follows the key principles summarized in Table 8.24.

Regardless of how well the acquirer follows these rules, the greater the difference between products, markets, management style and geography, the smaller the chance of the acquisition being successfully integrated. Acquisitions of new technology automatically start with a number of these shortcomings — the product is usually different, the markets are likely to be, and it is almost inevitable that the management style of the two companies will be substantially different. Grumbles of research and development teams within acquired companies are often legendary, revolving around such issues as the type of suits that they will be required to wear and restrictions on the use of the office photocopier. These differences will be further multiplied by size — the larger the acquisition is in relation to the acquirer, the greater the potential problems. Small acquisitions within clearly understood markets are less likely to pose problems and serve as a method of acquiring specific, clearly defined technology. Gaining technology via such small acquisitions is often, therefore, an important element of the implementation of particular innovation policies, but these will differ fundamentally from large market entry acquisitions.

The general conclusion from such considerations is that implementing innovation via acquisition is likely to have a high degree of risk associated with it unless the acquisition is small in relation to the acquirer. The acquisition of Jaguar by Ford in 1990 is an example of the risks that can be faced even by a company with substantial knowledge of the motor car market, though with limited exposure in the luxury sector. Here, a large multinational paid vast sums for a company with production and market problems that would require substantial further investment to correct. By contrast, the development of the Lexus range by Toyota as their method of entering the luxury car sector has initially been highly successful and appears to have been significantly more cost effective than the Ford venture with Jaguar.

Joint ventures

A range of alternatives exist apart from total acquisition, which are difficult to classify, but which can be considered under the general title of joint ventures. Here, two companies enter into some form of agreement which may range from a fairly loose understanding concerning the supply of components and access to markets (for example Honda and British Leyland) through to the much more formalized creation of a shared subsidiary designed to share development costs or gain access to particular markets. Equity partnership joint ventures have for long been criticized as effective channels of innovation with the chances of failure within five years, according to various studies, in the order of 55 to 70 per cent.

The reasons put forward are numerous. Firstly, few partnerships are equal: one partner will tend to provide more management or more capital than the other. In Japan, for example, many of the early joint ventures between Western and Japanese firms were staffed entirely by personnel provided by the Japanese partner. The Western firms should not have been surprised that the loyalty of the staff was in these instances entirely to the Japanese parent company, rather than to the legal entity that was the joint venture.

Secondly, the joint venture is outside the mainstream activities of either organization and is therefore likely to receive less-able staff (because they are not perceived as an attractive route to senior management). The inevitable result of this lower management status is that the venture is far less likely to receive a large allocation of resources. Where the company is involved in a whole range of joint ventures, such as Corning, it becomes increasingly difficult to decide which venture should receive high levels of investment support, and decisions may be made on 'political' rather than objective grounds, with the parent company deciding that joint ventures with large companies should receive more funding than those with small companies because of the possible long-term repercussions of low rates of investment in such ventures.

Many analysts of joint ventures have also commented on the existence of so-called 'hidden' agendas that one or both of the partners are entering into the joint venture with ulterior motives either to gain technological expertise or eventually to acquire a particular company. The existence of possible hidden agendas makes the parent companies often unwilling to provide the joint venture with all the information and expert knowledge necessary to compete effectively in the market, with the resulting loss of competitiveness. Where the joint venture is operating in areas central to either partner's long-term strategy, there may also be a tendency to police strictly the information or resources that are provided, further restricting the freedom of the joint venture to progress effectively.

Joint ventures as a positive strategic move, directed at achieving greater market penetration or innovative development, have become less popular, except where the costs of research in particular areas are astronomic and have been replaced by the joint venture as a defensive route. GEC in 1988 and 1989 entered into

Table 8.25 Joint venture rules

1. Don't rush into it
2. Make sure both sides stand to win
3. Don't micromanage
4. Don't stab your partner in the back
5. Tell him only what he needs to know

Source: Fortune, 27 March 1989

a whole series of joint ventures with Siemens, Fokker and General Electric of the United States — providing one of the best examples of the defensive joint venture. It is interesting that Scott Industries, at one time a most enthusiastic supporter of the joint venture concept has been unravelling its joint venture operations throughout the world. As market access improves, many of the reasons why joint ventures were inevitable (tariff barriers and other legal restrictions) will be progressively removed and reduce the need for companies to enter into such high-risk ventures. Where, however, joint ventures remain essential to successful innovation, they should consider the key rules summarized in Table 8.25.

Internal development

Using internal development as a vehicle for innovation has a number of benefits. First, it may be substantially cheaper. Even in the depressed stockmarkets at the end of the 1980s costs of acquisitions were high, with companies paying significantly over the stockmarket valuation for particular acquisition targets, and well in excess of the cost of greenfield ventures. There are additional costs of making the acquisition yield effective results. One example, the acquisition by BSN-Gervase-Danois of the HP sauce business from Hanson Trust for £160 million, illustrates this point. BSN, eager to become established in the UK market prior to the projected deregulation of markets in 1992 purchased the company, a manufacturer of ketchup and brown sauce, which did not have particular European-wide franchises. Had BSN decided to establish a manufacturing site for its milk products with associated distribution and sales support it is unlikely that the total investment would have been in excess of £20 million. The ease of acquisitions may overemphasize one particular market route for expansion. During the mid-1980s many British companies, for example, concentrated on the United States for expansion partly because of its ease of acquisitions rather than in the Pacific basin — where growth rates had been higher — or within high-growth markets inside the European Community.

Japanese companies have, in contrast, concentrated on internal development. This compelled them to train their staff, to acquire the particular skills necessary for particular developments and to plan carefully the introduction of new types of technology or new manufacturing ventures. Above all it necessitated examining all the alternatives available and choosing objectively the most strategically

Table 8.26 Comparisons of methods of acquiring intellectual property

Factor	Advantages	Disadvantages
In-house R & D	• Unique knowledge base • Full understanding of management/customer/product demands • Objective assessment of innovation requirements • Even failure builds experience and advances company • Builds core competence	•Time to introduction • Cost • Risk of project failure • Risk of prior competitive success
Licensing	• Calculable risk • Builds knowledge base at low cost • Speed to market	• No unique knowledge base • Reduces objective assessment of innovation requirements • Makes company externally dependent • Difficult to build core competence
Acquisition	• Little or no initial research required • Speed into production • Some unique knowledge acquired	• Substantial risk of management failing to understand implications • Cost of acquisition • Integration of technology complex • Can build core competence if management effectively integrated
Joint venture	• Shares cost and risk • Provides rapid diffusion	• Technology transfer • Difficult to develop core competence

Source: Author

acceptable route, rather than the direction which would be easiest to implement. Because management understood the implications of the directions in which the company was progressing by being intimately associated with it, the risk of taking the wrong decisions was automatically reduced.

In conclusion, each of the available methods of implementing innovative policies has advantages and disadvantages associated which need to be carefully weighed (see Table 8.26). It seems that the most sound policy for the effective overall management of innovation concentrates on internal development to search for new ideas and to manage their introduction within the confines of the firm, thereby ensuring fullest understanding of the demands of particular types of innovation. It also means concentrating on building up the resources necessary to achieve the goals that have been set, instead of relying on acquiring them in the marketplace. It will remain the most important route for the company to develop core competences throughout the late twentieth and early twenty-first centuries.

Such a general conclusion obviously has its caveats. Each circumstance should be evaluated on its merits, and the likely return from each particular route carefully assessed. A technique that can aid in this assessment is shareholder value assessment (SVA) which concentrates on the cash flows from each alternative. Many of the studies carried out suggest that acquisitions are unlikely to be the best available route for product or market development.

Notes

1. M.E. Porter, *Competitive Strategy*, (New York: The Free Press, 1980).
2. National Economic Development Organisation, *Restructuring the Cutlery Industry*, (London: NEDO, 1984).
3. W.G. Glueck, *Business Policy and Strategic Management*, (London: McGraw-Hill, 1980).
4. A.A. Thompson and A.J. Strickland, *Strategic Management, Concepts and Cases*, 3rd edn, (London: Business Publications, 1984).
5. A. West, *Understanding Marketing*, (London: Harper & Row, 1987).
6. T.J. Peters and R.H. Waterman, *In Search of Excellence*, (New York: Harper & Row, 1982).

9

Information management and protocol development

Introduction

Discussion has concentrated on how an understanding of the connection between market forces and company resources can help to identify areas for investment which will achieve competitive advantage through innovation. The implications of new product direction also have ramifications for the way companies search for product concepts and then bring them to market. Once the company has chosen a particular strategy it follows that it will need to concentrate on those parts of the information environment that will enable it to identify concepts from which it can gain competitive advantage. After their identification the company will need to structure the analysis and further development of the concept into a commercially viable proposition. The discussion in this chapter concentrates first on evaluating the type of information required for each type of innovation policy and then moves from concept to commercial proposition.

The changing information environment

The richness of the information environment creates previously unknown problems. The number of books and journals doubles every fifteen years, but until the specific implications of such an information explosion are actually spelt out they will not be easily understood. There are, for example, nearly 8,000 medical journals produced worldwide every year; estimates from the United States suggested that by 1988 there were over 450 abstracting services in operation and an abstracting service for abstract services was starting up. The EC produces nearly 900 metres of industry analyses every year, and this is likely to continue to expand exponentially. The development of databases within companies further adds to the vast oversupply of information available to the manager, with companies like Great Universal Stores holding literally billions of items of information on purchasing patterns, debt problems, population movements and the like.

This means that in reality even the most sophisticated and well-funded company has to be selective in choosing from the total available information areas on which to concentrate for future development; it cannot hope to use all the possible information concerning all aspects of the environment, or to afford it if total information access was deemed desirable. The increasing attractiveness of concentration within certain market sectors for new product development or synergy has already been mentioned in Chapter 5 (see pp. 96−8). Of the various synergistic factors, information management is one of the key issues in likely new product success (see Table 9.1). However, for many companies the range of information has already become too large, with the result that they tend to withdraw inwards and rely on internal idea generation. A survey of a large number of innovations in the 1960s revealed that this phenomenon was already well established (see Table 9.2).

Though it is hard to quantify the value of external information, first principles suggest that limiting access to relevant information produces steadily worsening

Table 9.1 Key success and failure criteria in industrial product introduction

Success	Failure
Product synergy with marketing skills	Too competitive
Product synergy with engineering skills	Low market research
High product quality	Concept not novel
Clear user benefits	Few benefits over competitors
Appropriate targeting policy	Poor salesforce
Distribution channel support	Poor promotion

Source: P. Link, *Industrial Marketing Management*, 16, 1987

Table 9.2 Key information inputs in innovation

Source	Percentage reported cases
Internal:	
• printed materials	2
• personal contacts	4
• individual expertise	41
• formal courses	0
• experimentation/analysis	7
External:	
• printed materials	6
• personal contacts	21
• individual expertise	7
• formal courses	2
Multiple sources	11

Source: D.G. Marquis, *Innovation*, November 1969

decisions, the apt quotation, 'knowledge itself is power', being no less true of the business world than politics. For fifteen years the information that nuclear power produced more expensive electricity than other forms of generation was kept out of any discussions on the future direction of energy policy in the United Kingdom — only the demands of privatization forced the information into the public domain. This example from national policy is supported by evidence from successful innovators which shows that a key difference between them and the less successful is that they concentrate on identifying and organizing coherently the most important information sources. Successful innovators have a far better understanding of industrial trends, and a significantly greater interest in all aspects of the industry in which they operate.[1] Such curiosity is nurtured by a company's working environment which encourages knowledge acquisition.

For an innovative company in an information rich environment the issue is to identify data for its relevance to a chosen strategic direction, to organize it so that individuals within the organization have access to the data and are able to contribute to the development of concepts. Even where the information gathering is matched to a particular innovation strategy it is as well to understand the strengths and weaknesses of the chosen information sources. These can be classified according to the volume of information available, the ease of access to that information, its comprehensiveness, the likely cost of using that particular information channel, and how unique or individualistic the information provided will be. Approaching information sources in this way provides the organization with an objective assessment of their data requirements. Other definitions, such as the unexpected, the incongruity, process need, changes in industry/market structure, demographics, perception and new knowledge, are largely unworkable as they can be generated from a wide range of information channels.[2] A detailed assessment of the total available information channels yields nearly thirty possibilities (see Table 9.3). For convenience these can be grouped into seven main categories, each with particular attributes (see Table 9.4).

Table 9.3 Total available information sources

Customer information	Working in user environment (active need experience)
Staff information	Simulation
Government information	Confrontation
Competitive information	Brainstorming techniques
Trade fairs	Morphological analysis
Literature	Progressive abstraction
Expert opinion (including Delphi approach)	Value analysis
User questioning	Bionics
Employing ex-users for product development	Scenario writing
Co-operation with end users	System analysis
Dealer/distributor questioning	Ecological analysis
Product safety analysis	Informal contacts
Resource analysis	Commercial developers
User observation	

Source: Author

Table 9.4 Types and characteristics of main categories of information sources

Source	Volume	Access	Completeness	Objectivity	Cost	Uniqueness
Competitors	Low	Low	Low	High	Low	Low
Technical journals	High	High	Low	High	Low	Low
Customers	High	Low	High	Low	High	Mod
Product analysis	High	High	Low	High	Low	Low
Technical staff	Low	High	High	Low	High	High
Non-technical staff	High	High	Low	Low	Low	Mod
Research institutions	Low	High	High	Low	Mod	Mod
Specialist new product development companies	Low	High	High	Low	High	Mod

Source: Author

Defining information demands

The information requirements of the pure researcher are clear. They are likely to receive the most valuable information from technical journals and the academic community. Previously quoted research supports the integration of the technical staff with the academic community (see pp. 48—9), where the greater the level of academic publication the more effective the innovation programme. Though German and US research programmes highlight the close interrelationships between the academic and business worlds, UK firms do not attempt to develop an integrated knowledge-based idea-generation programme. This general view is supported by research on the way medium-sized chemical companies use various information sources.[3] Of the firms studied, only around 10 per cent of the sample replying to the survey made significant use of any of the numerous information sources available (see Table 9.5). Anecdotal evidence supports the importance of academic links in specific types of innovation. Links between the president of Hoffman LaRoche and Professor Taddeus Rechstein of Basle University led to the introduction of Vitamin C in 1934; similar close contacts with the academic community in the United States led to the development of the benzodiazepines, Librium and Valium. One obstacle to this type of contact is security. Attitudes

Table 9.5 Use of various information providers for new product concepts

Factor	Research associations	Private R & D houses	Universities	Polytechnics	Government R & D
Not aware of	6	2	1	3	4
Aware of: not used	36	51	28	53	55
Slight use	50	30	52	32	38
Significant use	7	10	28	10	4
Not answered	31	37	21	32	29

Source: NEDO, *Research and Development in the Chemical Industry*, 1984

Table 9.6 Criteria for effective management of research centres

1. Scientists see themselves as responsible for project management
2. Scientists have significant power and influence within the organization
3. They are secure in their jobs
4. They are provided with a significant amount of freedom by their superiors
5. Projects are limited in size/duration
6. Scientists are involved in other areas such as teaching
7. Motivation is maintained at as high a level as possible

Source: Author

towards the openness of information transfer is a decisive factor in whether academic information transfer can be used effectively, as is the degree of freedom that the researchers have in applying the information. One major survey identified the factors listed in Table 9.6 as crucial to the cost-effective management of pure research. Much of Merck's success in the pharmaceutical sector is thought to lie in the relative openness of information transfer within the organization. This underlines the common room concept as being crucial to the success of such innovation strategies; not only must the firm maintain a sufficiently large critical mass of researchers, but it must also endeavour to encourage exchange of ideas both within the firm and in the larger pool of expert talent outside it.

These surveys emphasize that companies concentrating on coffee shop innovation routes will rely far more heavily on analysis of current products and customer contact rather than on concepts provided by either technical literature or developments initiated by customers' specific demands. This is supported by a survey which identified the most important sources for a wide range of consumer companies in 1985 (see Table 9.7). Companies following this particular route will have to pay particular attention to classic market research and internal development to generate new concepts. Internal idea generation can be developed in a bewildering number of ways, as Table 9.8 reveals.[4] The majority of organizations will need to define which of these techniques is best suited to the information problem that they are attempting to resolve.

Most studies show that these techniques are not widely used, even within the

Table 9.7 What is most useful in finding new product opportunities?

Factor	Percentage
Range extensions of current products	38
Ideas from abroad (competitors)	29
Lessons from past projects (non-technical staff)	23
Brand extension work	20
Mapping exercises to find market gaps	18
Group discussions to find consumer needs	17
Ideas from R & D	12
Studies of technological development	10
Study of packaging developments	10

Source: KAE

Table 9.8 Classification of creativity techniques

	Triggering principle	
	Association/variation	Confrontation
Stimulation of intuition	Brainstorming: • Classical brainstorming • Two-step brainstorming • Discussion 66 Brainwriting: • Method 635 • Brainwriting • Pin card technique • Gallery method • Delphi • Collective notebook method	Word analysis Excursion synectics Picture folder, picture confrontation, semantic intuition
Systematic structuring	• Conceptual morphology • Sequential morphology • Modifying morphology • Progressive abstraction	Morphological matrix TILMAG Effective stimuli development

Source: H. Geschka, *R & D Management*, 3, 1983

most creatively demanding environments, and diminish in importance as the organization gets larger and more diffuse, though there remain exceptions such as 3M, which, because of its decentralized structure and emphasis on customer problem solving, uses such techniques as an integral part of its innovation programme. In other large companies, use is spasmodic, and this leads to a self-perpetuating phenomenon of failure leading to less usage leading to greater failure, because such techniques, like other management skills, require practice. Thus, common failings are the inability to apply the technique at all through lack of understanding and the inability of most management used to fairly concrete action to induce the type of freewheeling group discussion characteristic of successful problem solving.

Much more commonly used to identify specific relationships and product opportunities is some form of dependence or interdependence analysis which looks for relationships between factors. Discriminant analysis is a modified form of multiple regression analysis which resolves the differences between characteristics of light and heavy users, and loyal and non-loyal customers. This involves the development of a weighted linear combination of the different variables involved so that they can distinguish between the relative importance of the variables. Once these differences have been established, the company can assess whether there are market opportunities available to meet specific requirements that are not currently served. Factor analysis does not rely on the weighting of the relative variables but identifies relationships between variables which are grouped in some arbitrary fashion; it is most useful in clarifying the key purchase attributes for particular products or services. One toiletries company has successfully used factor analysis over a number of years to determine key purchase attributes for particular

Table 9.9 Relative frequency of use of factor, cluster, and discriminant analysis; percentage of companies using particular technique

Type of company	Factor	Cluster	Discriminant
Consumer goods	36	21	31
Industrial goods manufacturer	15	9	6
Finance and insurance	17	10	10
Other services	20	20	—

Source: B.A. Greenberg, J.L. Goldstucker, and D.N. Bellenger, *Journal of Marketing*, 50, 1977

products and to generate new product concepts in areas of high purchase interest. Cluster analysis searches for groups by a certain set of attributes: attitude, income, or educational background. The coffee companies, for example, continue to use cluster analysis to identify groups of individuals that are particular consumers of freeze dried, filter coffee or particular types of coffee flavour. As might be expected, the use of these techniques is much more common in consumer goods companies than those producing industrial goods (see Table 9.9).[5]

In contrast, companies concentrating on performance extension, technological reorganization and process innovation routes will need to concentrate more closely on customer usage and customer requirements, rather than formulating product concepts requiring additional testing in the market. The importance of customer usage is supported by several studies. A typical one compares idea generation in equipment industries with the development of new chemicals (see Table 9.10).

Companies like Hewlett Packard and Digital (DEC) use their highly skilled salesforce as a major information source to identify customer requirements and act as a channel in the development of new products and concepts, by providing them with ready access to the central database. A similar role is provided by quality circles in many Japanese companies.

The conclusion is that the majority of companies do not effectively set about

Table 9.10 Pattern of product introduction in certain sectors

Product field	First device developed by	
	Product user	Manufacturer
Instrumentation:		
First of type	100	
Major functional improvements	82	18
Minor functional improvements	70	30
Process equipment:		
First of type	100	
Major functional improvements	63	21
Minor functional improvements	20	29
Polymers		100
Additives		100

Source: E. Hippel, *Technology Review*, 7, 1978

analysing their information needs for innovation, where this information is likely to be derived and how the company can most cost effectively collect, analyse and use it. As the volume of information grows the task of managing a competitive information system in this area will become steadily greater, with the view that perhaps the software programmers who design systems to manage the information will only just keep ahead of the information flooding into the majority of medium-to large-sized corporations. The ability of the company to provide their staff with adequate support in this area will become one of the most important in building and maintaining core competence.

Protocol development

Traditional approaches to innovation management favour specific responsibilities at each progressive stage from concept to commercialization, but tended to treat each stage in isolation and not as part of an integrated process to speed response time and improve the chances of likely commercial success. A major problem associated with rigid divisions is its inability to match accurately customer requirements with product offerings because idea generation and screening are strictly separated in the new product development process. Nevertheless, as earlier discussion has shown (see pp. 162−3), the majority of studies on effective innovation identify the need for a close contact between the needs of the customer and the proposed new product. One study of innovation in the chemical and electronic instrument market clearly showed companies' inability to measure ideas against customer needs and so assess their potential market effectiveness. The innovations, and their main reasons for failure are in Table 9.11.[6] Other studies like the detailed Sappho work (see Table 9.12) further emphasize the importance of the early influence of customer needs and requirements in the likelihood of success in product innovation. The matching of customer needs with detailed descriptions of the product benefits has been described as customer *protocol*. Where this concept of matching customer needs very closely to product performance in the early stages of product development has been successfully applied, the probability of success is considerably higher, as the correlations in Table 9.13 indicate.

Table 9.11 Failure points in chemical and instrument innovation

Factor	Chemical	Instrument
No inquiries at all	1	3
Too few/unrepresentative	2	4
Ignored/misunderstood answers	0	3
No on-the-spot investigation	0	3
Preconceived design	4	2
Total	7	16

Source: NEDO, *Design for Corporate Culture*, 1988

Table 9.12 The crucial determinants of success

1. Better understanding of consumer needs
2. More marketing/publicity
3. More effective development work (not necessarily faster development work)
4. More use of outside technology and assistance
5. More senior people involved

Source: R. Rothwell *et al.*, *Research Policy*, 1974

Table 9.13 Impact of protocol on three dimensions of performance prior to product development work beginning

Factor	Financial performance	Opportunity window	Market share
Target market was defined	378		183
Customers' needs, wants, preferences were defined	590		257
The product concept — the 'what' and 'how' were defined	420		
Product specifications were accurately defined	329		

Source: R.G. Cooper and E.J. Kleinschmidt, *R & D Management*, 17(3), 1987

The importance of such protocol development is also supported by the relative importance given to product acceptability by potential buyers. All the highest rankings are given to those products that meet discernible needs and are understandable by the purchaser. Speeding diffusion rates obviously leads to a much improved financial performance, reduced competitive pressure, and a longer market life. Further evidence of the importance of protocol development comes from comparing the emphasis various companies put at different stages in the product development process with their success rates. Seven broad types of development process were defined in one study, each with different time spans at each stage of the process (see Table 9.14).

Companies that gave most emphasis at the marketing stage tended to have a significantly higher success rate than those that concentrated on the development of prototypes or moved straight to the full-scale launch without a significant period of testing. Where time was spent in developing the concept in relation to the customer, the project tended to be far more successful than where this obviously crucial component of the innovation process was ignored. Idea generation on its own was not a good indicator of likely success. The likely impact of each method of organizing new product development is summarized in Table 9.15. All this research supports the need for companies to reappraise their approach to the early stages of the product development process. Firms considering any form of innovation policy should first concentrate on customer benefit rather than new product features. This is an old sales concept — that the sales representative ascertains what the customer wants from a particular product, relates the product features to the prospective buyer, and then identifies those features that provide the sought-after benefits. The key features are those that provide relative

Table 9.14 Characteristics of each cluster of projects: activity duration

Stage	Cluster 1	2	3	4	5	6	7
1				High	Low		Low
2		Low	High				Low
3				High			
4	Low	High	Low	Low	Low	High	
5		Low				High	Low
6	Low	Low			Low		High
7	High	Low			Low		
8		High				Low	
9		Low			High		Low

Notes: Stages as identified above
Cluster types:
1. Market oriented — with the main emphasis being developing ideas in relation to the needs of the customer
2. Design dominated
3. Balanced — with equal amounts of time being spent in the market, in design, prototype development and introduction
4. Front-end dominated — where idea generation was the most important aspect of the process without contact with customers
5. Minimum process — A short development process without too much time being allocated at any stage
6. Launch with prototype
7. Prototype dominated

Source: R.G. Cooper, *R & D Management*, 13, 1983

Table 9.15 Characteristics of each cluster of projects: project and firm descriptors

Characteristic	Cluster 1	2	3	4	5	6	7
Success of project		Low	High				High
Success of entire programme	High		High		High	Low	
Per cent sales of new products					High		
R & D as % of sales	Low		High				Low
Management strength	High					Low	High
Salesforce/distribution strength	High					Low	High
Advertising/promotion resources						Low	High
Market research strengths	High	High				Low	

Source: Adapted from R.G. Cooper, *R & D Management*, 13, 1983

advantage, and compatibility to existing products, though the most important factor will be the relative advantage of the product over existing concepts.

To the period of idea generation, managers must therefore add a rigorous period of customer benefit analysis. What should be included in such a customer benefit analysis extends beyond the purely technical issues of product performance to include non-technical and attitudinal factors that are often crucial in the purchase decision. Such an analysis is vital for the effective reduction of risk — products that have accurately defined benefits will have a significantly greater probability of success than those that do not. Strategically, the concentration on the development of protocol has significant value in building competitive advantage, by concentrating on the comparisons between existing products and the proposed company introduction. An additional advantage of such a rigorous analysis is that when the company comes to commercialize the product, it will not need to ascertain what are the factors that most appeal to the customer as *they will already be known*. A considerable element of the testing procedure can, as a result, be discarded. Some of the key components of such a customer benefit analysis are in Table 9.16. Obviously, no single product sector will have the same profile. Those with high intangibility such as perfume or wine will rely on the attitudinal aspects of product differentiation and customer appeal; whereas for basic industrial fasteners technical performance criteria will be crucial, though the non-performance aspects of the product must not be under-rated.

Such an approach to the generation of ideas shows clearly the true shape of innovation outlined in Chapter 3 (see p. 27) — should customers value attitudinal factors more highly than performance, *it will be the attitudinal innovation that will succeed, not the performance improvement*. Naturally, the only way that the company will ascertain the truth is if it searches for ideas in the right places and ensures that these ideas offer realistic benefits to the intended customer group. The successful innovator, whether involved in technical or non-technical advances, will be the one that can best engineer the required customer benefits, further emphasizing that artificial divisions caused by perceptions of the 'value' of improving product performance, with, say, improving customer attitudes via improved service or branding, will create inefficiencies within any commercially directed organization.

The other major consideration is the assessment of the consumer benefit offered. Is the benefit in prospect sufficiently different from others, does it meet *real*

Table 9.16 Customer benefit analysis

Factor	Project A	Competitor B	Competitor C
Technical:			
• size			
• weigth			
• speed			
• reliability			
• user friendly			
Non-performance:			
• ease of servicing			
• spare parts			
• delivery			
Attitude:			
• trust			
• image			
• aesthetics			
Price:			
• cost			
• finance methods			

Source: Author

customer demands, and can it be supplied at a price which matches the level of perceived benefit? Customer perceptions of benefit and novelty may not coincide with those of the company, but it is, nevertheless, those that must prevail in the effective management of innovation. Much depends on whether the company can accurately identify particular groups of customers with common requirements, or how the market is realistically segmented. For high levels of investment demanded by many types of innovation, careful and detailed segmentation will ensure that a group will remain stable over the expected life of the product and provide adequate returns to the company.

> The progress of Amstrad, the consumer electronics company is an excellent case study in the benefits of protocol development. The company started in the home electronics market by carefully identifying benefits that customers wanted, such as double tape decks, and providing them at a price the customer would pay. This policy continued to be highly successful in the early days of their development into the computer market. The technology of the Amstrad PCW, the word processor, was nothing special. What was important, however, from the customers' perspective was the offer of a complete ready-to-run system combining printer, software and monitor.
>
> There existed a segment of customers wanting a simple, reliable, easy to run system which did not require either sophisticated software, add-on features (such as networking) or service support. The eventual product offering provided significant and clear advantages over the competitive products available. A similar customer-led philosophy was behind the development of a combined telephone answering machine/fax system for 1990, simple to operate, cost effective and reliable. This similarly provides significant and clear benefits over the competitive products.
>
> When Amstrad moved into the manufacture of more sophisticated computers, it failed to appreciate fully that the protocol or product benefits went beyond the purely technical, and focused more strongly on the service and support areas. They were unable to match the clear and demonstrable benefits seen in the other products. Many of the serious problems that the group faced in the late 1980s resulted from their failure to appreciate the demands of this quite differing market sector.

The demands of synergy

Though companies should consider the replacement of idea generation with the far more detailed and demanding concept of protocol development, the requirement that the development meets the strategic goals of the company and matches its available skills still remains. Previous discussion (see pp. 96–8) has emphasized that product innovations that are synergistic are much more likely to be successful than those that are not. Screening techniques are well identified in the majority of literature on new product development, but the key is to identify those elements which must be closely investigated, the most important of which are listed in Table 9.17.

Where synergy is most important will be in the area of risk reduction and the creation of core competence. Previous discussion (see pp. 146–8) has highlighted the need for organizations to build core competences in specific areas. Concentrating on product development within these areas of specialization will

Table 9.17 Most
important synergistic
components

Strategic fit
Management expertise fit
Customer fit
Distribution fit
Production fit
Service/support fit
Promotional fit
Information services fit

Source: Author

help to further expand the expertise of the unit and its competitive advantage. Secondly, as the product is an evolution of the existing knowledge base of the company, however novel the product concept may be even in the case of sector-creating products, the risk involved in its introduction will be substantially reduced. For example, the development of Kevlar by DuPont built on its existing expertise in artificial fibres and minimized the risk that existed in defining exact markets and overcoming manufacturing problems.

The role of concept development in the product development process

Earlier discussion (see pp. 46–78) has clearly identified the need for commercial organizations to be better directed in the way they develop and screen new ideas. Research reveals a need for a new stage in the product development process which combines customer-needs analysis with the old concept of ideas generation. This would generate a clear description of the product in structural and performance terms. This can then involve the translation of customer benefit through engineering and production planning, in a stage-by-stage process which is outlined in Figure 9.1. This additional change to the product development process implies that the old and new product development procedures will look increasingly different, with the bulk of the time spent at the earlier stages of formalizing the *exact* criteria under which the product will be produced and how the benefits will be effectively achieved. An additional benefit is that this is a relatively low-cost approach to new product development and provides detailed information about all the logistics required — what type of equipment, the performance requirements of materials, the likely timing of particular parts of the development and where the major problems (or critical paths) are likely to be found. It will also provide financial information about the project — what the likely production cost will be and when funds will need to be committed to ensure that the venture is completed on time. This further reduces the risk element involved in the project failing to meet all its specifications.

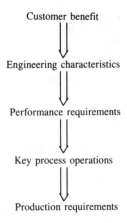

Customer benefit

Engineering characteristics

Performance requirements

Key process operations

Production requirements

Notes:
Engineering characteristics — what is the overall shape of the finished product that will meet the customer requirements?

Parts characteristics — what is the most efficient way of providing these performance requirements within the finished article?

Key process operations — how will these parts be assembled effectively into the final design so that the engineering characteristics are achieved?

Production requirements — what type of production machinery and layout does such a production process require?

The organization of the branding and service innovations can be developed along much the same lines, but replacing engineering characteristics with attitudinal or performance criteria.

Figure 9.1 Product to production

With the use of new technology in the design stage and the integration of project management software, managers are able to experiment on a far greater range of potential projects, as the expenditure at this early stage, prior to the development of prototypes, is relatively low. It also provides management with far greater control over the probable progress of the project, as many of the likely problem areas can be isolated and resolved before it starts. For example, one of the problems encountered with the development of the RB 211 jet engine was the failure at high speed of the carbon fibre materials used in the turbines. Had this problem been resolved before the commencement of the project, many of the delays encountered could have been avoided.

Finally, the close matching of the benefit with customer type will enable much of the marketing planning to be completed at an early stage, as the company will be aware exactly of the key buying criteria and will also know how the precise segment can be reached and serviced effectively. This alteration in the early stages of new product development demands that the company introduce new stages into the classic 'new product development' stage-by-stage process. The 'old' and 'new' product development procedures are compared in Table 9.18. This approach gives a far more rapid and clear-cut developmental path more attuned to the demands of the marketplace — much more specific and directional in the action that it proposes and significantly more integrated into company planning procedures.

Table 9.18 New structures in the development of new products

Old product development process	New process
Idea generation	Defining appropriate data
	Idea generation
	Customer benefit analysis
	Synergy analysis
Screening	Segmentation description
Prototype development	Structured design/production planning
Prototype testing	Prototype development
Prototype redesign	Prototype testing
Production model development	Commercialization
Production testing	
Production model testing	
Commercialization	

Source: Author

The early stages of new product development

The skier, once started downhill, often has a choice of routes and can control the speed at which he or she travels. They are not realistically in the position to decide during the middle of the descent that they would at that moment much rather be swimming in Florida. The innovation process is very similar. Companies once started can do little to alter fundamentally the direction of a project, and will generally incur greater and greater costs as it nears completion. The only way that such costs can be reduced is to cancel the project and write off the incurred expenditure. Choosing the right course at the earliest possible stage is therefore crucial to effective investment in new product development, and this further emphasizes the correct choice of information, the development of detailed and comprehensive protocol, how this relates to a precisely described and attainable market segment, and a full understanding of the likely synergistic or non-synergistic effects of the product proposal.

Notes

1. E. von Hippel, *The Sources of Innovation*, (Oxford: Oxford University Press, 1988).
2. P. Drucker, *Innovation and Entrepreneurship*, (London: Pan, 1987).
3. National Economic Development Organisation, *Research and Development in the Chemical Industry*, (London: NEDO, 1984).
4. H. Geschka, 'Types of Creativity Techniques', *R & D Management*, issue 3, 13, (1983), pp. 25–35.
5. B.A. Greenberg, J.L. Goldstucker and D.N. Bellenger, 'What Techniques Are Used by Marketing Researchers in Business', *Journal of Marketing*, 50, (1977), pp. 67–74.
6. National Economic Development Organisation, *Design for Corporate Culture*, (London: NEDO, 1988).

10

Testing

Introduction

Earlier discussion (see pp. 186–90) has highlighted the importance of protocol development in aiding the accurate definition of customers' requirements. Though early and exact specifications of product benefit does much to speed up both the manufacturing process and its acceptance by the consumer, there remains a number of potential areas of failure which will inevitably increase the risk involved in the commercialization of any new product. The first problem may be that the protocol concept developed is not an accurate reflection of the real demands of the consumer. For example, a machine-tool manufacturer found that though the individual elements of a new lathe had been accurately defined, the interaction of the components had not, and, as a result, the finished product was unacceptable. Testing also provides the company with evidence of which benefit is considered as most important by the customer among the range provided — the 'core' benefit of the product may differ from the initial protocol. Such revisions to product definition greatly aid in the eventual commercialization of the product by ensuring that minimal barriers to diffusion have been created. The inability to define accurately the particular customer segments and the likely benefits that would appeal to them will also be a potential area of failure that will be reduced by specific testing of the product or concept in the market.

Second, there may be specific performance limits which company management have not considered. This is a major problem with most computer software — the use that external organizations make of the software may be so significantly different from the intentions of the supplier's management/development team that a much higher than predicted level of errors (the famous 'bugs') appear in using the software. Testing is vital to define where the limits of performance are. Third, where the company is producing a novel product the likely safety implications also cannot be forecast effectively. This is obviously most apparent in the manufacture of pharmaceuticals and pesticides, which may have toxic effects which cannot be understood at the theoretical stage because of the complexity of the organisms on which they are used. The importance of product safety goes well beyond these narrow confines. The inclusion of enzymes in reformulated Persil Automatic caused major problems in the market because the potential effects on the skin of a small group of users had not been fully identified prior to full-scale commercialization.

Fourth, forecasting attitudes towards new products can also be extremely complex. One of the best examples of this was the introduction of 'new Coke' in the United States. Here Coca Cola was attempting to respond to their arch rival Pepsi by introducing a reformulated, sweeter product. The resulting furore forced them to reconsider the entire programme and re-introduce 'Classic'. A similar famous and much-quoted advertising campaign for Strand cigarettes, illustrating a man at the end of a bridge, with the title 'You're never alone with a Strand' led to a dramatic drop in consumption because of the consumer's (wrongly held) perception that smoking Strand cigarettes might lead to isolation. In highly price sensitive markets, the accurate definition of price may also be of prime concern. Black & Decker found that a very strong price point at £25 existed for the Workmate, and above that price sales dropped by 25 to 30 per cent. Such strong price points will often mean the difference between product success and failure.

Finally, no concept is ever translated direct from the drawing board (or in modern parlance the CAD screen) into full-scale production without minor or major engineering problems to be resolved before the product meets its performance or price targets. They are generally of two main types. Material and component performance often vary from initial specifications, and design modifications have to take this into account; the speed of equipment operation may also vary and lead to adjustments in either the design or the costing. Moreover, the initial design may fail to meet quality standards or performance criteria resulting in considerable changes either to production methods, components, or design.

Defining the testing requirements

Though all innovative concepts need some form of testing to resolve potential problems, the type and duration of the testing procedure should reflect organizational requirements. Obviously, the testing procedure for a new cancer-reducing drug must be more stringent than one for a new type of flower pot, with the one demanding vital and lengthy clinical testing and the other involving little risk to either company or customer. The level of investment and the potential risk of failure are crucial to decisions on the type of testing procedure used, but in the competitive environment of the 1990s the importance of the time constraint in getting a product into the market is often vitally important. Where a company is operating in a highly competitive environment, lengthy and sophisticated testing procedures provide competitors with accurate information about product developments enabling them to counter the product introduction by bringing rival products to market, or to develop tactical plans to counter the new products. Nevertheless, Procter & Gamble can continue to flourish with its heavy emphasis on detailed and comprehensive market testing because the resources at the final commercialization phase will be massive enough to swamp most competitive efforts. As one competitor has commented, 'the fact that one can see a steamroller from a long way off, doesn't stop it from being a steamroller.' Unfortunately, few companies are in the position of Procter & Gamble and have to be far more acute about how they test new products.

The historic insistence on a full and vigorous testing procedure made up of a number of steps, each having to be completed before moving to the next, is less and less appropriate. Classically, testing began with a concept test — comparing the proposed product's performance and physical criteria with competitive products, competitive pricing, competitive service criteria, and current usage patterns. Such a concept test, was as the name implies, carried out without the availability of the actual product. If it became clear that the concept offered significant performance advantages, samples were next produced for testing. This sample or prototype test would yield information about the cost of manufacture and likely market price and the volume that could be achieved at that price, and would confirm whether the performance levels promised at the concept stage were really achievable. After successful completion of the prototype trials, the company would then move forward to the final stage of testing with a full-blown analysis of price, product, competitive strengths, distribution and promotional components in a test market. Should the company find that this confirms the favourable findings of earlier tests, the full-scale introduction of the product throughout the markets in which the company operates will follow. The stages and the types of information that they have traditionally provided are summarized in Table 10.1.

Table 10.1 Testing stages and the issues that they will resolve

Issues resolved	Test type		
	Concept test	Prototype test	Test market
Sales volume: estimate		•	
Sales volume: detailed			•
Price	•	•	•
Technical performance: outline	•		
Technical performance: detailed		•	
Non-technical issues eg servicing	•		
Key or 'core' benefit		•	•
Attitudes	•		
Competitive perception: outline	•		
Competitive perception: detailed		•	
Distribution			•
Promotion			•

Source: Author

In the 1990s, the innovative company concentrating on a protocol approach to the market will have to alter its testing procedures to reflect the new investment levels, manufacturing techniques and market demands. High levels of investment in the new product venture will still demand accurate testing, but how this is achieved may need changing. For example, Ford did not invest sufficiently in testing one of the largest investments that it ever made, the Edsel. Its failure nearly led to the company's collapse. It has since then always heavily tested key introductions such as the Cortina and Sierra to ensure that this mistake will not recur. With advanced computer-aided design techniques, the company is able to move straight to the stage of testing prototypes, significantly cutting both the cost of the development process and the time that is taken. In contrast, Japanese manufacturers of audio equipment have used the protocol concept to move straight to test market, and to use the 300 shops in Tokyo's Akihabara district to test market their experimental products.

The lower costs of production for many such products, and the fact that it is speed rather than complete information about a product's performance that is crucial, has inevitably changed company perceptions of testing. With substantially lower costs of producing small batches of experimental product (one circuit breaker manufacturer reporting a fifteen-fold reduction with the introduction of new flexible manufacturing systems), a rapid action approach to product development is feasible rather than a reflective laborious, step-by-step development through concept, working model, and advanced prototypes. The result is that the traditional approaches to testing need to be replaced with techniques more appropriate to the competitive environment and the level of investment involved; higher levels of competition and lower levels of cost involved in prototype development requiring concentration on faster methods of testing.

Testing methods

This section gives an assessment of some of the relevant testing procedures for the resolution of particular types of problems, their advantages and their inevitable drawbacks. Each market and market sector will vary as to their applicability, depending on such factors as custom and local infrastructure. Carrying out consumer research in Middle Eastern and many African markets is, for example, a complex operation requiring detailed planning and organization because of constraints on the types of research that are locally acceptable.

Employee panels

Many consumer companies use a pool of employees to carry out product tests, a practice which is particularly common among food and detergent companies — the Wash Panel of Lever Brothers has been established for several decades, for example. The use of an employee panel has a number of substantial advantages;

it is quick, simple to administer, easy to retest the same respondents with a changed product for comparative purposes, and maintains a high level of security. The disadvantages are that the panel tends to be very 'expert' and knowledgeable about the product field — more so than the rest of the population — and it may not be particularly representative of the population in terms of age, sex or socio-economic groupings. Finally, the employee panel may fail to be objective about a product which is heavily promoted internally as essential to survival or substantial increases in profit. The most useful role for employee panels is in *product evaluation* in what is effectively a blind test, giving the company some idea of how the product, shorn of promotion, price and other elements of the marketing mix, is perceived in relation to products already available in the marketplace.

Focus groups

Focus groups are discussion panels structured to analyse a particular aspect of the product or the marketing mix. They can provide a large amount of information on attitudes towards new products and likely purchase levels, are quick to assemble and are of relatively low cost. Though focus panels can cover a much broader cross-segment of the population, the type of question structure used in focus groups will only provide broad qualitative data about the range of perceptions in the general population. For example, Birds Eye, the frozen foods group, uses focus groups to ascertain attitudes towards additives and healthy eating. The focus group will not provide detailed information about price, precise performance or servicing requirements and other quantitative issues in the development of new products.

User questionnaires

Industrial equipment manufacturers can develop much the same type of understanding about the broad issues that are of importance in purchase decisions by the use of questionnaires among their current customer base. This is a little-used testing route — though the companies using it report high response rates accompanied by some valuable information. Crossfield, the UK engineering firm uses a customer panel as a central part of its testing procedure to define what type of product benefit is most required and to check — at prototype stage — to maintain quality assurance and to ensure that all production problems have been solved. The user questionnaire or user panel is quick to establish, maintains a relatively high level of security, and provides a high level of objective information about the likely acceptability of particular product developments. It can, however, only operate with long-standing customers and will often require a technically proficient salesforce to administer and to select customer subjects who are most likely to be co-operative.

Hall tests

'Hall' tests or centralized location tests as they are sometimes called, involve testing product concepts in a defined locality: for example, off a street within a shopping precinct or at some form of social gathering. Hall tests allow the company to evaluate the likely effectiveness of alternative packs or concepts by providing a forum which brings possible customers into contact with the product in a cost effective and rapid fashion. For example, the company can explore the relationship between design, packaging and price or other criteria and define the likely best fit between the various variables under investigation where there will often be trade-offs (conjoint analysis); or examine the relationships between factors (cluster analysis or perceptual mapping).

A problem with hall tests is that the sample is unlikely to be representative of the population as a whole — for example, tests in shopping precincts will vastly over-report young married women, and members of social clubs are obviously self-selecting. The alternative to hall testing is to carry out full-scale quantitative research with a properly structured sample, but this is far more expensive and time-consuming to set up and administer.

Minivan testing

The previously discussed testing procedures are deficient in that products are being evaluated out of the normal usage environment and so the perception of the product will often be substantially 'coloured'. As a result, there are a number of low-cost methods of testing in-home usage. One of the most popular is the minivan system organized by some market research agencies that sell a range of household and grocery products to the householder and compare the offtake of the test product against commonly available alternatives.

Pricing of the product is often crucial to the successful conclusion of a minivan test; too low and the product is perceived as a free offer, too high and the product will not be taken up. Minivan tests are not suitable for products with a fairly long purchase cycle, and for such products the company will have to establish some sort of consumer panel to evaluate the product over a longer time span. Control of such panels is often a major problem.

User testing

The user panel is a similar technique in the industrial equipment market. It tests particular items of equipment in the working environment alongside other equipment. There are advantages for the manufacturer. It can choose those users with the potentially most extreme demands upon the equipment to define the product limits within the working environment. Secondly, it enables the company to clarify whether the initial protocol decisions are realistic, and that the 'core' benefit has been correctly isolated. User tests are most appropriate in industrial equipment which is relatively portable and freestanding: computers, software and medical diagnostic equipment all being good examples. Larger industrial equipment such as packaging machinery cannot be so easily tested. User tests may pose certain problems of security in so far as they often enable competitors to gain access to particular developments, but they certainly provide a rapid and effective check on quality, performance limits and competitive performance.

In-store testing

Where the company has the co-operation of a number of stores it can accurately measure the offtake of the product compared with direct competitors or similar products. In-store testing will also permit pre-test of promotional and packaging material. Side-by-side variance, comparing one pack with another over a period of twelve weeks, can produce statistically valid results with just six stores, though it will normally be calculated in two or more regions with a panel of ten stores. The statistical problem with side-by-side testing is the availability of sufficient data 'points' to enable a viable comparison to be made; the more data points, the shorter the length of the testing period. With the advent of electronic point-of-sale (EPOS) systems, this problem has been overcome provided that the manufacturer can gain access to the day-by-day information that such systems provide — a lucrative field that some of the larger market research companies have now entered. Where such store data-collection systems can be married to cable television systems, small local test areas of considerable value can be develolped. In the United States, where cable networks expanded early, a number of such integrated systems are offered to manufacturers as a low-cost and rapid market-evaluation system. Even where data capture of such types does not occur, a large concentration of stores selling test and competitive products provides the same volume of information for analysis as is the case for Japanese consumer durables.

Product or test markets

Concept tests provide valuable information but most of the input will be qualitative rather than quantitative. There will often be substantial areas of uncertainty about the new concept which can only be resolved by more extensive testing procedures. Two important issues must be addressed by any organization wanting to carry out effective full-scale test procedures: how to define accurately a representative test area and testing period, and how to clarify the problems that need to be resolved and create an information system which will then measure them.

Defining the test area

To provide accurate data, the test area must be both representative of the market as a whole and comparable with areas in which no activity is taking place, or control areas. It must also allow the entire test procedure to be carried out in as economic a fashion as possible. Establishing such representative test areas is a major problem in the majority of markets. Each market sector has its own anomalies: socio-economic distributions may differ, age structures may vary, family sizes, urban/rural distinctions, and other behavioural factors may show diverse patterns from those 'average' values within the national market. Choice of the particular area will then be a balancing act dependent on the weighing up of advantages and disadvantages of one area compared with another, and no test area can be considered as strictly representative of the market as a whole. For example, the consumption of prepared fish and flour is significantly higher in the north of England; and the Scots consume nearly double the average quantity of oatmeal in the United Kingdom and half the quantity of lamb; the South-West consumes a far larger weight of both wholemeal bread and fresh vegetables. Once the test area is established a decision must be taken on the duration of the test period. In an ideal world, the data that the company has will be absolutely accurate about such factors as market share, price and the like. The reality is that there will be considerable error in the data because of the size of the sample, and the frequency of the data collection. The greater the number of data 'points' (the quantity of measurement) and the greater the change expected, the shorter the length of the test procedure. This inter-relationship is given by the equation:

$$ N = \frac{(T1 + T2)2 \ \S2}{s2} $$

where:

N = number of data points (areas $\times$ observations)
$\S$ = variance or error of the data
s = expected market share or sales change
T1 & T2 = confidence limits

Establishing data requirements

How the company collects data about the test market will therefore have an important influence on the duration of the entire process. In addition, the demands of the company for other types of information not provided at earlier stages of the testing process also affect how the test is structured. The most important additional information needed concerns the expected sales level, marketing-mix issues such as delivery, servicing, price, and promotion, and for many types of innovation — such as branding or service alterations — customer perceptions about either the product or the company. Where precise volume forecasts are required, the company will have to measure the likely starting volume levels of the new product which will consist of a measure of market penetration (that is, the percentage of the total customer base that will be *initial* potential purchasers), and calculate the level of repeat buying (how many customers will be *repeat* purchasers of the product and at what rate). This calculation will be vital to determine how the market sales will change over time and what eventual sales plateau will be achieved. This measure cannot normally be provided by concept testing. Often the company will also need to identify response to specific attributes of the new product, broken down by purchase group, the image of the new product and how this affects the perception of the supplier company, and the level of awareness of the new changed product.

Within the marketing mix, the company may need specific information, again broken down by purchase group, concerning customers' perceptions about price levels: whether they can, for example, be raised (vital for profitability) or will need to be significantly lowered to achieve initial market penetration and required levels of repeat purchase. Customers' perceptions about distribution channels may also be important in certain circumstances: for example, whether the product should be available via the distribution intermediaries that currently handle it, or should it be stocked in a different way. Information about promotional effectiveness will be particularly important for many consumer goods: for example, what the recall of the advertising or promotional material has been, the degree of understanding of the potential consumer concerning the message or information contained in the advertising material, and reactions to packaging.

Structuring information for test markets

Some, but by no means all, of the necessary information will be available from extant company sources, and decisions must be made about which of four broad alternative sources of information could most effectively be used: current company sales data (available from within the company), an existing consumer panel, a special panel, or via post-test enquiry. Each of the data sources will provide information in specific areas, as detailed in Table 10.2.

No single source will provide all the data requirements, and each will have distinct advantages and disadvantages. Most companies will have to carry out

Table 10.2 The applicability of data types for particular problem areas

Data	Source			
	Company sales	Existing panel	Special panel	Post test enquiry
Sales	*	*	*	*
Penetration		*		
Repeat buying		*	*	
Likes/dislikes		*	*	
Image				*
Awareness				*
Pricing		*	*	*
Distribution		*		
Advertising impact				*
Advertising understanding				*
Trade reaction	*			

Source: Author

specific post-test enquiries because of the paucity of information from current sources. The main problem is that the timescale of the test period will then need to be substantial, and the analysis of the results lengthy in consequence — comparison between the test and control areas being often complex because of the large numbers of variables involved — and this is contrary to the requirements for rapid commercialization. In the future, with the advent of electronic point-of-sale data possibly becoming available from stores on a day-by-day basis, the need for special post-launch enquiries may be reduced. In the absence of such electronic sales data, some companies have attempted to shorten the testing process by developing methods of quick reading of test markets. One method utilized by Unilever in the consumer goods field uses a questionnaire approach to estimate total eventual market share by concentrating on the interrelationship between market share, penetration and repeat buying rate, with the assumption that the eventual market share will be the eventual penetration multiplied by the repeat buying rate. It is suggested that around twelve samples of 250 questionnaires over the test market period will provide a reliable estimate of the eventual market share and will provide much of the attitudinal information normally derived from a full post-test enquiry.

Summary

With the changing competitive environment and costs of prototype development, companies have to re-evaluate how they test products to limit the risks of failure in product performance, non-technical components, attitude, or delay to market. With the advances in manufacturing technology and data management available to many manufacturing companies, testing procedures that shorten the traditional lengthy process of concept, prototype and full test market procedures become more and more important. Different approaches to innovation also demand different emphasis within the testing programme and hence the concentration on particular parts of the testing procedure — branding innovation, for example, demanding a much longer-term testing process than reformulation. Each of the available methods of testing has particular advantages and disadvantages which are summarized in Table 10.3.

Table 10.3 Types of testing procedure and advantages and disadvantages

	Cost	Speed	Objectivity	Accuracy	Completeness	Secrecy
Employee panel	Low	High	Low	High	Low	High
Focus group	Mod	High	Low	Low	Low	High
User group	Low	Mod	High	High	Low	Low
Customer appraisal	Low	Mod	Low	High	Mod	Low
Hall test	Mod	Mod	Mod	Mod	Mod	Low
Store test	Low	High	High	High	Low	Low
Mini van	Mod	Mod	Mod	Mod	Mod	Mod
Test market	High	Low	High	High	High	Low

Source: Author

11

The golden rules of innovation

Introduction

This book has dealt in detail with certain key innovation issues. An important initial consideration is the fact of a highly competitive environment making it essential for companies to concentrate on understanding, and managing innovation and change. A second consideration is that innovation should not be perceived as part of a limited framework relating solely to product performance. It is far, far broader in scope and potential benefits. The company that can identify all the components of innovation in its environment is far more likely to introduce successful change than one that limits itself to historic concepts of innovation. Because innovation is so complex, and market/resource interactions so numerous, no single road to success will apply to all companies at all times and in all markets.

The key strategic innovation issues are identified as follows in the text:

* The type of innovation policy that best fits company and market positions.
* Its implications for the company infrastructure.
* Its implications in terms of information management.
* A common need to concentrate on defining accurately the performance criteria of the product at the earliest possible stage.
* Its implications in terms of choosing the appropriate testing procedure to meet the demands of the product.

Those who always remember that the product is a collection of consumer benefits — technical, non-technical and attitudinal — are likely to be the successful innovators. The golden rules of innovation originate from the detailed analysis of these factors and separate the successful from the unsuccessful.

Think strategic

In two respects all companies are equal: they all face changing markets and resource environments. What works for one company in one particular period may not continue to work as well, or another approach will be even more successful. There is no such thing as a universally successful concept or universally successful strategy. Business managers must fit the resources of the organization to the conditions of the market. The only way that this can be achieved is to continue to plan as objectively as possible, identifying those routes that best fit the company at a particular time, and — most important of all — determining where the goal posts are likely to be at the end of the planning cycle. This will identify the long-term objectives of the organization suiting short- and medium-term actions to achieving this long-term policy. Even where, as in some technical sectors, the environment is rapidly changing, the demands of strategic planning remain paramount — only the company that evaluates changes in the marketplace in terms of its resources can take advantage of new opportunities, when and wherever they occur. Thinking strategically, above all else, involves the organization in attempting to control the environment and competition rather than being controlled by it. *Remember to control your own destiny or someone else will!*

Think different

No company or organization has succeeded by exactly duplicating the competition. The dictum concerning Lord Lever, that where he led he conquered and where he followed he failed, is a significant one in the context of innovation. Organizations and their staff must maintain the questioning attitude that separates the successful innovator from the unsuccessful. There is, after all, no such thing as a definitive product. Corporate and departmental thinking often follows the three stages of mankind's thinking postulated by De Bono: an initial broad search for understanding — the 'why' phase; then an attempt to apply this knowledge in problem solving — the 'why not' phase; and finally, reaching the perceived wisdom of a particular problem which limits the entire set of possible solutions — the 'because' phase. Most organizations regrettably reach the 'because' phase early on in their existence, and accept the agenda set either by the market leader or by historic perceptions of what is acceptable and/or successful. Such thinking obviously accepts that the market leader will always continue to set the agenda. Companies should always concentrate on not following the crowd, developing approaches to products and customers that are demonstrably different from those currently on offer in the market. An insistence on novel approaches should also be made to extend to old concepts and products — to ensure that no possible avenue for both current and future development is ignored. This will emphasize the role of entrepreneurism rather than reaction. *Remember that surprise is the essence of most successful attacks.*

Think customer benefit

What is it that the customer wants? What are the real benefits that the company can offer in the way of new products and services? Are the benefits offered by the company perceived as real and effective by the customer base? The company that can produce the real customer benefit, however it is achieved, by a change in colour, design, image or components rather than the additional performance which is not perceived as a benefit, will be the company that has added real value to its products. It is, after all, only the customer's perception that something is new that makes it new. An accurate definition of customer demands in all aspects of the product — technical, support, attitudinal and price — enables many of the early stages of product development to be shortened and the product investment to be accurately placed within the developing company strategy. It will also target those products which will yield an effective commercial return by meeting demands for which the customer will be prepared to pay. *Remember that it is only the customer who pays your wages.*

Think detail

Detailed planning is the cornerstone of effective innovation, enabling the company to translate the required customer benefit profitably into the final effective innovative concept. Accurately defining the components of each stage of the process provides vital benefits: a high level of experimental capability within the organization; a great deal of control over the likely cash flow and overall costing of the eventual innovation; a significantly improved chance of a successful outcome to any particular developmental path; and far greater speed of effective introduction. The innovation planner should attempt to limit the uncertainty of the process by creating a specific and detailed protocol, developing from this a comprehensive engineering analysis, and integrating this with a predetermined testing programme that will identify the major potential problem areas. *Remember that the fast journey will only come from knowing the route in great detail.*

Think internal

Innovation is a difficult and complex operation that will best succeed if the company thoroughly and painstakingly appreciates the work requirements involved in each type of task, and builds on the existing strengths within the organization. Emphasizing internal issues will also prevent the company from making expensive mistakes with products, customers, technology, or markets, that the organization does not fully understand. Concentrating on internal resources forces management to make logical and objective assessments of where investment would be most appropriate. It creates a climate in which management will concentrate on the long-term rather than the short-term advances in total sales, looking for real growth in added value per employee rather than in total return on capital employed. *Remember that if you don't have a competitive advantage, don't compete.*

Think knowledge

In the 1990s, survival will depend on how clever a company is. Employee knowledge, properly applied will add value to products, enable high levels of reinvestment to be maintained, and lead to ever higher value added products and competitive advantage. Firms must give emphasis to the development of knowledge within the firm both by deciding what information is crucial for new product evolution and creating an internal environment through which the acquisition and retention of such knowledge can be maximized. This will involve the application of information technology and the appropriate recruitment, training and motivational systems. *Remember, knowledge itself is power.*

Think people

In the 1990s the winning firm will be the knowledge-intensive firm adding more value to the products than the competition. Knowledge only functions through company personnel and this makes employees a key resource for future development. Getting hold of the right people, ensuring they work efficiently, effectively and above all enthusiastically is vital to the management of innovation. The corporate dinosaurs of the late twentieth century will be those companies that fail to appreciate the personnel role in effective innovation. They will steadily lose their competitive edge, accepting that they will always belong in second place. The difference between the 'can do' and the 'can't do' organization will be the concentration on developing people, and the belief that senior management have to make particular and continuing efforts to change the organization to suit subordinates, rather than forcing subordinates to change to suit the organization. *Remember that most struggles are won first in the mind, and only then in the market.*

Think thin

Companies in the 1990s have to be more knowledgeable, more responsive and, in many areas of the innovation environment, quicker than their competitors. Getting change implemented, understanding the customer and producing more added value will be the central components of leadership in this brave new world. Meetings and conferences will become unaffordable luxuries. Getting closer to the market, sharing knowledge and information, and concentrating on action rather than reflection will all be the hallmarks of the effective innovator of the 1990s. *Remember that small organizations are simple organizations and simple organizations will spend less time on maintaining the organization, and more on task achievement.*

Index